Anthony Trollope

by

Arthur Pollard

Professor of English in the University of Hull

Routledge & Kegan Paul

London, Henley and Boston

First published in 1978
by Routledge & Kegan Paul Ltd
39 Store Street,
London WC1E 7DD,
Broadway House,
Newtown Road,
Henley-on-Thames,
Oxon RG9 1EN and
9 Park Street,
Boston, Mass. 02108, USA
Set in 11 on 12pt Bembo by
Weatherby Woolnough, Wellingborough, Northants
and printed in Great Britain by
Redwood Burn Ltd
Trowbridge and Esher

British Library Cataloguing in Publication Data

Pollard, Arthur, b.1922

Anthony Trollope.
1. Trollope, Anthony – Criticism and interpretation
823'.8   PR5687   77-30497

ISBN 0 7100 8811 6

To Phyllis

Contents

	Preface	ix
	Acknowledgments	xi
1	Life and Character	1
2	The Irish Novels and Stories	9
3	The Way They Lived Then	26
4	Barchester Chronicles	47
5	The Semi-Political Novels	75
6	Other Longer Novels, 1858-70	109
7	Shorter Novels, 1863-74	135
8	The Final Phase	155
9	Other Works	174
10	Conclusion: An Estimate	192
	A Note on *La Vendée*	200
	Bibliography	202
	Index	205

Preface

This is a labour of love and an attempt at justification. I have read Trollope with enthusiasm ever since I discovered *Barchester Towers* at school. I was therefore surprised when the late Bonamy Dobrée, first a revered teacher and then for long years a valued friend, challenged me to mention 'one thing that Trollope had contributed to the English novel'. The request to write this book gives me the opportunity. It is an author-guide, going systematically through Trollope's voluminous output, omitting only the ephemera.

Trollope was a pre-Jamesian who has suffered more than most from post-Jamesian assumptions. Yet, curiously enough, James is still one of his most perceptive critics, noticing Trollope's 'complete appreciation of the usual'. It is against this background of the usual that we must judge him. Trollope provides the fullest and most reliable picture of nineteenth-century society to be found anywhere in the novel of his time. That is one thing that he contributed, but, lest that be thought too merely sociological, I would claim another. In this setting he explores social behaviour, the ways in which characters react to pressures, opinions and *mores,* but this is not just external chronicling. As Beatrice Curtis Brown neatly puts it, 'he implies much of life that lies above and below behaviour'. (1950, pp. 47-8) In other words, we have to read Trollope and judge his characters with an eye and ear to inference and nuance of the kind we use all the time in everyday life. There is yet a third thing I would claim for him, his awareness of what we would perhaps call 'situation ethics'. Circumstances alter cases, and precept, however exemplary, has a bad habit of not fitting the particular example to which it may have to be applied. This results in dilemmas not only for the characters most closely involved, but more especially for those around, their friends maybe, their associates certainly, who are called upon to judge and perhaps to help them.

It is important that we should approach Trollope on his own terms, considering him in the light of the literary practice, and, even more vital, by the standards of personal and social morality, of his own time. I have therefore been concerned to stress precisely those values on which he himself set most store. He will never satisfy the post-Freudian or the post-Marxian or perhaps even the post-Jamesian. If, however, we are prepared to make an effort in historical transference of our imaginative requirements, we may be better rewarded. The Victorian age has always had a strong attraction in this regard (witness Dickens and Christmas), and this may be why both Trollope and Dickens have sustained a popular appeal when the tide of intellectual opinion has flowed against them.

Arthur Pollard

Acknowledgments

I should like to thank the Brynmor Jones Library of the University of Hull and its librarian (Dr Philip Larkin) for unfailing help in the provision of books and periodicals, the University authorities who granted me study leave in 1975 when much of this book was written, and colleagues in the English Department who assumed some of my teaching responsibilities at that time. I must also record my obligations to my wife for her patience and help and to Miss Ruth Green, who not only transformed my execrable hand into impeccable typescript but also detected errors that my own less scrupulous eye had left uncorrected. Needless to say, what follows with any errors and inadequacies still remaining is all my own and I must bear the responsibility for it.

1

Life and Character

Writing to Watkins about his photograph in April 1860, Trollope commented: 'I think the portrait as it now stands will do very well. It looks uncommon fierce, as that of a dog about to bite; but that I fear is the nature of the animal portrayed.' (*Letters*, No. 87) Twenty years later – and as the 1873 'Spy' cartoon in *Vanity Fair* amply demonstrates – Julian Hawthorne described him as

> a broad-shouldered sturdy man, of middle height, with a ruddy countenance and snow-white tempestuous beard and hair. He wore large, gold-rimmed spectacles, but his eyes were black and brilliant.... He spoke volubly and almost boisterously, and his voice was full-toned and powerful ... his words bursting forth from beneath his white moustache with such an impetus of hearty breath that it seemed as if all opposing arguments must be blown away.... Here was a man of abundant physical strength and vigor, no doubt, but carrying within him a nature more than commonly alert and impressible.... His character was simple and straightforward to a fault, but he was abnormally conscientious.... It might be thought that he was overburdened with self-esteem, and unduly opinionated; but, in fact, he was but over-anxious to secure the good-will and agreement of all with whom he came in contact.... He was never more angry than he was forgiving and generous. (*Confessions and Criticisms*, 1887, quoted Sadleir, 1961 p. 338)

I have selected rigorously from a long and perceptive estimation, but the essential Trollope, I think, is there – full-blooded, prejudiced, energetic, forthright, sensitive, sympathetic.

Trollope was born and died in London. After their marriage his parents set up house at 6 Keppel Street, Bloomsbury, and there in quick succession five of their children were born. Anthony, their fourth son, was born in 1815 on 24 April, some eight weeks before the battle of Waterloo. Two younger sisters completed the family, but, as with so many nineteenth-century families, two of the children died in childhood, and only Anthony and his eldest brother, Tom, survived into comparative old age.

Their parents were each the offspring of country parsons, the father coming from Hertfordshire and the mother from Heckfield in Hampshire, an area which Trollope celebrates in *Ralph the Heir* (ch. 11) as a 'county in which moorland and woodland and pasture are more daintily thrown together to please the eye' than anywhere else in England. Thomas Anthony Trollope, the father, was a scholar of Winchester and then Vinerian (Law) Fellow of New College, Oxford, before becoming a Chancery barrister. Through his mother's family he was the accepted heir to his uncle, Adolphus Meetkerke, the wealthy squire of Julians near Royston in Hertfordshire. Prospects could hardly have been brighter: ahead lay a career at the Bar, already rich in promise, and the succession to a country estate. One defect was sufficient to lose both – Thomas Trollope's uncontrollable irascibility. Attorneys ceased to come with their briefs, preferring other barristers who would not lambast them for their stupidity; and the lawyer's popularity with his uncle fell sharply as a result of their violent political differences. The crushing blow came when the uncle, following his childless first wife's death, quickly remarried and produced in his sixties a numerous family who thus destroyed the Trollopes' hopes of joining the landed classes.

There is a sour irony, therefore, in their move from London to Harrow in 1817 when, still possessing his great expectations, the elder Trollope leased 400 acres from Lord Northwick and built on it an expensive house which, in anticipation perhaps, he called Julians. It was the nearest he ever came to becoming a country squire and the nearest also that he ever came to Julians. Though he continued in chambers, work fell off, and his attempts at farming were as ill-fated as his practice of the law. One son (Arthur) died, and, both marvellous to relate and difficult to believe of a lawyer, the title deeds to some property in London were mislaid and Mrs Trollope's marriage-settlement was discovered to be invalid.

His irascibility vented itself also on his own family and worsened with the years. The boys were expected to follow their father to

Winchester and New College and he spared no effort and no rage in urging them on. Harrow School, however – and this was one of the advantages of the move – offered practically free education to local boys. Thither therefore the Trollopes went, surely one of the very few occasions when Harrow has been a prep school for Winchester! Of his years at Harrow Anthony has left his own account. It is of a piece with his remark that his 'boyhood was, I think, as unhappy as that of a young gentleman could well be'. He was a day-boy, not even a day-boarder as his brothers had been, and he records that his journeyings between home and school were a daily purgatory. He was also the dunce of his class and he was dirty, 'not only slovenly in dress, but his work was equally dirty', as a school-friend, later Sir William Gregory of Coole, recalled. Trollope tells of constant floggings from the headmaster, and what he suffered at Harrow he was to continue suffering at his brother's hands at Winchester, where Tom was a prefect and Anthony a junior boy. Of this latter experience he comments: 'That. such thrashings should have been possible at a school as a continual part of one's daily life seems to me to argue a very ill condition of school discipline.' There is obviously deep feeling in this detached remark. Another is more personal when he tells of being unjustly blamed for some misdemeanour at the school in Sunbury-on-Thames, which he attended for two years before going on to Winchester: 'All that was fifty years ago and it burns me now as though it were yesterday.' The seared childhood of a Dickens or a Charlotte Brontë went into their novels. Of Trollope's, if we had not had the *Autobiography*, there would have been not a word.

It was not just physical punishment; there was also poverty with all the deprivations and sense of exclusion which that entailed. Trollope tells of unpaid fees and how his credit from the college buttery at Winchester was stopped and of something more – 'The loss of a shilling a week would not have been much, – even though pocket-money from other sources never reached me, – but that the other boys all knew it!' The family fortunes went from bad to worse. Julians had to be forsaken for what he calls 'a wretched tumble-down farmhouse', Anthony was withdrawn from Winchester to Harrow again, 'What right had a wretched farmer's boy, reeking from a dunghill, to sit next to the sons of peers? ... The indignities I endured are not to be described.' His poverty made him the taunt of his fellows; his tutor took him without fee, but let everybody know it; Trollope says of himself: 'I skulked and

3

was odious in the eyes of those I admired and envied'; he longed to play cricket and racquets, but there was no money to equip him for these sports. (Quotations in this and the preceding paragraph from the *Autobiography*, ch. 1)

At home he lived alone with his father, for his mother and Henry, his brother, had gone off to America in furtherance of a hare-brained scheme of Anthony's father's to send 'pin-cushions, pepper-boxes and pocket-knives' to them at a store they opened in Cincinnati. This was in 1827, and later he and Tom went out, leaving Anthony, still at Winchester, to spend a gloomily memorable midsummer holiday alone in his father's chambers in Lincoln's Inn, 'wandering about in those old deserted buildings' and reading Shakespeare because there was nothing else to read. His father returned, Tom went to Oxford and Anthony was transferred to Harrow, alone once more with his father, who spent his time for the most part incarcerated in the parlour, working endlessly and pointlessly on his never-completed 'Encyclopaedia Ecclesiastica'.

At last fortune smiled, for though his father's writings were futile, Fanny Trollope's were not. Returning to England, she turned the American experience to some profit by publishing her *Domèstic Manners of the Americans*, which was an immediate success. The poverty of the Harrow Weald farmhouse, not one of the children with a pillow to his head, was changed for another Julians or, rather, Julians Hill, the Orley Farm of Trollope's novel of that name; and Mrs Trollope embarked, at the age of fifty, on a prolific and successful career as author.

Hardly had Trollope left school, 'a hobbledehoy of nineteen, without any idea of a career' (*Autobiography*, ch. 2), than further blows hit the family. Old debts caught up with Trollope's father and the bailiffs distrained on Julians Hill. Trollope himself was bidden to drive his father to London, and thence to the Ostend boat, in fact, though Anthony did not know it, for him to escape imprisonment as a debtor. The elder Trollope was ill and so too were Henry and Emily who, with all the family except Tom, joined their father at Bruges. There he and Henry died, and Emily quickly followed them after the family returned home, this time to Hadley (Herts), to a house which Trollope described in detail in *The Bertrams*. Anthony himself was to suffer, in 1840, a serious illness, whose outward manifestation was asthma, but, his mother wrote, the doctors say 'this can only be a symptom and not the disease'. It was probably an illness of psychosomatic origin.

By this time Trollope had been at work for six years in the Post Office, which he was to serve both in England and abroad until 1867. His mother's influence had secured him a nomination in the fashion of those days, and despite his imperfections in spelling and handwriting he was appointed clerk at £90 a year. He did not commend himself to Colonel Maberly, the secretary, and in general those first six years were far from happy. Drinking, smoking and cards were the distraction of himself and his friends. There was probably some occasional flirtation and there were certainly some debts. *The Three Clerks* is a fictional reminiscence of these years, and *The Small House at Allington* also owes much to this period.

'In dire trouble, having debts on my head and quarrels with our Secretary-Colonel and a full conviction that my life was taking me downwards to the lowest pits' (*Autobiography*, ch. 3) – this is the prelude to the turning point in Trollope's life. He volunteered to go as surveyor's clerk to Ireland. His reputation preceded him in a note from the Colonel, but the ten years there from 1841 to 1851 were a record of achievement and happiness. At Banagher and Clonmel he brought efficiency to his work in reorganising the postal rounds, he took up hunting which was to be a passion with him for over thirty years and, in general, he developed a love for and became a social success with the people among whom he worked. Even his marriage to an Englishwoman, Rose Heseltine, daughter of a bank-manager in Rotherham, was permitted to cast only a passing cloud over his social relations.

It was now that he began to write, not, be it said, with much success, so that by 1850 he could say with a certain sardonic air to his mother that at the forthcoming Crystal Palace Exhibition 'I mean to exhibit four 4 vol. novels – all failures! – which I look upon as a great proof of industry at any rate.' (*Letters*, No. 19)

From 1851 to 1853 he was engaged on the reorganisation of postal arrangements in South Wales and South-West England including the Channel Islands, and it was from Guernsey that he wrote in November 1851 suggesting the iron pillar-boxes that soon became and ever since have been a familiar feature of the British street-scene. He sought promotion in the Post Office, trying to gain the Superintendency of Mail Coaches in 1852 and ultimately being appointed Surveyor in 1854. He also continued to write and, though success came slowly, it came surely. The sojourn in the West Country inspired *The Warden*, but when it appeared Trollope was back in Ireland for another tour. Newby had published his first novel, *The Macdermots of Ballycloran*, in 1847. This yielded nothing, whilst his second, *The Kellys and the O'Kellys*, lost £63.10s.1½d. For his third novel, *La Vendée*, Trollope received the agreed advance of £20 and no more, presumably because not enough copies were sold. Even for the works that made his name he received at first only just over £20 for *The Warden* (1855) and an advance of £100 for *Barchester Towers* (1857). Longman published both these volumes, but Trollope was not satisfied with his terms.

For his next work, *The Three Clerks* (1858), Bentley paid £250 outright and in the same year Chapman & Hall outbid Bentley's offer by giving £400 for *Doctor Thorne*. They took a number of his other books, but in 1860 Trollope moved again, this time to Smith, Elder who serialised *Framley Parsonage* in the newly established *Cornhill Magazine*. For this he was paid £1000. Books followed one another with stunning rapidity, so much so that he published some novels (*Nina Balatka* and *Linda Tressel*) anonymously. He continued in his own characteristic vein in the Barsetshire series and in the Palliser or political novels. He exploited current fashions in such realms as the sensational and the mystery tale. What Mrs Braddon could do in *Lady Audley's Secret* Trollope would improve upon in *Orley Farm*. What made Wilkie Collins popular Trollope would try his hand at in *The Eustace Diamonds*. In addition, there were travel books, biographies and miscellanea. The story of Trollope's immense and methodical industry is too well known to need telling again. His own honesty in telling it and his meticulous account of the financial success of his writings did much to damn him in the eyes of his immediate successors. He claimed 'persevering diligence in [his] profession' and none would deny him that, but he went further, asserting 'that the work that has been done quickest has been done the best'.

After his final establishment in England in 1859 at Waltham House in Essex he still found time to go hunting three times a week, to carry on his duties in the Post Office, to undertake frequent trips abroad and to cultivate a host of literary and other acquaintances in London. In 1853 he had visited his brother Tom in Florence and again in 1857; the next year he went on Post Office business first to Egypt and then to the West Indies and in 1861-2 to the United States after a final visit to Italy in 1860. There he met Kate Field, an intelligent young woman, later to be a champion of women's rights. It was the beginning of a friendship of many years. Their correspondence (see Sadleir, 1961, pp. 218-25) includes some candid and sensible advice about writing from Trollope, and also touches on the Civil War (Trollope's visit coincided with the early months of that conflict). The attractive and intelligent girl of the Italian visit, though remaining very dear to Trollope, was seen to be turning into a militant Boston female, and there is something of this later persona in Wallachia Petrie of *He Knew He Was Right*.

Trollope's return to England in 1859 and his association with the *Cornhill* opened the way to literary London. He established a friendship with Thackeray, who edited the new periodical. He knew George Henry Lewes and George Eliot, whose work he admired and who acknowledged that her own *Middlemarch* owed much to Trollope. At their house he met Browning and Tennyson, Herbert Spencer, Tyndall and others prominent in the intellectual life of the time. He was a member of the Garrick Club and was elected to the Athenaeum. He stayed with the artist Millais, who was one of his illustrators, at the latter's house in the Highlands; he visited Sir Henry James (later Lord James of Hereford) in Kent and also at his shooting box in Wiltshire; he was entertained at the country houses of Lord Lytton at Knebworth and Lord Houghton at Monk Fryston; and in his last years – a result of his book on South Africa – he formed a close friendship with Lord Carnarvon and stayed at Highclere. Trollope's London life became even fuller after 1873 when he moved to 39 Montagu Square.

This, however, is to anticipate. In 1867 he resigned from the Post Office, feeling amongst other things that his talents and services had not received their due acknowledgment. His later years in the service had been marked by a running animosity between him and the secretary, Rowland Hill. He was none the less asked to make one further trip to the United States, where he arranged the Anglo-American Postal Treaty. While he was away, he missed nomination as a Liberal to the safe parliamentary seat of South-East Essex. Instead, he had to contest Beverley at great cost both in money and nervous frustration. He came bottom of the poll, but such had been the bribery and corruption that the election was declared invalid and the constituency disfranchised. Trollope's experiences in the election form the readable parts of what he himself recognised as a poor novel, *Ralph the Heir*. In the *Autobiography* he describes himself somewhat elusively as an 'advanced conservative liberal', but the tone of all his work shows how the remarks of his first biographer, Escott, about him make sense: 'Whatever at different periods Trollope might think and call himself, his natural prejudices were always those of aristocratic and reactionary Toryism.' (Escott, 1913, p. 166) In the last year of his life he parted decisively from the Gladstonian Liberals over Home Rule for Ireland.

Excluded from active politics, Trollope returned to his work as editor of *St Paul's Magazine* and there published *Phineas Finn* – the first, as he put it, of a series of semi-political tales. The 1870s were even more prolific and more lucrative than the 1860s, but the last years marked some falling-off in popularity, such that, for instance, his publisher Chapman lost £120 on *The Duke's Children* in 1880, a sum which the novelist resolved to repay. (*Letters*, No. 796) He was little less active in his travels. In 1875 he went to Australia, where the younger of his two sons was engaged in sheep-farming. The journey was tiresome and the conditions hard, but Trollope went into it with his characteristic zest. The result was a book about the country, and two novels which have Australia for some part of their setting. In 1878 he went on his South African trip, found Olive Schreiner's *Story of an African Farm* and was impressed by Jameson 'who has just started in medical practice in Kimberley, and in whom I see qualities that will go to the making of events in this country'. (Quoted in Escott, 1913, p. 284) He visited Ireland in May 1882, shortly after the murder of Lord Frederick Cavendish in Phoenix Park, Dublin; he was in Ireland for the last time, in August. He was writing about what he called the 'lamentable' condition of that country in his last unfinished novel, *The Landleaguers*.

Trollope had left London in 1880 and moved to Harting (near Petersfield), to what he called 'a little cottage here, just big enough (or nearly so) to hold my books, with five acres and a cow and a dog and a cock and a hen'. The last years were marked by increasing deafness and increasing asthma: 'great spasmodic want of breath is the evil that affects [? afflicts] me'. (*Letters*, No. 908) He was in London, however, staying at Garlant's Hotel in Suffolk Street when he was struck down by a seizure on 3 November 1882 dining at an evening party at his brother-in-law's house in Pimlico. He lingered speechless for five weeks and died on 6 December. He was buried at Kensal Green Cemetery a few days later.

2

The Irish Novels and Stories

(Letters to the *Examiner*; Short Stories; *The Mac-dermots of Ballycloran*; *The Kellys and the O'Kellys*; *Castle Richmond*; *An Eye for an Eye*; *The Landleaguers*)

From his base, first at Banagher and then, after 1845, at Clonmel, Trollope sallied forth to investigate complaints about the postal service and to check the work of sub-postmasters in that brusque fashion that always characterised his dealings; and then, when he had despatched the duties of the day, he went off hunting! 'It was altogether a very jolly life that I led in Ireland.' (*Autobiography*, ch. 4)

For Ireland as a whole the 1840s was a traumatic decade, split in half by the onset of the great famine in 1846. Even before this disaster, however, things were far from well. Between 1816 and 1842 the potato crop had failed no less than fourteen times and 'every year a large section of the population was, for a period of two or three months, practically destitute'. (Beckett, 1966, p. 336) This is not surprising when one recalls that Ireland was one of the most densely populated countries in Europe, where the number of inhabitants had increased from 6.8 million in 1821 to over 8 million twenty years later. Land-hunger was an inevitable consequence, and this led to high rents, an evil exacerbated by the practice of tendering, and also to the fragmentation of holdings by the habit of dividing among the sons at death. There were enlightened land-owners like Lords Palmerston, Headley and Farnham who assisted in building, in providing plans for cottages, laying roads and drainage and employing agricultural experts, but there were also pauperised landowners,

> clinging to their estates with incomes eaten away by settlements, living like the poorest farmers, but scorning to bring up their children to any sort of business and screwing out of their miserable tenants in addition to rack-rents, butter, eggs and fish. (McDowell, 1956, p.8)

9

In addition, the country was afflicted with the political agitation of O'Connell's Repeal Movement. The one hopeful sign was state provision; in the 1830s a large number of dispensaries and hospitals were established, the reorganisation of the Poor Law ensured that 122 workhouses were ready by 1842, there was an efficient police force numbering 9,000 in 1845, and in that year also £1 million was paid in loans and grants by the Board of Works, mainly for road improvements.

Ireland's sorrow fell on her in a single week between 27 July and 3 August 1846. The first official response was a public works programme: in September 30,000 were being employed, by December the figure was half a million. The government, however, made several mistakes. It refused to subsidise private estate work such as land reclamation and drainage; it refused to stop the export of grain from Ireland; at first it insisted that the food that it had prudently imported should be sold at market prices; it refused to ratify the Lord Lieutenant's firm measures for dealing with disorder. As things got worse, subsidised work was followed by the soup kitchens, these latter at first largely the result of voluntary effort. The workhouses were, however, the inevitable recourse in the end, and even they could not cope with the suppliants. Large numbers still had to be supported by outdoor relief. In 1848, with continuing potato failures, discontent expressed itself in abortive insurrection. Death and emigration reduced the population drastically: by 1851 it was down to 6.5 millions. As W. Steuart Trench, himself an Irish land-agent, wrote:

> It drove some millions of people to the other side of the
> Atlantic and sent many thousands to an untimely grave [but it
> also] broke up to a great extent the small farms of Ireland. It
> relieved the plethora of the labour market. It removed the
> needy country gentleman ... It unlocked millions of capital,
> since then laid out on the improved cultivation of the land.
> (1966, p. 50)

Towards the end of the crisis Sidney Godolphin Osborne, with his radical self-confidence, as ill-informed as it was unqualified, wrote a series of letters to *The Times* analysing on the basis of a brief and superficial acquaintance what he thought was wrong with Ireland. Trollope answered him in the *Examiner,* opposing ten years' experience to less than ten weeks'. He had no difficulty in showing that Osborne's assertions failed to take into account such facts as the time of the year and that the agricultural cycle involves leaving acres untilled as fallow. Osborne, the visitor, complained of 'old roads spoilt, of ground cut up to make new roads, which are still unfinished ... and of a curious mountain of wheelbarrows'; Trollope, the resident, the man who knew, could testify to seeing 'famine arrested in its wild career by the measure which set all those barrows trundling'.

His first letter was published on 25 August 1849. Six others followed between 30 March and 15 June 1850. They provide a survey of the Ireland of the famine years from the time when 'early in the autumn of 1846 the disease fell upon the potato gardens like a dark mantle; before the end of September entire fields were black, and the air was infected with the unwholesome odour of the blight'. There is no doubt of Trollope's compassion: his feelings were seared:

> Those who lived in the country during the period will never forget the winter of 1846 and the spring of 1847. The sufferings of the poor were awful; very awful in their extent and severity, but almost more tremendous from the patience, nay, the apathy, with which they were borne.

He hits out at the clamour of the Irish gentry in petitions for relief, matched by no sacrifices on their part – 'no carriages were abandoned, no hounds destroyed, no retinues reduced'. By contrast, the clergy, both Established and Roman, 'exerted their energies with a unanimity that surprised us all'. (*Examiner,* Letters, No. 2)

The third letter examined the philosophy and practice of relief. The problem was immense, but 'the supply provided should not be gratuitous, for dependence on charity for daily bread destroys the feeling of independence'. He next discussed (in the fourth letter) the effects of poor relief which no less than half a million were receiving by the end of 1848, with the resultant crippling burden on the rates. Trollope pays tribute to the efforts of the Irish gentry (by contrast with a little time before) in employing men and getting the land back into cultivation. But the Poor Law charges fell hardest on those least able to pay: the need for relief was greatest precisely where the properties were most heavily mortgaged and the landlord was left 'utterly powerless; he can neither live himself, nor allow others who are dependent on him to do so'.

The result is best expressed in Trollope's own words:

11

He is blamed for the rapacity with which he demands that which the land cannot produce; he is called harsh, hard and heartless; he ejects the poorer of his tenants, and is held up to execration in the provincial newspapers; the better sort of farmers quit his land, carrying the rest with them to America; his acres lie on his hands, and he has not capital to farm them; by degrees his horses, his carriage, his car, his gig, vanish out of his sight; his coat and hat become worn and shabby; he takes to his house, and locks his door, fearing unfriendly visitors; here, within doors, the lack of luxuries is quickly followed by the want of necessaries, and at last his wife and daughter sob to find themselves without the comfort of a cup of tea . . . .

They do not suffer alone: the ruin spreads itself widely . . . those living on their properties are pauperised, and the workhouses are filled while the land is idle. (*Examiner*, Letters, No. 5)

He concluded that the continuing trouble of Ireland was apathy, the feeling 'that there is no longer any hope; that an easy death is a good thing; and that toil and trouble are useless, as ruin and desolation are imminent'. (*Examiner*, Letters, No. 7)

The fate of many of the landlords was that of Jack O'Conor in one of Trollope's short stories – 'Poor Jack! I fear that the Encumbered Estates Court sent him altogether adrift upon the world.' 'The O'Conors of Castle Conor' is a slight piece, a mere anecdote about the amusing consequences of the hero's arriving at an Irish country house without his dancing-pumps, but in it Trollope suggests much of a way of life, hospitable, forthright and easy-going. The tale manages to include both Trollope's love of hunting and his delight in Irish social life of the 1840s. But the main point of the story is the joke – the hero's amusing discomfort and embarrassment from the odd pumps he all but compels the Irish butler to let him have and the butler's troubles in trying to serve dinner in the hero's top boots!

Trollope's other Irish story, 'Father Giles of Ballymoy', is about a misinterpreted incident in which the narrator, retiring to his bedroom in a small Irish hotel, finds it invaded by another man. There follows an encounter in which the intruder is thrown downstairs. He is Father Giles, the much-loved parish priest, who, unbeknown to Archibald Green, the narrator, had agreed to share his bedroom with Green. Giles is hurt, the populace is roused, Green is taken to the police cells for the night for his own protection. Trollope conveys excellently the Irish small-town atmosphere with its down-at-heel intimacy, its staunch Catholic loyalty and indeed that characteristic casualness which is the source of all the trouble. Likewise, he suggests concisely the generosity of Father Giles, the hostility of the natives from the doctor downwards and the considerable apprehensions of the unfortunate Green.

Ireland was the subject of Trollope's first two novels – *The Macdermots of Ballycloran* (1847) and *The Kellys and the O'Kellys*. As the inspiration for the first he has told us in the *Autobiography* of a walk near Drumsna (Co. Leitrim) when he and John Merivale came upon 'a deserted gateway along a weedy, grass-grown avenue ... to the modern ruins of a country house. It was one of the most melancholy spots I ever visited.' (ch. 4) That house was Ballycloran of the novel:

> The entire roof was off; one could see the rotting joists and beams, some fallen, some falling, the rest ready to fall, like the skeleton of a felon left to rot on an open gibbet ... The doors of the ground floor would not open; the ceiling above me was all gone ... everything that wanted keeping was gone; everything that required care to preserve it had perished. Time had not touched it. Time had evidently not yet had leisure to do his work. He is sure, but slow. Ruin works fast enough unaided, where once he puts his foot. Time would have pulled down the chimneys – Ruin had taken off the slates ...
> Round the outhouses I saw clustering a lot of those wretched cabins which the poor Irish builds against a deserted wall.
> (ch. 1)

Elsewhere there are other vignettes of Irish social conditions. There is the powerful chapter (9) on the small town of Mohill with its occasional slated house 'and the long spaces intervening are filled with the most miserable descriptions of cabins – hovels without chimneys, windows, door, or signs of humanity, except the children playing on the collected filth in front of them'. Inside one such,

> A sickly woman, the entangled nature of whose insufficient garments would defy description, is sitting on a low stool before the fire, suckling a miserably dirty infant; a boy, whose only covering is a tattered shirt, is putting fresh, but, alas, damp turf beneath the pot in which are put to boil the

13

potatoes – their only food. Two or three dim children – their number is lost in their obscurity – are cowering round the dull, dark fire, atop of one another; and on a miserable pallet beyond – a few rotten boards, propped upon equally infirm supports, and covered over with only one thin black quilt – is sitting the master of the mansion.

The sardonic final phrase rounds off the pathos of the passage. By contrast, we have 'the big house, with such pretensions to comfort, and even elegance' – but *there* lives only the agent. Lord Birmingham is an absentee landlord, of whom we hear in two paragraphs largely of rhetorical questions, the first half a series, uttered in apparent disbelief, telling of his philanthropic concerns, the second seriously directing us to the plight of the peasants on his Irish estate. The peasantry everywhere were desperate with poverty and driven to such devices as illicit distilling and even to violence and murder. The events of Trollope's story issue from this setting.

Ballycloran House is a symbol of the ruin and disaster which has come to its inhabitants. Larry Macdermot, the father, is in the last stages of physical decline, accelerated by addiction to whisky. His daughter Feemy is 'ardent and energetic, if she had aught to be ardent about ... addicted to novels ... passionately fond of dancing'; 'with all his faults, Thady [the son] was perhaps a better man than his father', but the circumstances of his life make him ever 'more gloomy and more tyrannical'. (ch. 2)

The other crucial character is the hated Protestant excise officer, Ussher. His twin successes against illicit poteen-distilling and in gaining Feemy's love are the engines of the novel's disasters. The peasants are goaded into conspiracy against him, Thady is persuaded to join them by their accounts of Ussher's conduct towards Feemy. Trollope succinctly states the significance of what was happening: 'The fall of high and fine feelings, when once commenced, is soon accomplished, even when the fall is from a higher dignity than those of Thady's ever reached.'

Thady surprises Ussher, about to take Feemy away. He strikes him a violent blow and Ussher falls dead. Trollope spares us nothing in hideous immediacy – Thady had 'shattered his brains .... He had felt the skull give way beneath the strike.' (ch. 20) The chapter is ironically entitled 'How Captain Ussher Succeeded'. The brutality here is matched, even exceeded, elsewhere, particularly in the harrowing account of the ambush of the hated attorney,

Keegan, and the amputation of his foot with an axe. One suspects that in some of these instances Trollope is writing of incidents he knew of, but he does not always dispose them well or tell them economically. This applies particularly with the long trial scene. It is too nearly verbatim either to sustain suspense about Thady's fate or to emphasise the sympathy which surrounded him. The suspense comes out much better in the account of the protracted deliberations before verdict, and the sympathy is more effectively evoked, without any trace of exaggeration, in Father McGrath's ministrations to the condemned prisoner.

The scene between Thady and Feemy immediately after the murder is memorable. He is aware of his deed and its all but certain consequences; he would kiss her before he tries to escape:

> Fanny shuddered horribly as she felt his hand upon her. Thady quickly withdrew it, for he saw it was all covered with blood; Feemy, however, had seen it, for she screamed loudly – she had raised her head to answer, and at last she said – 'Kiss you! no; I hate you – you're a murdherer; You've murdhered him because you knew I loved him'. (ch. 21)

Feemy is pregnant (Trollope has given several hints about this before we know for certain). She sustains her animosity against Thady, but it appears in the trial that her evidence may be used to help him. She is to be the last witness but, terribly changed in appearance and strength, she is destined never to testify. Before she is called, she collapses and dies. It is a feeble end to a character all too feebly conceived. Feemy is too faint. By contrast, Thady with his sullen hatred of Ussher makes us feel that he is doomed from the start. Trollope informs the novel with a finely realised tension between the occasional outbursts of fragile gaiety and the entrapping powers of debt, drink, poverty and fecklessness in Irish life. In this situation Thady has no chance at all.

The next work, *The Kellys and the O'Kellys* (1848), shows a decided advance in Trollope's abilities as a novelist and deserves to be better known. It does not possess the tensions of the earlier novel, but, it must be added, it is not afflicted, either, with the barely relevant *longueurs* of its predecessor. Trollope here uses the double plot that later becomes so familiar. In one line he traces the trials and triumph of the love-affair between Francis O'Kelly, Lord Ballindine, and the heiress, Fanny Wyndham, ward of Lord Cashel, who intends to make her the wife of his dissolute son, Lord Kilcullen. In the other he tells us of Martin Kelly and Anty (Anastasia) Lynch another heiress, joint inheritor with her brother, Barry, another dissolute character, who in seeking to gain control of her portion tries first to get her certified insane and then to murder her. Anty is protected by Mrs Kelly, the most lively character in the book. Martin falls in love with Anty after originally planning to marry her only for her money.

The novel is firmly set in the Ireland that Trollope knew. It begins, for example, with an actual historical situation, O'Connell's trial, early in 1844; and in the course of a few paragraphs we feel the passion, perhaps it might be better called the frenzy, of the time. Trollope then distances it with a paragraph of comment, indicating the speedy realisation by many of the participants of the unwisdom of their attitude. And there is the shrewdness of the author's own remark inserted in all this: 'Nothing ever so strengthened the love of the Irish for, and the obedience of the Irish to O'Connell, as his imprisonment; nothing ever so weakened his power over them as his unexpected enfranchisement.' (ch. 1) But though the novel begins in this fashion, it is but little concerned with actual social conditions, by contrast with its precursor. It is none the worse for that.

The novel is quintessentially Irish in the way it grasps and presents the idiosyncrasies of the social structure there in the mid-nineteenth century. Nowhere is this more evident, perhaps because it was so easy to achieve, than in the presentation of two minor characters, Protestant clergymen. One is Armstrong, the parson of Ballindine, 'good-natured and charitable [who] lived on friendly terms with all his neighbours', the ludicrous nature of whose situation Trollope remarked upon with mild humour:

> How could a Protestant rector be a good parish clergyman, with but one old lady and her daughters, for the exercise of his clerical energies and talents? He constantly lauded the zeal of St. Paul for proselytism; but, as he himself once observed, even St. Paul had never had to deal with the obstinacy of an Irish Roman Catholic. (ch. 21)

In this brief comment Trollope neatly combines the man's real difficulties and the fact that he made the most of them. The other cleric is O'Joscelyn, Cashel's chaplain, 'a most ultra and even furious Protestant. He was, by principle, a charitable man to his neighbours;

but he hated popery, and he carried the feeling to such a length, that he almost hated Papists.' (ch. 38) A significant segment of the history of Ireland is condensed in this short statement.

Lord Cashel mistook Armstrong, believing that all parsons must be like O'Joscelyn. Cashel is a triumph of characterisation as a blinkered, unimaginative person, totally ignorant of his own defects. Trollope is careful to demonstrate that he is not an evil man, rather indeed one whose motives may seem worse than they really are. He rejects Lord Ballindine as a match for Fanny Wyndham, his ward, on the grounds of his profligacy. He does so just when he has heard of Fanny's vastly increased fortune, following the death of her brother, and also of his own son (Kilcullen)'s profligacy, vastly greater than that of Ballindine. Trollope comments:

> Poor Lord Cashel! He wished to be honest to his ward; and yet to save his son, and his own pocket at the same time, at her expense .... The devil and mammon were too strong for him, particularly coming as they did, half hidden beneath the gloss of parental affection. (ch. 28)

Only 'half hidden', it will be noted; the conscience does not have to be wicked; it is often more interesting when it is merely frail.

The old man is more interesting than the young people. Frank Ballindine is careless, but we are to assume a nobility that will blossom with his union with Fanny Wyndham. She is resolute, like many another Trollope heroine, but also like them rather too much in the background to be very impressive. Kilcullen is a *roué*, but, though he obeys his father in proposing to Fanny, even he has sufficient honesty in him to realise that there is no point in such action in face of Fanny's firm refusal. He also has courage and good nature sufficient to tell his father that it is Ballindine, and not he, who has won Fanny's heart.

The racy quality of Irish life comes out in the Kelly part of the story. It is there in Martin Kelly's candour about his intentions towards Anty Lynch. (ch. 3) It is there supremely in the fiery outbursts and determined protectiveness that Mrs Kelly exercises over Anty against the predatory intentions of her brother:

> 'Lies!', screamed the widow; 'av' you say lies to me again, in this house, I'll smash the bones of ye myself, with the broom-handle. Lies, indeed! and from you Barry Lynch, the biggest liar in all Connaught – not to talk of robber and ruffian!' (ch. 7)

Yet, paradoxically, good as this is, Trollope's faithfulness in rendering Irish idiom and accent may have been partly responsible for the novel's lack of success. As with Scott and Kipling, such dialectal faithfulness can be overwhelming in excessive doses.

In this novel we have what is to become the familiar Trollopian tale of love and money, a tale, be it said immediately, of manifold variations. In later works the examination will be more subtle, but in this Trollope has conveyed a sense of vigorous life and powerful, even vehement, passions set against a background that strikes the reader as rich and authentic.

His years in Ireland were to provide Trollope with the material for another novel, *Castle Richmond*, which, however, would not be written and published until 1860. In the final chapter Trollope wrote: 'I might have called this "A Tale of the Famine Year in Ireland"', and Michael Sadleir thinks it is merely a 'documented essay on distress'. (1961, p. 144) It is this, but it is also something more; alas, at times too much more. The main plot is economically constructed. The staid Herbert Fitzgerald and his cousin Owen, a young man with a reputation for wildness, are rivals for the hand of Lady Clara Desmond. Herbert's father is being blackmailed by his wife's first husband, a worthless character presumed dead at the time of the marriage of Sir Thomas and Lady Fitzgerald. Herbert looks like losing both his estate and his beloved, and the pressure of the blackmail does, in fact, kill Sir Thomas. Owen, however, refuses to take the estate that now appears to be his. The outcome is not unexpected: the 'husband', Mollett, is discovered to have been married before his bigamous union as Talbot with Lady Fitzgerald, and so all is well.

The appearance of Prendergast, the Fitzgeralds' man of business, in the middle of the novel with his belief in Mollett's story, but 'it was necessary that this should be proved' (ch. 19), gives the first hint of a release for the stricken family. It does not much matter that we know this: Trollope maintains the suspense. He might, however, have done better, had he improved his pace. This is altogether too leisurely, and the other strand of the plot, the rivalry for Clara's hand and the developments arising in this regard from the consequences of the blackmail, is not sufficiently interesting. The two young men are 'wooden' and Lady Clara, with and perhaps in spite of her admirable single-minded devotion to Herbert, is little more than a cipher. Even the potential inherent in the rivalry of

Owen and Herbert, though described at length, is never realised: Trollope never ventures beyond the bounds of the conventional.

Of the other characters, Aunt Lotty is a bigotedly Protestant minor version of Jane Austen's Aunt Norris in *Mansfield Park,* while the two Molletts, Matthew and Aby, father and son, have about them much of that melodramatic villainy which we more usually associate with Dickens. They are vicious, but also slightly comic and therefore never wholly fearful – that is, to us. They are fearful enough to Sir Thomas, whose taciturn, withdrawn and gloomy state of mind Trollope conveys perfectly. Aby Mollett's prolonged and merciless bullying of Sir Thomas, his 'freshening up of the old gentleman' (ch. 15) as he at first calls it, is a masterpiece of its kind. The contrast between the father and the son is one which both Sir Thomas and the reader makes. The scene itself presents another contrast of old and young, Sir Thomas and Aby, oppressed and oppressor, cultivated man and criminal boor. Mollett turns the screw of Sir Thomas's agony as he openly refers to Lady Fitzgerald's position. He eventually states his demands:

> Poor Sir Thomas was now almost broken down. His head swam round and round, and he felt that he was in a whirlpool from which there was no escape. He had heard the sum named, and knew that he had no power of raising it ....
>
> But Aby had not yet done ... 'There's one other point, Sir Thomas,' he continued, 'and hif I can bring you and your good lady to my way of thinking in that, why, we may all be comfortable for all that is come and gone. You've a daughter, Hemmeline.'

That is too much for Sir Thomas who requires him to go.

The characterisation of Sir Thomas is an achievement within what is often a difficult area, namely, the successful portrayal of a predominantly passive and suffering character. Another success, though of a lesser order, is that of the imperious Lady Desmond, intent on a successful marriage for her daughter, an intent arising from ambitions matched only by her poverty. That is why Herbert is preferred, but when his prospects appear to have changed, so also have Lady Desmond's views. He is callously rejected without a word of sympathy for his family in their distress. 'That match no longer suited her greed, and she could throw from her without a struggle to her feelings the suitor that was now poor and the family of the suitor neither grand nor powerful.' (ch. 26) This is con-

vincing enough: what it misses and what Trollope suggests elsewhere but never fully develops is Lady Desmond's fierce materna
passion, without which her concern for Clara's wealth and position
is meaningless.

We come finally to the famine which takes up the greater par
of several chapters. Trollope's description bears out the authenticity
which he suggests in the first sentence of the first of these: 'They
who were in the south of Ireland during the winter of 1846-47 wil
not readily forget the agony of that period.' (ch. 7) There follow
an analysis of the changes the famine brought in its train. Trollope
felt that

> It was not the absence of the absentees that did the damage,
> but the presence of those they left behind them ... a class who
> looked to be gentlemen living on their property, but who
> should have earned their bread by the work of their brain, or,
> failing that, by the sweat of their brow.

These men were the rack-renters, tenants themselves who sub-let a
exorbitant rents which reduced the peasants to abject poverty and
agriculture to a single-crop subsistence pattern. Trollope, however
praises the relief efforts of the landed classes and the clergy, th
former in spite of the fact that their own incomes were decimated
by the tenants' inability or refusal to pay their rents at the very time
that poor-rates levied on the landlords had soared.

The most moving passages, as in such near-contemporary novel
as those of Mrs Gaskell, are those in which Trollope presents u
directly with scene and dialogue – the scene, for example, which
confronts Herbert Fitzgerald as he enters a cabin: no fire, no
furniture and, squatting on the wet floor, a woman with a child in
her arms, both covered only in rags, dirty, the child with sores, the
mother in the last stages of apathetic misery (ch. 33); or the repor
which comes straight from human suffering in such speeches as:-

> 'It's the worst vittles iver a man tooked into the inside of
> him ....'
> 'It's as wake as cats we all is ....'
> 'And the childer is worse, yer honor ....'
> 'Six mouths to feed; and what's eight pennorth of yally meal
> among such a lot as that; let alone the Sundays, then there's
> nothing?' (ch. 25)

Trollope believed that good had come out of evil. (ch. 31) In hi first reference to the famine he deprecated the attribution of the suffering to God's anger and also the use of prayers to deflect it. Indeed, he seems to have found the famine more explicable in terms of God's mercy:

> When men by their folly and by the shortness of their vision have brought upon themselves penalties which seem to be overwhelming ... then God raises his hand, not in anger, but in mercy, and by his wisdom does for us that for which our own wisdom has been insufficient ... If this beneficent agency did not from time to time disencumber our crowded places, we should even be living in narrow alleys with stinking gutters, and supply of water at the minimum. (ch. 7)

Trollope was a realist, but he was also a sympathetic realist: 'Those who saw [the famine's] course and watched its victims, will not readily forget what they saw.'

Not until late in life did Trollope again return to Ireland for a novel. *An Eye for an Eye* was written in 1870 but not published until 1879. It is altogether a more subtle work than its Irish predecessors, though we notice likenesses in such characters as the possessive mother (Mrs O'Hara and Lady Desmond) and the seduced girl (Kate O'Hara and Feemy Macdermot). Fred Neville, Lieutenant of the 20th Hussars and heir to the earldom of Scroope, seduces Kate O'Hara and is then haunted by the dilemma of his double promise – to marry her and yet to be faithful to his uncle's request not to make her Countess of Scroope. He seeks escape from marriage by pressing his inability to marry someone with such a rascally father as Captain O'Hara turns out to be. But this is a mere excuse. The end is melodramatic, with the maddened mother pushing Fred over the cliffs to his death.

The plot is commonplace and at the end bathetic, and it may therefore seem strange that I have called it a more subtle book than its predecessors. It is so in its realisation of the central character, a type found frequently in Trollope's later work – the weak young man who means better than he does, who allows himself to drift into a situation whose depths he has not recognised and whose perils he lives to regret. Fred's uncle, the Earl, is a shadowy figure, almost a recluse, and the gloom of his house is the mark of the man. Scroope does not appeal to Fred, but its way of life is one that dignifies its master and makes demands on his heir. Fred's dilemma is between the claims of duty and rank and those of love and moral obligation. The Earl puts the contrast, not explicitly but yet very obviously, between himself and Fred when he says:

> You do not suppose that wealth is to be given to you, and a great name, and all the appanages and power of nobility in order that you may eat more and drink more, and lie softer than others. It is because some think so, and act upon such base thoughts that the only hereditary peerage left in the world is in danger of encountering the ill will of the people. (I, ch. 12)

A page or two earlier Trollope has summarised Fred's character: 'He was not a villain – simply a self-indulgent spoiled young man who had realised to himself no idea of duty in life.' The passage continues: 'He never once told himself that Kate should be his mistress' and with aptly romantic fantasy, 'His yacht should be made a floating bower for her delight'. At the very moment that, recalled to Scroope, he should be realising his responsibilities, he writes her an indiscreetly affectionate letter. Then, hardly has he seduced her but 'her pricelessness in his eyes was gone for ever' and he is seeking a means of escape by use of her father's reputation. But he is no unfeeling reprobate; he recognises the damning paradox – 'Having dishonoured this woman's [Mrs O'Hara's] daughter, should he shelter himself behind the dishonour of her husband?' (II, ch. 3) Trollope then in a single sentence elaborates the confusion of Fred's mind and soul: 'That he meant to do so ultimately is true; but at the present moment such a task would have required a harder heart than his.'

Kate O'Hara is just a silly girl. Her letter (II, ch. 6) shows it and her welcome to Fred, 'Am I still to call you Fred? ... I was thinking whether I would call you – my Lord' (II, ch. 10), emphasises it, so that when Trollope states: 'To her he was godlike, noble, excellent, all but holy. He was the man whom Fortune, more than kind, had sent to her to be the joy of her existence, the fountain of her life, the strong staff for her weakness', one can only suspect deliberate over-writing to suggest her starry-eyed romanticising. The mother and the priest are a different proposition: Fred has good reason to fear them. On our first introduction to Mrs O'Hara she is associated at length with the steep cliffs, the rough sea and the wild winds. (I, ch. 5) She is aggressively protective towards her daughter and calculating in her designs on Fred Neville. It is

Father Marty who introduces Neville to the O'Haras and his one purpose in this is clear: 'Why shouldn't she be his wife? How many of them young officers take Irish wives home with 'em every year.' (I, ch. 6) He uses every variety of verbal coercion against Fred and in one scene we are treated to the comedy of his upbraidings whilst Fred is wondering, crassly, whether Father Marty might be persuaded to act as go-between for one of his impractical schemes of accommodation. (II, ch. 2) Marty's calculation is mingled with genuine feeling for Kate. It contrasts unfavourably, however, with the restrained and conscience-stricken questionings of the Countess of Scroope, aware of the conflicting and irreconcilable demands on Fred and the advice she had given him not to marry Kate:

> In the agony of her spirit she threw herself upon her knees and implored the Lord to pardon her and to guide her. But even while kneeling before the throne of heaven she could not drive the pride of birth out of her heart. That the young Earl might be saved from the damning sin and also from the polluting marriage – that was the prayer she prayed.
> (II, ch. 7)

The claims on Fred Neville were both absolute, neither completely irreproachable, yet irreconcilable to each other, and he himself incapable of responding to the demands of either. To the extent that he has conveyed this Trollope has succeeded in elaborating what would otherwise have been a hackneyed theme.

Trollope ended his career as he had begun – with a novel about Ireland. Stimulated by his own recent visit and by the renewed troubles, he wrote *The Landleaguers,* incomplete with only forty-nine of its intended sixty chapters and published posthumously in 1883. The new civil troubles in Ireland naturally interested him with his long association with that country. *The Landleaguers,* like *Castle Richmond,* attempts to combine story and history. Sadleir described it as a 'sad account of wretched actuality in which characterisation is submerged in floods of almost literal fact'. (Sadleir, 1961, p. 144) Certainly, a chapter such as 41 is pure fact and comment (Bradford Booth has surmised that it may have been intended as the preface (Booth, 1958, pp. 110-11)), and elsewhere there is plenty of description of contemporary events, but *The Landleaguers* differs from *Castle Richmond* in that the events have a more direct bearing on the lives of the main characters than in the earlier work. This is because, whilst the aristocracy contributed to the relief in the famine times of *Castle Richmond,* in the land agitation they were the victims; their lives were affected and altered by it.

Trollope shows a distinct bias. He places the blame for recent troubles emphatically on American influence and money. He repeats his belief that the famine had been a God-directed means of remedying man's ill rule and that 'the country was on its road to a fair amount of prosperity, when the tocsin was sounded in America, and Home Rule became the cry'. He announces his final break with the Liberals because of their Home Rule policy, and with his characteristically sound common sense he recognises the realities of economics and politics:

> The tenant who undertakes to pay for land that which the
> land will not enable him to pay had better go, – under
> whatever pressure.... Men finding their power, and beginning
> to learn how much might be exacted from a yielding
> Government, hardly knew how to moderate their aspirations.

The Land Law of 1881, he felt, was false economics and feeble politics. The Landleaguers were being allowed to operate successfully by threat and revenge. 'In order that the truth of this may be seen and made apparent, the present story is told.' (all ch. 41)

The main plot centres on the Landleaguers' persecution of the Jones family, beginning with the flooding of their meadow land. The most interesting member of this family (and rare in Trollope) is a child, the altogether too precocious ten-year-old, Florian, who has become a Roman Catholic and who knows something about the crime. Trollope notices the new generation of 'political' priests and Florian's lack of frankness ('It's a great thing in our religion to be able to hold your tongue' – ch. 2). Eventually, Florian confesses what he knows, but on his journey to give evidence he is shot dead. The other members of the family serve to show the suffering inflicted by the boycott, whilst, in addition, they supply the love-interest of the novel. This latter is tedious enough. Frank, the elder son, is in love with Rachel O'Mahony, but will not marry her whilst his family's troubles persist. In the meantime, she follows a successful career as a singer and is pursued by two unconvincing characters of the theatre, Mr Mahomet M. Moss, an all-too-conventional Victorian seducer, and Lord Castlewell, an aristocratic nonentity. Her father personifies the new American-Irishman who, in Trollope's view, was causing so much trouble. There are two Jones sisters – Ada, in love with the policeman Captain Clayton, and Edith, for whom he eventually declares his affection.

The tale maintains a certain tension until the death of Florian, but after that it is both slow and disconnected. It includes more assassinations. Rachel's history in London meanders on to the point where she rejects Castlewell and in a melodramatic scene stabs Moss. Clayton himself is shot, but not fatally. A postscript note by Trollope's son states that his father intended Clayton to marry Edith Jones, Rachel to marry Frank and the assassin, Lax, to be hanged.

The Landleaguers is a failure. This may be, in part, the result of Trollope's ill-health, but whatever the reason, its weaknesses are everywhere apparent. Trollope was more interested in the politics than in the tale he had to tell. The tale was thin, anyway, so thin that the later narrative interest lies more in the ridiculous Rachel O'Mahony story than in the main plot. The novel represents a sad end to the career of a fine story-teller. The skill remains, but it is taxed unfairly in being made to work so hard on material so poor, about which the author obviously felt so little.

3

The Way They Lived Then

(The New Zealander; The Struggles of Brown, Jones and Robinson; The Way We Live Now; The American Senator; Hunting Sketches)

In recent years Trollope's reputation has received a boost from the rediscovery of *The Way We Live Now* which has been read as some more or less left-wing indictment of Victorian society. It is nothing of the sort, but it is an indictment of certain manifestations of that society, and not the only one which Trollope made either. All the works in this chapter, with the exception of the last, are criticisms of society. He found much that was tawdry in many areas of his world, but to measure the extent of his dislike and indeed to understand the underlying moral and social basis of all his work we must first of all look at those he admired and loved – the landed gentry. Theirs was a world with a well-integrated social fabric and set of accepted *mores*. When these began to be questioned, the individual was liable to lose himself in a flux of moral relativism.

Trollope wrote in the last fine Indian summer of the landed gentry's ascendancy. The superior forces of industrial and commercial wealth and a widening franchise were at their destructive work. As Bagehot noted, 'the aristocracy cannot lead the old life ...They are ruled by a stronger power. They suffer from the tendency of all modern society to raise the average, and ... to lower the summit.' (1904, p. 94) The decreasing profitability of land could no longer sustain their way of life and what had thus begun the pernicious effects of estate duty in the early twentieth century would inexorably complete.

There thus disappeared a way of life which, as Bagehot noted, centred upon deference, 'the habitual respect which the upper classes, in particular the landed classes, were accustomed to receive from the community at large'. (Thompson, 1971, p. 184. I should like to acknowledge my indebtedness to this excellent study in much of what follows in this survey of English landed society.) It was a world in which authority was firmly established, universally acknowledged and mildly administered. As Professor Thompson goes on to say, 'the real heart went out of deference with the passing of the age of Trollope'.

This was the world Trollope knew and depicted so lovingly and so well. It was headed by the landed aristocracy, dukes and earls, the lords of rolling acres. Some, like the Devonshires, had, besides their vast agricultural acreages, valuable London estates, mining rights and the ground-rents of developing resorts like Eastbourne, whilst the Duke of Portland's income in 1850 was £180,000 per year. Next to the aristocracy came the gentry or squirearchy, followed by the yeomen and tenant farmers. Nobles and squires had often lived on their land for several generations or even centuries. If, like the Greshams in *Doctor Thorne* or a Carbury of Carbury (*The Way We Live Now*), the period was of centuries, they might look with scorn on newcomers who merely reckoned by generations, people like the Longestaffes or even the noble de Courcys.

Ownership of land gave status and influence. Hence the wealthy *parvenu* sought to establish himself as a country gentleman. A railway king like George Hudson could buy Londesborough Hall in the East Riding of Yorkshire; a Roger Scatcherd (in *Doctor Thorne*) would build his own house on the estate he had bought, or a Melmotte might attempt to buy his way into Pickering Park at a knock-down price at the expense of the impoverished Squire Longstaffe. Once on his estate, such a man would seek to find a place in county society. One way to do this was to make himself sufficiently acceptable to be made a Justice of the Peace: another was to marry his daughters into old-established families. Often enough, these latter were looking around to recoup their fallen fortunes. The Monson heir of the 1850s was told that his aunt would like to see him 'married to a nice girl with a good fortune'. We remember that the aunt in *Doctor Thorne*, Lady de Courcy, is insistent that 'Frank must marry money'.

The influence of the landed classes was exercised through their possession of power at local and national level. The great families were often not only represented in the House of Lords, but also, until the widening franchise lessened and ultimately extinguished it, had several seats in the House of Commons in their gift. Phineas Finn sat for two such pocket-boroughs. Even till late in the century, however, the influence of the local landowner, especially if he were a peer, might still count for much, and Trollope makes the Duchess of Omnium's attempt, and the Duke's refusal, to use it of some importance in the Silverbridge election in *The Prime Minister*. Outside politics, the landed aristocracy and gentry exercised widespread patronage in the Church (the parson was often a younger brother of the squire) and in the Civil Service, and many a younger son held a commission in the Army. Local influence came through the magisterial bench and, of course, through the actual ownership of land and control thereby of the tenantry from the most prosperous farmer down to the meanest labourer. It is this ethos that Trollope everywhere reflects, whether it be in the nice social gradations of the *fête champêtre* at Ullathorne (*Barchester Towers*) or the frustrations of a Marquis of Trowbridge over a miller who unfortunately lives just outside his own estate and control (*The Vicar of Bullhampton*).

Not least in the armoury of their influence was the close-knit relationship between landed families. They might marry outside the clan to fortify their fortunes, but, generally speaking, they inter-married. Aristocratic matrons arranged marriages as in the case of the eventual Lady Glencora Palliser. The eldest son mattered most because he would inherit both estate and title. Such expectation might lead to great profligacy as in the case of Lady Glencora's son, Silverbridge (*The Duke's Children*). The system also led to friction and discontent, but by maintaining the estate inviolate from father to son it ensured the continuing place of the landed family in English life. That is what death-duties and the dissolution of the great estates destroyed.

Society revolved round the great houses with their hunting and shooting, their garden parties and balls. The great house was the hub of the community, having not only the estate within its care under the steward, but also employing a large indoor staff under the head butler and an outdoor staff stretching from the head gardener and gamekeeper down to labouring boys, all of them either living in or housed in estate cottages. Each had his place, amid a host of dependants, and possessed thereby security and a role.

The gentry commanded respect not only or mostly by virtue of their position but mainly by their character and values. The atmosphere of life in an aristocratic household instilled a social and moral code. I cannot improve on Professor Thompson's summary:

Honour, dignity, integrity, considerateness, courtesy and
chivalry were all virtues essential to an English gentleman, and

> they all derived in part from the nature of English country
> life. Not only did the stability and permanence of country
> society foster the subordination of personal whims to these
> traditional and enduring values. But also the intimate nature
> of country society, its lack of openings for anonymity; its
> necessary exposure to the public eye of many of the doings of
> the landowners, called forth these very virtues which made
> for good feelings, neighbourliness and absence of friction.
> (1971, p. 16)

This is Trollope's world. This is what gives his novels their firm
moral sub-structure. In such well-mapped country, temptations to
wander are easy to identify and fascinating to contemplate. They
are all the more interesting when the signposts are just beginning to
disappear. By the last years of Trollope's life 'an air of rich vulgarity
and indecent opulence was beginning to permeate society'.
(Thompson, 1971, p. 300) That was bad enough, but it was worse
still when the deceit of speculators lured none-too-scrupulous but
impoverished aristocrats into mistaking, as Trollope made them do
with Melmotte, a charlatan's fake house of cards for a palace of
largesse.

The first work to be considered here, though written in 1855, that
is, at the beginning of Trollope's career as a successful novelist, has
only recently seen the light. *The New Zealander* (edited by N. J.
Hall, Oxford, 1972) is not a novel, but a panoramic survey of
England some two decades before *The Way We Live Now*. The title
is taken from Macaulay's prophecy of the 'New Zealander standing
on the ruins of London Bridge' and, in the words of Longman's
reader, the object was 'to show how England may be saved from
the ruin that now threatens her'. (Sadleir, 1961, p. 169) He advised
against publication and that was the last that was heard of the work
until its recent appearance. It was not, however, the last that
Trollope did with it, for he used a long passage on the establishment, proceedings and results of a parliamentary committee for the
chapter entitled 'The Parliamentary Committee' (ch. 32) in *The
Three Clerks*, and Mr Hall opines that the missing chapter on Trade
may have been incorporated in the early part of *The Struggles of
Brown, Jones and Robinson*. (1972, p. xxi)

Longman's reader also remarked that 'All the good points have
already been treated of by Mr Carlyle, of whose *Latter Day*

29

Pamphlets this work, *both in style and matter*, is a most feeble imitation.' Trollope would not have disowned the affinity. In the *Autobiography*, talking of *The Way We Live Now*, and referring to the dismissal of such views, he says ironically of his contemporaries: 'But then we do not put very much faith in Mr Carlyle', adding 'It is regarded simply as Carlylism to say that the English-speaking world is growing worse from day to day.' (ch. 20) Yet Trollope, despite his manifest imitation of Carlyle in various passages of *The New Zealander* with its sharp exhortations, exclamations, commands and rhetorical questions and its use of the archaic second-person singular, is no mere slavish follower of the master. He does not have 'the loudness and extravagance of [his] lamentations, the wailing and gnashing of teeth' (*Autobiography*, ch. 20); that was part of his failure in the eyes of Longman's reader. He does, however, share Carlyle's belief in a natural aristocracy 'Take any sporting marquis who is that and *nothing else*, and any great working Railway Contractor, and it will be found that of the two, the Railway Contractor has the most to say towards the ruling of the country' – (*The New Zealander*, ch. 2); hence the admiration that one can detect for the in many ways repulsive Sir Roger Scatcherd. Like Carlyle, he sees the task of aristocracy as the due governance of labour and, like him again, he rejects the cash-nexus or money profit, as he calls it, as the sole relationship of master and workman.

He does not, however, hold the past in the same unqualified reverence as Carlyle. In an article in the very first volume of the periodical, *St Paul's Magazine*, 1867, which Virtue invited him to edit, Trollope considered Carlylism and noted that the 'age from which we have so sadly degenerated' (p. 303) (to use his ironic phrase) was one in which 'buccaneering' was rather common and that men like Gladstone, Russell and Derby have to be acknowledged at least 'as patriotic as was Cecil, and ... infinitely more honest and true'. (ibid., p. 304) But, though this was so, the burden of Trollope's complaint was just that in many spheres of the national life the situation was quite different. The epigraph and the conclusion of *The New Zealander* is the quotation 'It's gude to be honest and true', and by the time he reached *The Way We Live Now* he was overwhelmed by the shamelessly impudent flauntings of a new 'dishonesty magnificent in its proportions'. (*Autobiography*, ch. 20)

In the several chapters of *The New Zealander* Trollope covers the press, the law, the Army and Navy, the Church, Parliament and the

Crown, society and the arts. Many of his criticisms are familiar from the novels. The aspersions on the law remind us of *Orley Farm*; what Trollope regards as the bamboozling of the jury and the bullying of witnesses by Mr Allwinde, the equivalent here of Chaffanbrass in the novels (ch. 4), is just another instance of his failure to understand the adversary system of English legal pleading. Similarly, his remarks on the mock hostilities of parliamentary polemics (ch. 7) anticipate what he has to say in the political novels, whilst the case of Stonor (ch. 7), convicted for bribery in promising to pay a publican's bill outstanding from a previous election, is reproduced in Romer of *Doctor Thorne*. (ch. 22) When Trollope tells us that 'Men think, and speak, and act the Times newspaper' (ch. 3), it is not only the *Jupiter* of *The Warden* that comes to mind, but, more generally, the insidious power of the press, whether in influencing the rise and fall of governments as in *Framley Parsonage* or dredging the gutters of politics in Quintus Slide's 'The People's Banner' of the semi-political novels. He attacks the Sabbatarianism and the anti-Romanism of the Low Church Mr Everscreech (ch. 6), demonstrating indeed the anti-Romanism more fiercely than in any of the novels, but he also castigates the fripperies of Tractarian ritualism (ch. 6) with a fervour entirely absent, for instance, from his portrayal of Oriel in *Doctor Thorne*.

There are other things, however, that do not figure so much in the novels. For instance, what is often there implicit, the dullness of English society, is here openly and vigorously criticised. The *vignette* of Mrs Gingham Walker's 'at home' is in the best Trollopian manner, with its awkwardnesses and its abortive attempts at conversation. (ch. 10) 'As to that relaxation and unbending of the bow which should be the special comfort of all social hours – who ever dreams of finding such in an English drawing room?' As with Mrs Furnival in *Orley Farm*, far better those early days before Gingham Walker's prosperity and their rise in the world. Trollope is protesting against a society whose members are not equipped to fulfil the role to which they aspire, but he is also criticising them for their presumption in aspiring. As always, he sees the proper social distinctions, not just as mere outward show, not just as matters of wealth, power and status. In arguing that there should be a charge for admission to the National Gallery at least on certain days of the week, he refutes the view that this might be called class-distinction. He believes that 'four fifths care nothing for the pictures', lacking the education and refinement necessary to appreciate them. He

31

continues: 'This is not at present a popular doctrine. It is now in vogue to speak of the poor as if they were in all things equal to the rich except in their poverty.' (ch. 12) Trollope finds this just as dishonest as many of the other things he has considered, but he also adds: 'God forbid that we should use such an argument to the injury of the poor. But God forbid also that we should injure any class by a false argument in favour of the poor.' (ch. 12). Clear-eyed, unsentimental – and downright honest.

The Struggles of Brown, Jones and Robinson was intended as 'a satire on the ways of trade'. (*Autobiography*, ch. 9) The fate of this work was little better than that of its predecessor. It was serialised first in the *Cornhill* in 1861, but Smith, Elder did not choose to publish it in book-form until 1870 'and then it passed into the world of letters *sub silentio*'. (ibid.) Trollope himself admitted that he 'attempted a style for which [he] was certainly not qualified', but he added: 'Still I think that there was some good fun in it, but I have heard no one else express such an opinion.'

The tale is told largely from the standpoint of Robinson and consists in the brief and ill-starred history of a haberdashery firm, basing its commercial practices on the new-found 'principles' of large credit and spectacular advertising, with the usual Trollopian love-interest in the rival suits of Robinson and a butcher, Brisket, for the hand of Maryanne Brown. In this sub-plot there is 'some good fun', to use the novelist's own phrase, not least in the opposition of the burly butcher and his more diminutive and fragile opponent. The reiterated self-comparisons with Hamlet give to Robinson's passion an amusingly inflated artificiality and his final rejection of Maryanne achieves a fine ridiculous sense of pomposity, masquerading as dignity:

> When first I did so at the dancing room, I was afraid of your brute strength .... When I wrote that paper the second time .... I was afraid. My heart was high on other matters, and why should I have sacrificed myself? Now I renounce her again; but I am not afraid, – for my heart is high on nothing. (ch. 18)

But dignity soon gives way to slapstick when Robinson, terrier-like, 'flew at the butcher's throat'. These two characters are simple enough. Ironically, it is with the more developed portrait of Maryanne that we are less satisfied. She is obviously a girl 'with an eye for the main chance', prepared even to contemplate ousting her father from his home, but, despite repeated comparisons with Regan, we do not get a sufficiently vivid sense of her ruthless self-seeking. In any case, it was probably a mistake to include a character of such apparently purposeful intensity in a novel of this kind. The other possibility is that she also was intended as a burlesque character and that the references to Regan are to show that. If so, Trollope has indeed fallen heavily between two stools.

It is, however, the satire on trading methods which is least satisfactory of all. What Trollope regarded as small-scale trading seems generally, even though it was cheap and nasty, to have provided occasion for comedy. Moulder and Kantwise illustrate this best in *Orley Farm*, but the grandiose dreams of little men in *The Struggles of Brown, Jones and Robinson* are also typical. The most grandiose are those of Robinson himself with the painting of the premises at 81 Bishopsgate Street in the latest colour, magenta, calling the shop Magenta House and adopting the inane slogan 'Nine Times Nine'. Then there is the sensation-serial of the defalcation of Johnson of Manchester on his contract to supply printed cloth, a whole succession of false announcements to stimulate interest in the firm. Robinson even writes the advertisement for the firm's ultimate receivers in bankruptcy: 'Wasteful and Impetuous Sale'. By contrast with the older man, Brown, Robinson is the advocate of extensive credit: 'When you order goods, do so as though the bank was at your back. Look your victim full in the face, and write down your long numbers without a falter in your pen.' (ch. 5) Much of the firm's failure seems due to Jones and his wife, Maryanne's sister, who embezzle the takings, but again these characters are neither drawn in sufficient detail nor endowed with sufficient motivation for us to do anything more than take them on unwilling trust. Robinson is a naïve character who by the end has apparently learnt nothing and forgotten nothing. Again, we seem to confront Trollope's divided mind on the matter. What he is dealing with is too serious for the tone he adopts through a narrator, who is himself, however stupidly, one of the villains of the piece.

Trollope's divided mind had concentrated itself wonderfully by the time he made another attempt at a similar subject in *The Way We Live Now* (1875). The *Autobiography*, introducing the section on *The Way We Live Now*, shows that Trollope was still turning

33

towards Carlyle and his pessimism and, though he dismissed much of Carlyle and Ruskin as disproportionately sensationalist, he continues:

> Nevertheless, a certain class of dishonesty, dishonesty
> magnificent in its proportions, and climbing into high places,
> has become at the same time so rampant and so splendid that
> there seems to be reason for fearing that men and women will
> be taught to feel that dishonesty, if it can become splendid will
> cease to be abominable. (ch. 20)

That dishonesty is embodied in Melmotte. In choosing him Trollope pinpointed the significant change that had happened in England which Disraeli also noted when he wrote in *Endymion* (1880): 'Forty years ago the great financiers had not that commanding, not to say predominant, position in society which they possess at present.' (ch. 38) Melmotte's feasts are frequented by the 'leaders of the fashion [who] know, – at any rate they believe, – that he is what he is because he has been a swindler greater than other swindlers'. (ch. 55) These words are spoken by Melmotte's polar opposite in the novel, the staunch country squire, Roger Carbury. With pointed juxtaposition Trollope follows the paragraph in which they occur with:

> Roger dined with the Bishop of Elmham that evening, and
> the same hero was discussed under a different heading. 'He has
> given £200,' said the Bishop, 'to the Curates' Aid Society. I
> don't know that a man could spend his money much better
> than that.'

Pope's words about Vice come to mind:

> Her Birth, her Beauty, Crowds and Courts confess,
> Chaste Matrons praise her, and grave Bishops bless ...
> All, all look up, with reverential Awe,
> At Crimes that 'scape, or triumph o'er the Law.
>
> (*Epilogue to the Satires* I, 145-6, 167-8)

No wonder the title is so cynical. Dr Ruth ap Roberts makes the interesting suggestion that it derives from Cicero, whose *Life* Trollope was to write a little later: 'Sed quid agas? Sic vivitur' (*Ad Familiares* II, 15) [What do you want us to do? That's the way we live now]. The title of Lady Carbury's novel, spoken about in the work itself, 'The Wheel of Fortune', would also not have been inapposite, for the tale shows clearly enough how those who live on such shaky moral foundations as it exhibits are always at the mercy of the fickle goddess. Few get what they want, most are grievously disappointed, and practically every good – and there are not many of them – is a damaged good.

The Way We Live Now is a truly panoramic work, taking in a host of characters (twenty-three mentioned in the chapter-titles alone) and a whole series of relationships. Towering over the novel is Melmotte himself, cashing in on the great speculative enterprise of the non-existent South Central Pacific and Mexican Railway, rising to such eminence in society that he entertains royalty, getting himself elected to Parliament (Trollope the Liberal makes sure he is a Conservative), then overstepping himself in his fraudulent dealings with forged signatures to documents that lead to the collapse of his empire and his own death.

Besides his principal topic of commercial dishonesty, Trollope listed three other vices which he was seeking to deal with – 'the intrigues of girls who want to get married ... the luxury of the young men who prefer to remain single, and ... the puffing propensities of authors who desire to cheat the public into buying their volumes'. (*Autobiography*, ch. 20) The last of these is demonstrated in Lady Carbury, but her role covers much more than this. Though her amorality extends to several doubtful actions in furthering the suit of her worthless son, Sir Felix, for the hand of Marie Melmotte, the condemnation of these is mitigated by the fervour of her maternal feelings both for him and, misguided, even cruel, as she is towards her at times, for her daughter Hetta and her possible marriage to her cousin, Roger. Hetta, however, favours Paul Montague, Roger's friend and the most intriguingly ambiguous character in the novel. His former involvement with the mysterious American, Mrs Hurtle, is never fully explained, but in her, too, we have a character of reverberating depth who makes someone like Hetta look altogether too pale and uninteresting. Paul is sucked into the group of young men at the Beargarden Club – Sir Felix, Dolly Longestaffe, Nidderdale, Miles Grendall *et al.* – who in their futile wastrel lives illustrate the 'luxury of the young men who prefer to remain single'.

Dolly's sister, Georgiana, principally exemplifies 'the intrigues of girls who want to get married'. Beyond these are other minor lines of interest such as that centring on Ruby Ruggles, the beloved of the Bungay meal-dealer, John Crumb, who thrashes Felix Carbury for his affair with her; and the peripheral ecclesiastical references involving the Bishop and, rather more prominently, the Roman Catholic convert, Father Barham. He, too, shows one of the ways in which we live now with his fanatical alienation from his family and his sense of masochistic satisfaction from the 'persecution, worldly degradation, and poverty' (ch. 16) which he chooses to magnify as the consequence of his conversion.

Melmotte, married to a Bohemian Jewess, is a man of obscure origins. Trollope never allows us to place too much trust in his boast that he had been born in England. He speaks 'his "native" language fluently, but with an accent which betrayed at least a long expatriation' (ch. 4), and his speech on the launching of his company is the occasion for a broad irony:

> Mr Melmotte may have been held to have clearly proved the genuineness of that English birth which he claimed by the awkwardness and incapacity which he showed on the occasion .... It was a great thing, – a very great thing; – he had no hesitation in saying that it was one of the greatest things out. He didn't believe a greater thing had ever come out. (ch. 10)

Though he may make fun of this, the rest of Trollope's portrayal of Melmotte is of 'dishonesty magnificent in its proportions', such that one must sympathise with Mrs Hurtle's suggestions of Napoleonic stature: 'Such a man rises above honesty ... as a great general rises above humanity when he sacrifices an army to conquer a nation.' (ch. 26) His aspirations are matched by his arrogance. When he is chosen to entertain the Emperor of China, he demands a prior introduction in a situation in which it is obvious that established society is happy to use him but not very easily disposed to admit him fully within its circle. (ch. 54) The dinner represents the zenith of his ascent, but, rocket-like, the moment of his greatest brilliance is also that of his imminent destruction. The aftermath of the banquet is symbolic: 'Within the hall the pilasters and trophies, the wreaths and the banners, which three or four days since had been built up with so much trouble, were now pulled down and hauled away. And amidst the ruins Melmotte himself was standing.' (ch. 68) He does not fall without a fight. His final gesture, an attempt to address the House of Commons, drunk, stumbling and incoherent though it is, has about it the character of a giant falling, and his suicide by prussic acid is given Roman and senatorial overtones by Trollope's earlier reference to his having perhaps 'wrapped his toga around him better had he remained at home'. (ch. 83)

Beside him all the rest are pygmies and some resemble leeches. This is nowhere better illustrated than in the dinner and in the attitude of Lady Monogram towards it. Julia Triplex, originally no better placed than Georgiana Longestaffe, despises the latter for choosing not to miss the London season at the cost of being a guest with the Melmottes; but circumstances alter cases considerably and she is glad enough to accept tickets from Georgiana when she discovers that the *beau monde* will all be there. Society, however, scatters as quickly as it had congregated. The rumours of Melmotte's crime leave empty places at the banquet, and like the proverbial rats hastening from the sinking ship, his erstwhile associates disappear, his closest confidant, Lord Alfred Grendall, first among them. (ch. 83) This too helps to provide Melmotte's death with something of its lonely magnificence.

People like these represent the rottenness of English society, and none shows its decadence more than the Longestaffes. They are appropriate victims of Melmotte's rapacity. The father, squire of Caversham, 'was intensely proud of his position in life, thinking himself to be immensely superior to all those who earned their bread .... He was a silly man, who had no fixed idea that it behoved him to be of use to any one.' (ch. 13) Beset with debts, he rents his town house to Melmotte and, could he gain his son Dolly's consent, would sell him one of his country properties, the deeds of which do actually pass as a result of Melmotte's forgery. Nothing upsets him and Lady Pomona more than Georgiana's engaging herself to the Jewish merchant, Brehgert. He is filled with aristocratic distaste on meeting him (ch. 88), but Brehgert is, in fact, one of the most upright characters in the novel. The scene in question, after Georgiana under parental pressure has reneged on the engagement, provides a marked contrast between Brehgert's dignity and Longestaffe's mere hauteur.

Georgiana, like some of the other girls in the book, is endowed with a fair amount of spirit. Trollope makes fun of her aspirations and especially of the way by which the passing years had modified them from wealth and a coronet through 'Twenty-five and six ... the years for baronets and squires' (ch. 60) to the acceptance of Brehgert. He exposes the single-mindedness required by the essential business of marriage – and its pathos. By contrast, Marie Melmotte, also a spirited girl, is plagued by an embarrassment of suitors, all after her money. She chooses to fall, inexplicably, in love with Sir Felix Carbury, or explicably perhaps only because he is unacceptable to her father. None the less, having bestowed her love, she is tenaciously faithful to her choice. She is the leader in the plans to elope, she gets to Liverpool while Sir Felix merely gets drunk, and when she is caught and brought back, she resolutely withstands her father's tyrannous attempts to make her marry Nidderdale and equally resolutely his plans to appropriate her money. At the end we read:

> She had really loved; – but had found out that her golden idol was made of the basest clay. She had then declared to herself that bad as the clay was she would still love it; – but even the clay had turned away from her and had refused her love! (ch. 82)

Sir Felix Carbury must surely be one of the most despicable characters in all literature, a thorough degenerate, who battens on all around him. He has no qualms in begging from his mother when he knows that she has hardly anything left to give. His life consists of drinking and gambling and – surely the only reason for including yet another spirited girl – attempting to seduce Ruby Ruggles. The Beargarden (the name is significant) is his spiritual home and is itself a parody in miniature of the great world of Melmotte, even down to the cheating by Miles Grendall. Sir Felix is a knave but an incompetent one. Dolly Longestaffe is simply a fool. One should perhaps say utterly a fool, and Trollope was right to single him out as 'very good'. (*Autobiography*, ch. 20) His conversation is superbly vacuous. The idea of Sir Felix consulting him on Miles Grendall's cheating is laughable; it constitutes a moral problem altogether beyond Dolly's ken: 'I shouldn't believe my own eyes. Or if I did, should take care not to look at him.' (ch. 28) The closure of the Beargarden is like the end of the world: 'I think everything is going to come to an end .... One can't even get up a game of cards.' (ch. 74), and his letter to his father about Georgiana's engagement is brief and pointed: 'The fellows say so; but I can't believe it. I'm sure you wouldn't let her. You ought to lock her up.' (ch. 78) Yet by a perfect irony it is he who brings about Melmotte's downfall. Only someone as stupid as Dolly could be absolutely sure that he had not signed the document he said he had not.

Paul Montague is more interesting than the others because he is a mixture of strength and weakness and because there is an element of mystery in his background. More of this resides in Winifred Hurtle than in himself, but his association with her produces one of the more complex issues of the novel. Her stormy and uncertain marital experiences in America have a later parallel in *Dr Wortle's School,* but whatever her husband may have been, she herself gives an impression of a wild animal, not least in her bursts of intended vengeance on Paul for their broken engagement. That she might have used a pistol on her husband is not hard to believe. The depths of passion within her contrast markedly with the absence of that quality among most of the other young women of the novel. Her conduct represents a mixture of the feminine desire to get her man back and a nobility that is prepared to suffer and let him go (cf. her letter, ch. 47). These two conflicting inclinations fluctuate in their predominance. Trollope ultimately judges her as 'a good-natured woman' (ch. 97), but that is altogether inadequate. She was more than that. It is a measure of her stature that she alone was able to admire Melmotte. In her in proportionate measure was the same courage, the same inclination to ruthlessness and the same ability to suffer.

Paul Montague, though involved with both, measures up to neither. Capable enough by contrast with his fellow-directors, he has yet only the capacity to get out of the firm, not to oppose Melmotte; and with Mrs Hurtle he wins more because she only fights half-heartedly than for any other reason. Nevertheless, his qualms of conscience, especially in relation to her, and his helplessness before her endow him with more interest than the rest of the young men. He at least would do as well as he could, and he is all too well aware that he both has done and sometimes still does that which falls below his own highest standards. And if he does not remind himself of this, Roger Carbury is always there to supply the deficiency.

Roger, the unbending *laudator temporis acti* in the face of present laxity, is always right to such an extent that he stands often like an Athanasius *contra mundum.* He does not ape his neighbours in their London life, but resides as squire of Carbury 'on his own land among his own people, as all the Carburys before him had done'. (ch. 6) He loathes Sir Felix and reproves Lady Carbury for her indulgence and he scorns the attempts to entrap Marie Melmotte for Sir Felix. He both regrets and condemns Paul Montague's involvement with Mrs Hurtle, even going so far as to say: 'If you make a bargain with the Devil, it may be dishonest to cheat him, – and yet I would have you cheat him if you could' (ch. 39); and, to the point of stuffiness, he supports John Crumb in his pursuit of Ruby Ruggles. He is Montague's rival for the hand of Hetta Carbury, but she with similar, but, one is to take it, more refined, determination than Marie Melmotte's, opposes her mother in persistently preferring Montague. The end of Roger Carbury's history is consistent with what goes before, but in its generosity more noble than his preceding behaviour often appears. He accepts the inevitable but, in addition, with a degree of self-gratification, he alienates his estate from Sir Felix to, we are to assume, Hetta's and Paul's offspring. Even then, however, he believes he is best performing his 'duty to those who live on his land and [his] duty to his country'. (ch. 100)

Of Lady Carbury's literary pretensions we need say little. Trollope doubtless knew people like her and like Mr Alf, Mr Broune and the reviewer, Jones. The *Westminster Review* wished that Jones might have written a slashing review of *The Way We Live Now,* and it suggested that he might have contrasted the book with *Vanity Fair,* its 'flabby sentences' against the latter's 'terse epigrams', its Sir Felix against Rawdon Crawley and its Lady Carbury against Becky. Even if one concedes the point in part, it must none the less be said that the Regency era of Thackeray's novel provided more spectacular villainy than the mid-Victorian period as the opposition of Lady Carbury and Becky makes only too apparent. Contrast Trollope with Dickens in *Little Dorrit* and, more painstaking, even, if you like, more plodding though he may appear, Trollope is fuller, more exact and more penetrating in his analysis of the contemporary commercial and social scene. Some have complained that there are too many characters and too many plots, and there may indeed be a superfluity when we get among the bakers of Bungay, but, especially if one remembers Trollope's self-confessed lack of interest and of skill in plot-construction, the result in *The Way We Live Now* is a tribute to his mastery in handling a very large canvas. He paints a dark picture, but his satire is never sardonic. His temperament was too sanguine for that, and in the next novel for us to consider he emerges out of the shadows into the sunshine of humorous criticism.

If *The Way We Live Now* examines prevalent modes of life in the metropolis, it may be said that the somewhat perversely entitled *The American Senator* (1877) does the same for life in the counties and small towns. Indeed at the end trollope suggested that the book might have been better named *The Chronicle of a Winter at Dillsborough*. (ch. 80) The criticism of England is made most explicitly through the comments of the American Senator, Elias Gotobed, but the book as a whole takes in the life of Dillsborough with its small-town professional men and traders and the life of the county stretching through the hierarchy from Lord Rufford at one end to the disgruntled smallholder Dan Goarly at the other. The public interest of the novel is centred on the poisoning of foxes and the private takes in the two contrasting love-stories of Arabella Trefoil and Mary Masters. Arabella, an undisguised fortune-hunter, is engaged first to the diplomat John Morton, then pursues Lord Rufford, but eventually has to settle for marriage and Patagonia with the newly appointed ambassador, Mounser Green. Mary, quietly in love with Reginald Morton, though he appears to have shown no interest, rejects the offer of the perfectly suitable but unacceptable Larry Twentyman and persists in doing so despite, particularly, the pressures of her step-mother. Patience is rewarded; at the end she becomes Reginald's wife and mistress of Bragton Hall.

Arabella is hunting a man of sufficient social standing to make her

> a great lady – one who would be allowed to swim out of
> rooms before others, one who could snub others, one who
> could show real diamonds when others wore paste, one who
> might be sure to be asked everywhere, even by the people who
> hated her. She rather liked being hated by women, and did
> not want any man to be in love with her, – except as far as
> might be sufficient for marriage. (ch. 12)

She has recently been damned as 'frigid, calculating, cruel, selfish' (Roberts, 1971, p. 183), whilst Trollope himself anticipated that she would be regarded as 'unwomanly, unnatural, turgid'. (*Letters,* No. 643) She quite ruthlessly drops John Morton to pursue Lord Rufford, but Morton is obviously a cipher to whom Trollope attaches the mocking title, The Paragon. Her manipulation of Rufford, however morally and socially objectionable, is a masterpiece of strategy and, at the crisis in the carriage on the way back from the hunt, of tactics. (ch. 39) There is no doubt that he did declare his love for her, though it was she who drove him to it, and he later has to acknowledge as much. (ch. 45) The financial settlement he makes to escape his embarrassment reflects more upon him than upon her; it is 'a low-minded idea', as Trollope tells us. (ch. 61) Her boldness in striking for Rufford is matched in her subsidiary and contributory dealings with such people as her aunt, the Duchess of Mayfair. Her spirit achieves its final triumph when, after he has rejected her, she goes and confronts him in his own hall in an interview in which he is worsted at every turn. (ch. 67) This incident, which reminds us that hell hath no fury like a woman scorned, is followed by the expected announcement of Rufford's engagement to Miss Penge, a favoured nonentity of his sister's. It is the contrast between *The Claverings'* Julia Ongar and Florence Burton – magnified.

Arabella was heartless. Trollope himself says: 'There certainly was no man for whom she cared a straw.' There are lines that almost suggest the prostitute,

> Even when he was kissing her she was thinking of her
> built-up hair, of her pearl powder, her paint, and of possible
> accidents and untoward revelations. The loan of her lips had
> been for use only .... But there was a future through which
> she must live. (ch. 49)

Her creator, however, does not begrudge her a limited reward:

> Will such a one as Arabella Trefoil be damned, and if so why?
> Think of her virtues; how she works, how true she is to her
> vocation, how little there is of self-indulgence, or idleness. I
> think that she will go to a kind of third class heaven in
> which she will always be getting third class husbands. (*Letters*,
> No. 643)

She is all that Ruth ap Roberts says she is, but we must not ignore the 'virtues' that Trollope thought that she so manifestly possessed.

Arabella is rootless, and this, as with Melmotte and his kind, contrasts with the settled nature of English society at practically every level. Trollope devotes the first chapter of *The American Senator* to Dillsborough, a dull place with no attractions and 'no character of its own', one long main street with a market square. The very minuteness of the description gives a sense of solidity and customary ways. Trade is represented by the innkeeper Runciman and the butcher Ribbs, the professions by the attorney Masters.

They meet regularly with others to exchange gossip, to discuss local developments and to comment on the activities of their betters. These latter in descending order of social standing include Lord Rufford, John Morton, the squire of Bragton, and Lawrence Twentyman 'who was quite the gentleman farmer'. (ch. 1) Trollope may have written better novels, but in none has he shown the comprehensive range and subtle gradations of English society so skilfully as in *The American Senator*. Those gradations reveal themselves with especial minuteness in the case of Twentyman. The phrase quoted above by its very assertiveness leads us to question its truth. Larry is 'Esquire', he contributes handsomely enough to the Hunt, he has been at Cheltenham College. Trollope even picks his public school with a sure sense of its standing relative to others, a place with some reputation but not in the top class. Yet he is Larry to some who should call him Mr Twentyman; and there are men with whom he is familiar enough and he is glad of it, but they do not invite him to their houses. If Twentyman is striving upward, Arabella is struggling at least not to fall. She and her mother, members of the cadet branch of an aristocratic family, saddled with a ne'er-do-well father and husband, wander from house to house in their struggle to maintain the level in life which they believe is theirs.

They provide a contrast with the basic foundation of English social stability as Trollope saw it in his day and as it had existed through centuries. 'Land was the one proper possession for an English gentleman of ancient family,' (ch. 57) and as such it must descend to 'the proper heir', the eldest son or the nearest relative in succession. That is why its alienation by men who believed so strongly in this doctrine is so important in *The Way We Live Now* and *Sir Harry Hotspur*. To the American senator, Gotobed, this system of primogeniture is 'damnable and cruel' (ch. 78); and certainly on younger sons, bred up in the way of life of the great house and estate only to find themselves subsequently unable to maintain or enjoy it, it had a disastrous impact. Gotobed opposed it, however, on the other grounds – that it maintained a feudal tyranny in the hands of the landed aristocracy.

That way of life included hunting and shooting from September to March, and August spent shooting in Scotland.

During the other months he fishes, and plays cricket and tennis, and attends races, and goes about to parties in London.

His evenings he spends at a card table … It is the
employment of his life to fit in his amusements so that he
may not have a dull day. (ch. 30)

Thus we see the senator, who adds also that 'the man who is born
a lord, and who sees a dozen serfs around him who have been born
to be half-starved ploughmen, thinks that God arranged it all', but
even he had to add that 'they do their work as vicegerents with an
easy grace, and with sweet pleasant voices and soft movements,
which almost make a man doubt whether the Almighty has not, in
truth, intended that such injustice should be permanent.'

Gotobed's criticisms embrace the hereditary composition of the
House of Lords, the discrepant size of parliamentary constituencies
and the practice of buying and selling military commissions (chs
77-8), but it is, appropriately, hunting which engages his closest
attention. Trollope himself was an inveterate hunter. He used to
keep at least four horses and to hunt three days a week, usually in
Essex. He found it difficult to analyse his delight in the sport, being,
as he put it, 'too blind to see hounds turning' or 'the nature of a
fence', but with that persistence that characterised so much of his
endeavour, he rode

with a boy's energy, determined to get ahead if it may
possibly be done, hating the roads, despising young men who
ride them, and with a feeling that life can not, with all her
riches, have given me anything better than when I have gone
through a long run to the finish, keeping a place, not of glory,
but of credit, among my juniors. (*Autobiography*, ch. 9)

Elsewhere in the same work he declared: 'I have written on very
many subjects and on most of them with pleasure, but on no subject
with such delight as that of hunting.' (ch. 4) In his little collection
of *Hunting Sketches* (1865) he succinctly characterises several
hunting types, the ostentation of 'the man who hunts and doesn't
like it' (Edwards, 1952, p. 44), the trials of the man who does
(ibid., p. 54), the cunning and knowledge of 'the man who hunts
and never jumps' (ibid., pp. 94 ff.), the lady rider and the hunting
parson, but his most informative pieces are devoted to the hunting
farmer and the master of hounds. He recognises the tyranny of the
independent 'proper master' and the shortcomings of the paid
itinerant and would settle for a compromise, 'a country gentleman

who takes a subscription, and who therefore on becoming auto-cratic, makes himself answerable' (ibid., p. 122). He acknowledges the debt that the hunting fraternity must always owe to the farmer who suffers his young grass and growing corn to be ridden over, but at the same time he points out the wickedness of the man who puts up wire, a crime that leads to ostracism by his neighbours. He is 'frequently, a small proprietor new to the glories of ownership' (ibid., p. 81); such was Scrobby in *The American Senator*, who persuaded the wretched Goarly to plant the poisoned herrings for the foxes and the hounds.

Many of the novels contain hunting scenes, but apart from those in *Orley Farm* (chs 28-9) there are none to compare with those of *The American Senator*, chapters which, in the view of Lord Willoughby de Broke, 'set forth in a few touches but with unerring precision, almost every point of view from which foxhunting can be regarded'. (1921) With his transatlantic philistinism, Gotobed cannot understand why fifty couple of hounds are required when ten or twelve would apparently do, but, worse than that, he takes Goarly's side against the rest and even spends money in defending him, ignoring the fact that the Hunt pay for the losses men like Goarly sustain. (ch. 19) He remains obdurate, saying that it would be impossible to make Americans

> believe that a hundred harum-scarum tomboys may ride at
> their pleasure over every man's land, destroying crops and
> trampling down fences, going, if their vermin leads them there,
> with reckless violence into the sweet domestic gardens of your
> country residences. (ch. 78)

Not for Gotobed to realise the skill and exhilaration of the pursuit, which Trollope brings out from the angles of the several different riders, each with a different philosophy and strategy. Nor for him either to appreciate the character and cunning of the huntsman, the varying turns, excitements and disappointments of the chase, the physical strength and moral courage it requires. Elsewhere Trollope had described hunting accidents such as Felix Graham's in *Orley Farm*, but here the dangers of the chase take in Major Caneback's fatal injury, battling with a horse of renowned recalcitrance which finally rushes a fence, falls into the ditch, pitches him off and kicks him on the head.

Trollope wastes no improper grief upon him. Indeed, he makes his survival an ironical embarrassment.

Nobody in that house really cared much for Caneback. He
was not a man worthy of much care. He was possessed of
infinite pluck, and now that he was dying could bear it well
.... But, nevertheless, it is a bore when a gentleman dies in
your house, – and a worse bore when he dies from an accident
than from an illness for which his own body may be supposed
to be responsible. (ch. 23)

The way that Trollope uses the word 'bore', the very one that Lord
Rufford and his set would have used in colloquial understatement
that was, however, not all that far from the truth, is telling. So, too,
is the way in which Caneback's practically only virtue is cited to
dismiss the need for overmuch sympathy for him. It is a reminder
that Trollope did not fail to distinguish men's characters, even in
the hunting field. Indeed, as the *Hunting Sketches* show, it is there
that a man's character often reveals itself most fully.

The American senator did not see this, but even what he did see
he could not properly evaluate. The inescapable impression did not
always harmonise with the rational conclusion:

Everything he heard, and almost everything he saw, offended
him at some point. And yet, in the midst of it all, he was
conscious that he was surrounded by people who claimed and
made good their claims to superiority. (ch. 51)

In the two lectures which he delivers at the end he attacks the
irrationality, if not downright stupidity, of various English practices
and institutions, but his second is cut short by popular demon-
strations. His final words to himself are that 'the want of reason
among Britishers was so great, that no one ought to treat them as
wholly responsible beings'. (ch. 78) Trollope, however, treats him
as a man out of his element. He ridicules Gotobed's earnest but
uncomprehending criticisms, and the overall impression is to
counterbalance the gloom which pervades the portrait of London in
The Way We Live Now with a delight and enjoyment in the
unobtrusive but resilient rhythms of life in provincial England.

4

Barchester Chronicles

(Clergymen of the Church of England; The Warden; Barchester Towers; Doctor Thorne; Framley Parsonage; The Small House at Allington; The Last Chronicle of Barset; The Two Heroines of Plumplington)

Whatever be the fame or fashion of his other novels, Trollope is and will remain best known for his Barsetshire series. The map of the county did not spring forth in full detail from Trollope's head, and indeed the efforts of different topographers, among them Trollope himself, have not produced unanimity about the various geographical locations. None the less, the details are both full enough and exact enough to have provoked these several attempts. The panorama is on the first page of *Doctor Thorne* – 'its green pastures, its waving wheat, its deep and shady – and let us add – dirty lanes, its paths and stiles, its tawny-coloured well-built rural churches; its avenues of beeches and frequent Tudor mansions.' Some of the places we know in detail – Plumstead, the archdeacon's parish, the very name resonant of prosperity; Framley with its comfortable parsonage and even more comfortable Court; remoter Hogglestock, by contrast, poverty-stricken and isolated; above all, Barchester itself, Hiram's Hospital, the Deanery and the walk from there to the cathedral, the chapter reading-room, and the bishop's palace, down to the very chair on which the bishop sits or, perhaps more memorable, the sofa on which the siren Signora Madeline Vesey Neroni careers so destructively across the Proudies' drawing-room. This list reminds us how Trollope has skilfully varied the extent and depth of his detail. He has created a recognisable world. He tells us in the *Autobiography* of the genesis of *The Warden*, of how he 'stood for an hour on the little bridge in Salisbury, and had made out to [his] own satisfaction the spot on which Hiram's Hospital should stand'. (*Autobiography*, ch. 5) Yet Barchester is not Salisbury, nor Winchester, nor Wells, nor anywhere else; it is itself, Trollope's own vivid creation.

The second point to be made about these novels arises from the

first. They are a group, or more properly, a series, expanding and
developing, the reader ever learning more, just as he suspects that
the writer's own acquaintance and experience is itself ever widening.
Trollope was original in this: no other novelist before him had
exploited the idea of a single, gradually more fully revealed (or
self-revealing) community. Speaking of his clergymen in the novels
he uses a sentence that might well apply to the chronicles of Barset
on the widest scale: 'I had to pick up as I went whatever I might
know or pretend to know about them.' (ibid.) Yet this empirical
procedure was not so haphazard as it might seem, because on the
central issue Trollope knew what he was doing. He had not lived
in a cathedral city, he had not known any real archdeacons. He was
probably all the better fitted in consequence. He started off on the
same level as his readers, not burdened with an over-specialised
knowledge, not in entire ignorance, but having some awareness of
the ethos of the world he was presenting. His novelist's imagination,
that ability to concentrate and refine the ordinary, did the rest. It
is not, however, accidental that, in speaking of this effort with
special reference to Archdeacon Grantly, Trollope should call it 'the
simple result of an effort of my moral consciousness'. (ibid.) Integral
as is the clerical setting in much of the Barsetshire series, what
Trollope is surely saying is that psychology and morality are the
same the world over, that particular men in particular positions will
behave in a particular fashion. Barchester may provide the local
habitation and the name; the fundamental imaginative achievement
has a more universal significance.

We must not, however, underestimate the local habitation. By
the time that Trollope was beginning to write *The Warden*, the
novel as a genre was already well established as a literary mode of
setting forth topical problems. What Trollope chose he has summarised for us in the *Autobiography*:

> The first evil was the possession by the Church of certain
> funds and endowments which had been intended for charitable
> purposes, but which had been allowed to become incomes for
> idle Church dignitaries.... The second evil was its very
> opposite.... I had also often been angered by the undeserved
> severity of the newspapers towards the recipients of such
> incomes. (ibid.)

That ability to see both sides of the case is not only unusual among
social-reform novelists; it provides the clue also to much of

Trollope's tone and to the relationship in which he stands with the reader.

The clerical community of the mid-nineteenth century was a brilliant choice for a novelist to make, for it was not only of central concern in the eyes of the nation – it is difficult for a reader nowadays to realise how much the Church mattered then – but it was also at that particular period beset by enemies without and within. Wesley had done his work in the eighteenth century, and that work had bequeathed to the Church of England a revitalised section of Evangelicals and a schismatic split of Methodist dissenters. These latter with other nonconformist sects became ever more influential throughout the nineteenth century, but though this happened, and happened the more evidently at every widening of the parliamentary franchise in the successive Reform Acts, giving more power to the lower and urban classes, for all practical purposes the Dissenters made no significant impact on English society until after the Act of 1867. Their influence was not only limited; it was, as Matthew Arnold pointed out in *Culture and Anarchy* (1869), essentially provincial and lacking in standards.

The ecclesiastical world, then, that Trollope portrays, between the Reform Acts of 1832 and 1867, manifests the late flowering glories of the Church of England, but it is one also in which the shape of things to come is both evident and unwelcome. It was a world envisaged at a precise turning-point in its history, and Trollope was enough of a romantic to view with sorrow the world that was passing, even though there was much in it of which he could not approve. It is just such an environment that leads him into nostalgic raptures and sad regrets as he describes a typical cathedral close with its 'modest, comfortable clerical residences':

On one side there is an arched gate, – a gate that may possibly be capable of being locked, which gives to the spot a sweet savour of monastic privacy and ecclesiastical reserve; while on the other side the close opens itself freely to the city by paths leading, probably, under the dear old towers of the cathedral, by the graves of those who have been thought worthy of a resting-place so near the shrine.... It is true, indeed, that much of their glory has now departed from these hallowed places. The dean still keeps his deanery, but the number of resident canons has been terribly diminished. Houses intended for church dignitaries are let to prosperous tallow-chandlers,

49

and in the window of a mansion in a close can, at this
moment in which I am writing, be seen a notice that lodgings
can be had there by a private gentleman – with a reference.
(*Clergymen of the Church of England*, 1866, pp. 38-9)

That had not happened to Archdeacon Grantly's Barchester, but it
is the imminence of change – and its unwelcome distastefulness –
that gives so much vigour to *Barchester Towers*. In old Bishop
Grantly's time Barchester was a city of easy-going decorum: the
archdeacon was *de facto* ruler of the diocese; the prebendaries and
minor canons did their job – or didn't, as they chose. There were
fashionable and not over-zealous clergy, as Mark Robarts is shown
to be in *Framley Parsonage;* there were underpaid and overworked
clergy like Crawley at Hogglestock; and there was Mr Harding in
his leisured but innocent ease at Hiram's Hospital. Each had his
place, and peace, even if it was of lethargy, spread, comfortably for
the most part, over the diocese.

The change comes with the arrival of a new bishop, a friend of
Evangelicals, if not an Evangelical himself. Those Anglicans who
had been filled with the new spirituality which had inspired Wesley
came mainly from Cambridge, where Charles Simeon exercised a
lengthy and remarkable influence from 1782 to his death in 1836.
Evangelicalism emphasised the need for deep personal commitment,
and its earnestness resulted in vast new missionary endeavour
abroad and social concern at home. Saintliness, however, was easily
imitated by sanctimoniousness, and the enemies of the Evangelicals
were not slow, nor disinclined, to confuse the one with the other.
Mrs Trollope herself did this in what can only be regarded as a
libellous portrait of J. W. Cunningham, Vicar of Harrow, in her
novel, *The Vicar of Wrexhill*. Trollope himself confessed that he
might 'have inherited some of [his] good mother's antipathies
towards a certain clerical school'. (quoted in Escott, 1913, p. 11) He
possessed, however, somewhat greater self-control than she did in
expressing them.

By the 1850s the Evangelicals were at the zenith of their power
in the Church of England, and by their influence the whole tenor
of English social life had been transformed. Inevitably, there was
hypocrisy masquerading as piety; Thackeray in *The Newcomes* and
Charlotte Brontë's Mr Brocklehurst both remind us of this. There
was also the tremendously dynamic urge to social reform which is
associated with the names of men like Shaftesbury. The novelists

either did not see or else had no use for this. For Trollope, Shaftesbury merely recalled 'the last decade of years in which bishops are popularly supposed to have been selected in accordance with the advice of a religious Whig nobleman'. (*Clergymen of the Church of England*, 1866, p. 18) Hence the power which he derives in the opening pages of *Barchester Towers* from the suspense as to which will die first, the bishop or the ministry.

The earlier dissolution of the latter brings Bishop Proudie to Barchester, and with him Mrs Proudie. The bishop is a liberal. His wife, however, in this, as in other ways, is made of sterner stuff. She is probably in Trollope's eyes an Evangelical: she is certainly a Sabbatarian. In other words, Trollope shrewdly took one aspect of Evangelical profession and chose to emphasise that alone. The attack on Mr Slope, the bishop's chaplain, is mounted from other angles. (*Barchester Towers*, ch. 4) He is personally repulsive with red hair and clammy hands, Trollope probably remembering Uriah Heep in *David Copperfield*. Slope 'had been a sizar (i.e., a poor scholar) at Cambridge'; and one remembers Samuel Butler's jibe in *The Way of All Flesh* about the sizars of St John's, 'unprepossessing in features, gait and manners, unkempt and ill-dressed beyond what can be easily described'. He too is a Sabbatarian, but he is also more recognisably a Protestant with his dislike of Puseyites and their practices, preaching in the cathedral, for example, tactlessly indeed but with sentiments widely shared at the time, against the intoning of the service. Trollope's sympathies lie elsewhere, as can be seen when he speaks of the energy he attributes to the Tractarian Movement, which between 1833 and 1845 flourished in Oxford and from which the Anglo-Catholic element in the Church of England traces its origins:

> Dr Newman has gone to Rome, and Dr Pusey has perhaps helped to send many thither; but these men, and their brethren of the Tracts, stirred up throughout the country so strong a feeling of religion, gave rise by their works to so much thought on a matter which had been allowed for years to go on almost without any thought that it may be said of them that they made episcopal idleness impossible, and clerical idleness rare. (*Clergymen of the Church of England*, 1866, p. 25)

Yet in *Barchester Towers* it was the other party that was active, and that Trollope portrays, with some animosity, in part for being so. The dangerous activities of Mr Slope have to be countered by importation of Mr Arabin from Oxford. By contrast with Slope, Arabin has the right background – son of a country gentleman, Winchester and New College; not a double first because he had been involved in the politics of Puseyism, 'but he revenged himself on the university by putting firsts and double firsts out of fashion for the year' (*Barchester Towers*, ch. 20); Fellow of Lazarus, 'richest and most comfortable abode of Oxford dons' (surely Christ Church, whose Dean at the time, Gaisford, receiving a note from the Dean of Oriel, is said to have commented: 'Alexander the coppersmith sendeth greeting to Alexander the Great'!). He retreated (as Newman did to Littlemore) to a remote Cornish parish to battle in agony of soul with his inclinations towards Rome. Unlike Newman, he returned 'a confirmed Protestant' and an established Oxford man, 'ready at a moment's notice to take up the cudgels in opposition to anything that savoured of an evangelical bearing.' The Oxford Movement stressed the spiritual integrity of the Church against what it saw as the dangerous liberal Erastianism of the period after 1832. It exalted the office of the priest and sought to dignify the externals of worship. Trollope, however, is not concerned with these: he would have claimed an inability to be so. For him it is High Church against Low, Arabin against Slope.

Arabin, moreover, represents the establishment against the *parvenu*. Trollope may deplore the poverty of curates (*Clergymen of the Church of England*, 1866, p. 103, and cf. the portrait of Mr Saul in *The Claverings*), but he can still look with approval upon the wealth of the upper clergy:

> A poor archdeacon, an archdeacon who did not keep a curate or two, an archdeacon who could not give a dinner and put a special bottle of wine upon the table, an archdeacon who did not keep a carriage, or at least a one-horse chaise, an archdeacon without a man servant or a banker's account, would be no where, – if I may so speak, – in an English diocese. (ibid., p. 44)

One reason for deploring the poverty of curates is that it brings into the Church 'men of a lower class in life, who have come from harder antecedents ... all modern Churchmen will understand what must be the effect on the Church if such be the recruits to which the Church must trust.' (ibid., p. 104) Such men will probably be mere 'literates' from theological colleges, and the result

– 'an altered man, and as a man less attractive, less urbane, less genial, – in one significant word, less of a gentleman.' (ibid., p. 60) Such was Thumble of Barchester, who could so brusquely attempt to intrude himself into Mr Crawley's duties at Hogglestock: by contrast, poor as he was, Crawley was learned and a gentleman.

Trollope's Church was a church of gentlemen within an established and recognised order. As Ronald Knox put it in his introduction to the Oxford edition of *The Warden* (1855), Trollope 'could not save the old order of things, the world of privilege he so intimately loved, but his sympathies have embalmed the unavailing conflict'. (p. xviii) It is to that novel we must now turn, or rather to the scandals out of which it grew.

> The wellknown case of the Hospital of St Cross has even come before the law-courts of the country, and the struggles of Mr Whiston, at Rochester, have met with sympathy and support. Men are beginning to say that these things must be looked into. (*The Warden*, ch. 2)

At St Cross the Earl of Guildford had held the mastership since 1808 in plurality with several livings, including Alresford and St Mary's, Southampton. He was receiving £1200 per year from St Cross, but he had also paid out annually more than half the receipts in upkeep and, like Trollope's Mr Harding, he had voluntarily raised the stipends of the inmates. The visiting commissioner agreed with the Earl that, if the payments in kind were commuted to money, 'new grounds for dissatisfaction would not fail to occur in the minds of men utterly without occupation'. The Rochester case involved the persistent attempts by Whiston, the headmaster of the cathedral school, to compel the chapter to make the statutory payments for four scholars at university not just at the rates specified in the charter but at a rate grossed up to achieve in the nineteenth century what had been the founder's intention. He went on to extend the scope of his accusations at Rochester and in *Cathedral Trusts and their Fulfilment* (1849) to cite similar cases elsewhere, including Canterbury, Worcester and Ely. Whiston was dismissed from office, but eventually after much ecclesiastico-legal tergiversation he was reinstated, and the various statutory disbursements were all handsomely increased. (For these and other 'scandals' see Arnold, 1961; Martin, 1962; and Best, 1961-2, pp. 135-50.)

Barchester is a quiet place, on which has lain undisturbed the peace of generations. It is threatened by 'those whose impiety would venture to disturb the goodly grace of cathedral institutions'. (*The Warden*, ch. 5) So at least Archdeacon Grantly formulates the danger that is posed by the reforming zeal of the young middle-class surgeon John Bold, who would enquire too closely into the extent and disposal of the revenues accruing to Hiram's Hospital, a charitable institution housing twelve old bedesmen under the care of the archdeacon's self-effacing father-in-law, Mr Harding. To add to the piquancy of the tale, John Bold is also made to fall in love with Eleanor Harding and thus to set up not only the pulls of conflicting loyalties within himself but also to present difficulties for the archdeacon, condemning the possibility of such a marriage, and for Mr Harding, anxious not to frustrate what may well be his favourite daughter's hopes.

It is, however, the public theme, not the private one, which predominates. It would have been easy for Trollope to use bold colours and to take up a definite position. That is what both the chief protagonists do, and indeed Trollope suggests that he might have been better ranging himself alongside one or the other: 'Any writer in advocating a cause must do so after the fashion of an advocate – or his writing will be ineffective. He should take up·one side and cling to that.' (*Autobiography*, ch. 5) He thinks that Harding should have been either 'a bloated parson, with a red nose and all other iniquities' or good, sweet, mild (as Harding was), but also hard working and ill-paid. He concludes, however: 'Neither of these programmes recommended itself to my honesty.' He was right, and his novel, far from being ineffective, was all the more effective for its honesty. Harding is not a villain; indeed, his agonies of mind as soon as the validity of his right to so large a salary as he receives as warden is questioned (ch. 3) quickly indicate the very opposite. It is chief among Trollope's purposes to show the ill-considered effects of public outcry upon a sensitive soul. It could not have been better expressed than by suggesting Mr Harding's own sympathy for the Earl of Guildford, his 'inward weeping of the heart' for none 'more than that old lord, whose almost fabulous wealth, drawn from his church preferments, had become the subject of so much opprobrium, of such public scorn, that wretched clerical octogenarian Croesus, whom men would not allow to die in peace.' (ch. 5)

But Bold is no villain either. Ignorant and arrogant he may be, he yet lies in the grip of an *idée fixe*, 'comfort[ing] himself in the warmth of his own virtue' as he speaks of 'the duty of righting these poor men' (ch. 6) and all the time trying not to see the impact of his campaign on Mr Harding by persuading himself that because he is attacking a public abuse, he can somehow escape liability for personal distress. (ch. 11) Paradoxically, it is those who do not know Mr Harding who are cast as the real villains, and all the more surprisingly in view of Trollope's assertion in the *Autobiography* that it would have been more effective to take up one side of the case unequivocally. With sustained and damning irony Trollope attacks *The Times* in the guise of the *Jupiter* issuing from Mount Olympus with words from the pen of Tom Towers. Page after page of the fourteenth chapter is full with question and exclamation to impress upon the reader the opposite of the claim that 'the *Jupiter* is never wrong', merely incorrigibly arrogant in its belief in its own infallibility. Likewise, Carlyle and Dickens are superbly parodied as Dr Pessimist Anticant and Mr Popular Sentiment for their prejudiced and uninvestigated outbursts on the subject. (ch. 15) Trollope's contempt for such instant opinions is aptly put into the mouth of one who approves of them. Tom Towers (and Trollope was perhaps thinking of Dickens's brief descent upon Preston to get the 'feel' of an industrial dispute and then to write *Hard Times*) says Sentiment's novel will 'go a long way to put down Rochester, and Barchester, and Dulwich, and St Cross, and all such hotbeds of speculation. It is very clear that Sentiment has been down to Barchester, and got up the whole story there.' (ibid.) Bold is trying to persuade Towers to stop the *Jupiter's* attacks on Mr Harding personally. Typically sanctimonious, Towers claims that 'the public is defrauded whenever private considerations are allowed to have weight'. Trollope immediately seizes on these very words to say: 'Quite true, thou greatest oracle of the middle of the nineteenth century, thou sententious proclaimer of the purity of the press – the public is defrauded when it is purposely misled.' The novelist's use of the archaic second-person formula is always critical. How could a writer as clear-sighted as Trollope is here have been content to adopt just one side of the question?

He must therefore also be critical of the other side. The archdeacon is introduced as 'a personal friend of the dignitaries of the Rochester Chapter', who has written against Whiston and for the Earl of Guildford (ch. 2), with 'an overbearing assurance of the virtues and claims of his order and an equally strong confidence in the dignity of his own manner and the eloquence of his own words'. (ibid.) 'He is a moral man, believing the precepts which he teaches, and believing also that he acts up to them' (ibid.), but 'he did not believe in the Gospel with more assurance than he did in the sacred justice of all ecclesiastical revenues.' (ch. 5) In fact, he personifies the 'church militant here in earth', a man of pious worldliness, of whom also Trollope might have said, as he did of the parish-parson: 'Though he is a bigot, he is not a fanatic, and as long as men will belong to his Church, he is quite willing that the obligations of that Church shall sit lightly upon them.' (*Clergymen of the Church of England*, 1866, p. 62) 'The tone of our archdeacon's mind must not astonish us; it has been the growth of centuries of church ascendancy.' (*The Warden*, ch. 5) That is where the sympathy enters. When Trollope apologises for giving us too much of the archdeacon's 'weak side' at the end of the novel, we feel that he protests too much. It is, in fact, a mark not of the novelist's failure, but of how much he has fallen in love with his creation. The passage quoted above follows a paragraph of raptures about the beauties of Winchester, Hereford and Salisbury. Both *The Warden* and *Barchester Towers* are full of a temperate, nostalgic affection for a world that was passing, elbowed out by a new world, reforming, thrustful, competitive and distasteful. Trollope's emotional conservatism was revolted at the prospect. Thus arises the quiet pathos to match the quiet dignity in Mr Harding's single and ultimate act of independence in resigning the wardenship. In his difference with his son-in-law, the archdeacon, one feels that they were both right. As the latter, outraged at the decision, exclaims, 'Well – I have done my duty' (ch. 18), Trollope makes the reader recognise the impossibility of any compromise. Those who should have been allies could not be reconciled, for their duty differed, and not one, but both, had done that which was incumbent upon them.

' "New men are carrying out new measures, and are carting away the useless rubbish of past centuries!" What cruel words these had been; and how often are they now used with all the heartless cruelty of a Slope!' (*Barchester Towers*, ch. 13) If Trollope felt that he had been too impartial in *The Warden*, he need not have thought so about his attitude in its successor. In the account of the battle between the old order represented by Grantly and the new by Bishop Proudie or, more accurately, his domineering wife and devious chaplain, *Barchester Towers* (1857) leaves no doubt as to where Trollope's own sympathies lie. With the death of the archdeacon's father a new regime is ushered in under his Low

Church successor, a man associated with 'new measures' in every sort of way. After 1832, as Geoffrey Best has put it,

> one after another, the keys of the storehouses of the English inheritance were handed over to the reformers; public administration and finance, prisons, poor law, parochial clergy, parliament, charities, chancery, municipal corporations, bishops, deans and chapters in turn yielded, and ... even Oxford and Cambridge surrendered. (Best, 1961-2, p. 136)

Proudie himself is said by Trollope to be a member of the 'University Improvement Committee' (one notices the typical 'progressive' penchant for euphemism). He is a thorough Whig in the succession to Whately and Hampden, whose promotions had caused so much trouble in the 1830s.

Grantly, by contrast, is High and moves Higher. He, 'if he admits the Queen's supremacy in things spiritual, only admits it as being due to the *quasi* priesthood conveyed in the consecrating qualities of her coronation.' (ch. 4) Under attack he resorts to Oxford, and to Arabin who is Higher than he. Neither of them, however, has yet espoused any form of ritualism. Indeed, it is Eleanor, when married to Arabin, who moves Highest and who is said to have contributed to the expenses of a recent ecclesiastical case in Bath (a reference to the attempted prosecution of Archdeacon Denison for his claim that the wicked partake of the inward reality of the sacraments in contravention of Article XXIX of the Church of England – see Chadwick, 1966, Part I, pp. 491-5, who claims, I think wrongly, that Denison is probably the prototype of Grantly).

Much of this ecclesiastical furore now seems to us a storm in a teacup. It no doubt seemed so to many in the mid-nineteenth century, but to many more it was deadly serious. Trollope plays on this division in the public mind. Thus Eleanor (and how change in personal circumstances changes opinions!) to Arabin before their marriage: 'You wage your wars about trifles so bitterly. . . . Do not such contentions bring scandal on the church?' and his reply: 'More scandal would fall on the church if there were no such contentions.' (ch. 21) Trollope maintains a balance between comedy and seriousness. We cannot help laughing at the 'noble wrath of the archdeacon', which Trollope wished with mild irony to have commemorated in 'epic verse', after the interview with the bishop and the harangue from Mrs Proudie; but Trollope makes this the occasion for raising our sympathy for him, for whatever we may think of his self-confident, domineering ways, better be domineered graciously by him than ungraciously by a 'bishopess'. Even his perversity, as he determines his strategy in opposition to Proudie, is acceptable because it is so understandable, so natural.

Grantly, however, is ultimately sufficiently sympathetic because, whatever the faults of his own character, he is the proponent of a decorum that the newcomers, with the possible exception of the nonentity bishop himself, so notably do not recognise. To intrude herself and to preach at Mr Harding and the archdeacon is Mrs Proudie's fault; to censure, patronise and condescend is Mr Slope's. These two are therefore the butts of Trollope's dramatic satire. If the interview at the palace is the first main set-scene of the novel, the Proudies' reception is the second, and it is there that Mrs Proudie has a fall when the ineffable Bertie Stanhope propels his sister's sofa across the drawing room – with Mrs Proudie's lace-train firmly attached to one of the castors. It is there too that this siren-sister inveigles Mr Slope to the outrage of Mrs Proudie and the first mark of dissension within the Low-Church ranks. Meanwhile, Bertie is engaging the bishop with a series of embarrassing inanities such as 'I once had thoughts of being a bishop myself', culminating in the astounding and unanswerable 'I was a Jew once myself'. (ch. 11)

The Stanhopes are exotics, exiles in Italy suddenly recalled to Barchester. Trollope places them exactly as the happy victims of the *far niente* life, in whom is found a mixture of heartlessness and good-nature. Worthless they may be, they yet know what should be. (Incidentally, for such detail is never accidental in Trollope, we should note the contrast between the genealogies of Prebendary Vesey Stanhope (note even the name) and his wife – 'He himself was the brother of one peer, and his wife was the sister of another' (ch. 9) – and that of the Proudies – 'He was the nephew of an Irish baron by his mother's side, and his wife was the niece of a Scotch earl.' (ch. 3), in more ways than one, that is, more remotely related to the peerage.) The Stanhopes, or at any rate Bertie and Madeline, the only two who matter, are not just comic characters. Madeline especially, the *femme fatale*, even to Arabin, is shrewd and helpful. She is used by Trollope to gauge another aspect of the contest in the novel, the suits for the hand of Eleanor Bold, for a long time thought, unjustly, by the Grantlys and her father to be encouraging Slope, but ultimately to be won by Arabin. Madeline first makes Slope fall in the eyes of Mrs Proudie, then taunts him in his professions of love for her, next plays with Arabin, but all the time recognises the difference between him and Slope and refrains from making him so stupidly miserable. Finally, she makes clear to Eleanor that, shy as he is, Arabin loves her but will find it hard to tell her so.

Trollope does not intervene excessively in *Barchester Towers*, far less, for instance, than in some of his later novels and far less than his contemporaries, Thackeray, or even at times, George Eliot. Nevertheless, it is one of the strengths of the novel that we always know where the author himself stands. Where there might be any doubt, Trollope does come into the novel himself to dispel it. Some have criticised such authorial intrusion, especially when it serves to destroy suspense, but at the end of the fifteenth chapter Trollope springs to the defence of her he calls 'my Eleanor' to say that she would neither bring herself to marry Slope nor would she 'be sacrificed to a Bertie Stanhope'. In so doing he increases our sympathy for her as she continues to be sorrowfully suspected by her father and wrongly accused by the archdeacon.

They are, of course, right in so far as Slope has designs upon her, designs which, like those of Bertie, find expression in the last great set-piece of the novel, the Ullathorne Sports, where Trollope moves firmly into the world of the squirearchy and aristocracy. Squire Thorne, heir to a lineage stretching back to Saxon times, is a Tory of the Tories, for whom the 1852 vote, signalling as it did the final Tory surrender to free trade, was the ultimate apostasy; 'Now all trust in human nature must for ever be at an end'. (ch. 22) His sister is even more reactionary, 'not yet reconciled ... to the Reform Bill' and still regretting Catholic Emancipation [in 1829]. Trollope describes their house in loving detail, and Miss Thorne's *fête champêtre*, with its quaint attempts to revive medieval sports such as archery and tilting, in a tone of good-natured amusement. (The Earl of Eglinton actually staged an enormous medieval tournament at Eglinton Castle in 1839, described by Disraeli in *Endymion*. See also Martin, 1962, pp. 83 ff.)

It is at the Sports that Trollope first confronts us with the difficulties in determining the fine social-hierarchical distinctions that made for the stability of Victorian country society:

Who were to dispose themselves within the ha-ha, and who without? ... Oh, the bishop and such like within the ha-ha; and Farmer Greenacre and such like without. True, my

unthinking friend; but who shall define these such-likes? It is
in such definitions that the whole difficulty of society consists.
(ch. 35)

The aspirations of Mrs Lookaloft and her successful 'gate-crashing'
to the chagrin of Mrs Greenacre are proof enough of that. It is not,
however, at the level of the Lookalofts and the Greenacres that
Trollope finds most to interest him, but rather that of their hosts.
Blood, rank, class, gentility – and money: these will increasingly
occupy his attention.

In the *Autobiography* Trollope claims that 'there are places in life
that can hardly be well filled except by "Gentlemen" ', going on to
say how hard it is for any one attempting it to define that term:

> But he would know what he meant, and so very probably
> would they who defied him. It may be that the son of the
> butcher of the village shall become as well fitted for
> employments requiring gentle culture as the son of the parson.
> Such is often the case. When such is the case, no one has been
> more prone to give the butcher's son all the welcome he has
> merited than I myself; but the chances are greatly in favour of
> the parson's son. The gates of one class should be open to the
> other; but neither to the one class nor to the other can good
> be done by declaring that there are no gates, no barrier, no
> difference. (ch. 3)

This is brave in its candour and honesty. Trollope was writing
about competitive examinations for the Civil Service, a topic which
he treated in *The Three Clerks*, the novel that preceded the next in
the Barsetshire series, *Doctor Thorne* (1858). In this passage Trollope
is enforcing the difference between social and cultural *mores* on the
one hand and merely intellectual and, one suspects, ultimately
financial achievement on the other. The self-made man was the
product of a new national ethos.

Trollope saw that England was becoming a commercial country.
It was in *Doctor Thorne* that he came face to face with the clash of
birth and wealth, land and money. He declared his own position
right at the outset:

> The old symbols remained, and may such symbols long remain
> among us ... to him who can read aright, they explain more
> fully, more truly than any written history can do, how

Englishmen have become what they are. England is not yet a commercial country.... She might surely as well be called feudal England, or chivalrous England. If in western Europe there does exist a nation among whom there are high signors, and with whom the owners of the land are the true aristocracy, the aristocracy that is trusted as being best and fittest to rule, that nation is the English.... Buying and selling is good and necessary; it is very necessary, and may, possibly, be very good; but it cannot be the noblest work of man; and let us hope that it may not in our time be esteemed the noblest work of an Englishman. (ch. 1)

Generally speaking, it is not the aristocracy in the sense of those of the highest rank who represent Trollope's ideal. It is rather the gentry, 'the owners of the land'. Just as in Mrs Gaskell's *Wives and Daughters* Squire Hamley looks down from the heights of an ancient lineage on the Earls of Cumnor, so in Trollope the Thornes trace back a family-tree to before the Conquest, and the Greshams of Greshamsbury link family to soil in a way that makes their more magnificent neighbours like the de Courcys and even the Duke of Omnium look like vulgar *parvenus*. In this context Trollope's descriptions of country houses should never be disregarded. Greshamsbury is 'in the purest style of Tudor architecture ... and a multitude of trim gardens and stone-built terraces.' (ibid.) By contrast, Courcy Castle 'was a huge brick pile, built in the days of William III, which, though they were grand days for the construction of the Constitution, were not very grand for architecture of a more material description ... a dull place to look at,' (ch. 15) whilst Gatherum Castle 'was a new building of white stone, lately erected at an enormous cost ... would probably be called Italian in its style of architecture ... a vast edifice; irregular in height – having long wings on each side too high to be passed over by the eye as mere adjuncts to the mansion, and a portico so large as to make the house behind it look like another building of a greater altitude,' (ch. 19) and the inside was as overpowering as the outside.

The Greshams are an impoverished family. Significantly, they have been impoverished by Squire Gresham's marriage to an extravagant de Courcy, Lady Arabella. The initial situation is therefore that Frank, the heir, in the insistent phrase of his aunt, the Countess de Courcy, 'must marry money'. Unfortunately, Frank is in love with Mary Thorne, who not only does not have money but does not have birth, either. She is the ward of Doctor Thorne and the illegitimate daughter of his brother and the sister of wealthy but uncultivated Sir Roger Scatcherd. In *Doctor Thorne* Trollope places personal worth in the form of proper pride, honour, honesty, love and happiness against the pressures represented by considerations of birth, family, land and money. He plays wryly on the contortions and contradictions in which birth finds itself involved in achieving the necessary connection with money.

First, there is Augusta Gresham, engaged to Mr Moffat, 'a young man of very large fortune ... the son of a tailor'; 'She did not pretend, had never pretended, that she loved Mr Moffat.' (ch. 4) Her father calls him 'a griping, hungry fellow', (ibid.) and indeed he demands £6,000 to take her. 'Girls cost nothing', the Countess has just said! Moffat deserts her when he thinks there is a chance of marrying the ointment heiress, Miss Dunstable, but all he gets for his treachery is a horse-whipping from Frank. Poor Augusta later considers the solicitor, Mr Gazebee, but is advised against the match by her cousin, Lady Amelia. She duly acknowledges that 'rank has its responsibilities as well as its privileges' (ch. 38) – and then Lady Amelia marries him herself four years later. Such is the difference, to take the chapter's title, between 'De Courcy Precepts and De Courcy Practice'.

They have rank; Martha Dunstable only has money. It attracts Moffat, and in the casual way, of which he is alone capable, it also attracts a proposal from one of the worthless de Courcy sons, George. Frank Gresham, too, is made to be attracted by it under the careful and unscrupulous tutelage of his aunt: 'The countess had claimed her prey, in order that she might carry him off to Miss Dunstable's golden embrace.' (ch. 14) The imagery is worthy of note. Frank's advances are half-hearted and ridiculous, and Trollope brings the affair to a neat climax in which two honest people, the one misled, the other sure, recognise themselves as the intended victims of other people's machinations. (ch. 20) Miss Dunstable manifests an endearing honesty, in contrast with the de Courcys and their like. She focuses our attention on money and shows that possession of it need not make for a reprehensible character, even though other figures such as Moffat and Louis Scatcherd who do possess it are reprehensible. She focuses our attention also on birth and shows that there is no necessary equivalence between good birth and good character: indeed, rather the opposite. Finally, and by inference from these others, she demonstrates the worth of integrity.

If *Doctor Thorne* can be summed up in a single phrase, that phrase must surely be integrity of thought and action. It is the demands of honesty to oneself and to others amid the complexities of the social world that produce the personal dilemmas and the conflicts in the book. Frank, once he has realised the error of his advances to Miss Dunstable, becomes rebellious in his dismissals of birth and wealth and property (e.g. chs 30, 44). Mary cannot but admit her love for him (ch. 29), and when he returns after a year's absence, she faces the ostracism of his family yet more firmly. Trollope's words are worth noting: 'Honour, honesty, and truth, out-spoken truth, self-denying truth, and fealty from man to man, are worth more than maiden delicacy; more, at any rate, than the talk of it.' (ch. 36) It is such feelings that serve to demonstrate Mary's courage, dignity and tenderness at their best in the climactic scene with Lady Arabella when she resists the latter's demands that the engagement be broken. (ch. 42) She, none the less, writes to Frank, asking whether he wishes to release her from her promise – and is all the more noble for that.

Doctor Thorne, no less than Mary, acts as a moral touchstone in the novel. Thorne, however, has to tread delicately, for he is the honest man entrusted with decisive secrets. He knows the truth of Mary's birth; he knows the possible consequences of Scatcherd's will; he knows that Mary, if she marries Frank, will thus be able to disembarrass the Greshamsbury estate; but he can only remain completely honest by not telling. Indeed, by revealing the details of Mary's birth before he can reveal the rest he makes matters apparently more difficult to resolve. In addition, he has to risk the danger of Mary's disinheritance by his refusal even to contemplate a marriage between her and Sir Roger's son, the worthless Louis. Everything comes right in the end; indeed, the novel has often been criticised for this as a kind of fairy story, with Mary cast as a modern Cinderella.

I believe that this is a serious misreading of *Doctor Thorne*. We know how it will end, and Trollope, I am sure, did not bother about that. He had little enough regard for plot in itself. What interested him was the moral problem, for, true though it is that the doctor and Mary are moral touchstones and have all the constancy that that role requires, they are in no sense morally static. In fact, they point out the lower standards of others only by the way in which they have to wrestle so strenuously for their own. This is why the social background matters. It gives rise to that series, for instance, of anxious and agonised questions beginning: 'Why had she not obeyed her conscience and her better instinct in that moment when the necessity for deciding had come upon her? Did she not know that there was everything against such a marriage as that which he proposed? ... ' (ch. 33) Mary asks these questions because she has 'asked others earlier, and it is these that take us back to Trollope's concern with gentility. I venture to suggest that they give us a better answer than any that he gave elsewhere:

> If she were born a gentlewoman! And then came to her mind these curious questions; what makes a gentleman? what makes a gentlewoman? What is the inner reality, the spiritualised quintessence of that privilege in the world that men call rank? ...
>
> And she answered the question. Absolute, intrinsic, acknowledged individual merit must give it to its possessor, let him be whom, and what, and whence he might. So far the spirit of democracy was strong within her. Beyond this it could be had but by inheritance, received as it were second-hand, or twenty-second-hand. And so far the spirit of aristocracy was strong within her. (ch. 6)

That is why at the end there has to be from Doctor Thorne a touch of the inevitably apologetic about Mary's marriage to Frank in his wish 'that her birth were equal to her fortune'; but he goes on, 'as her worth is superior to both'. (ch. 46)

In the *Autobiography*, after speaking of the next novel in the Barsetshire series, *Framley Parsonage* (1861), Trollope states that it was his aim to impress his readers

> with a feeling that honesty is the best policy; that truth prevails while falsehood fails; that a girl will be loved as she is pure, and sweet, and unselfish; that a man will be honoured as he is true, and honest, and brave of heart; that things meanly done are ugly and odious, and things nobly done beautiful and gracious. (pp. 133-4)

This is plain, straightforward and modest, as Trollope always is. He summarised the plot of *Framley Parsonage* as

> a morsel of the biography of an English clergyman who should not be a bad man but one led into temptation by his own

youth and by the unclerical accidents of the life of those
around him. The love of his sister for the young lord was an
adjunct necessary, because there must be love in a novel.
(ibid.)

To these he added the past – the Proudies, Grantlys, even Dr
Thorne and Miss Dunstable of the preceding novels in the series –
and what was to turn out to be the future – the social and political
life of London, and the Crawley family.

Framley Parsonage was Trollope's first attempt at the serialised
novel, and, as several contemporary critics complained, it gave his
tendency to long-windedness even greater rein than before.
Trollope claimed that the handling of the characters ensured its
success, and certainly one must concede that Mark Robarts, his
sister Lucy and Lady Lufton are strongly delineated and help to
produce some memorable scenes. Even Trollope, however, felt that
it was 'a hodge-podge', and when one takes Booth's convenient
summary of what he calls

> the narrative fragments describing Mark Robarts' financial
> problems, Lord Lufton's and Lucy Robarts' matrimonial
> problems, Josiah Crawley's problems of survival, Harold
> Smith's political problems, Nathaniel Sowerby's legal problems,
> Mrs Proudie's problems of social and ecclesiastical control, and
> Martha Dunstable's problems of fending off insincere suitors,
> (p. 50)

it is possible to concede to him that, narratively speaking, these
several lines 'merge naturally and easily', but, as one looks at them
thus listed, one recognises that only the first two matter throughout,
the third has an episodic intensity which preludes better things to
come, and the rest are nowhere.

Mark Robarts is a combination of ambition, inexperience and
lack of self-knowledge. Trollope illustrates the ambition that makes
Robarts want to gain the acquaintance of a rising Member of
Parliament, Harold Smith, and that makes him rashly and with a
touch of assertive independence disregard the views of his patroness,
Lady Lufton, who had given him all the considerable advancement
he had already so precociously obtained. This 'young flattered fool
of a parson' (ch. 4) is drawn into a visit to the Duke of Omnium,
representative to Lady Lufton of all that was evil. He is led also into
the stupid signing of a bill by the worthless Sowerby. Thereafter his

history is that of suffering for his brief folly – falling into the hands of moneylenders, his home invaded by bailiffs, his agony of spirit as he confronts and confides in his wife. Robarts's dangers of impoverishment have been dismissed by some critics, who have pointed to the support on which he was able to call. These critics seem not to have noticed his staunch refusal to appeal to Lord Lufton for help; but in any case, as usually with Trollope, it is not the outcome that matters but what the characters endure before the outcome is reached.

Part of the interest also derives from the sort of people with whom he becomes involved. Robarts does obtain the preferment his ambition led him to seek – a prebendal stall at Barchester, but it comes through Sowerby, whose note he signed and it looks suspiciously like a reward for favours dispensed. Through Sowerby Robarts falls into the hands of Tozer; the country clergyman in the power of the London moneylender. For the first time the dark shadow of the metropolis casts its baleful influence over Barsetshire. Even within the county, Trollope suggests, the old order is breaking up. The Greshams had stood to lose their property, Sowerby is actually on the way to doing so; Gatherum Castle is about to act up to its name. Trollope writes elegiacally of Sowerby as he walks through Chaldicotes Woods and 'how they had roamed there time out of mind ... father and son and grandson in regular succession'. (ch. 37) The estate is saved from the Gatherum maw, but it is lost to Sowerby. There is surely irony as well as satisfaction in its purchase by Miss Dunstable. London wealth has bought it, even though she does marry Doctor Thorne.

'Now as to this Chaldicotes set. After all, there was nothing so very dangerous about them; for it was in London, not in the country, that Mr Sowerby indulged.' (ch. 2) Thus thinks Lady Lufton at the beginning of the novel, and how wrong all that follows proves her to be! She is the representative of the old order, patriotic, faithful to her Church, materialistic towards her dependants. Typical of her kind, she is forthright in thought and speech, but she is quick to withdraw hasty words. Robarts's excuses for going to Gatherum are dismissed as hypocrisy (ch. 5), but she soon apologises to his wife for speaking thus harshly to her. She deplores her son's involvement with Sowerby, but unhesitatingly sells stock to save him from having to part with any of the family estates.

Trollope is unfair to himself in describing the love of Lord

Lufton and Lucy as just a necessary adjunct. It is a variation on the theme that Frank Gresham and Mary Thorne had played, for, though Lucy is like the latter in her generosity and spirited character, the parts played by Lord Lufton and his mother provide new depth in Trollope's treatment of the relationship. Whereas the de Courcys and Lady Arabella opposed Mary for purely mercenary and therefore debased motives in a conflict of wrong against right, Lady Lufton's maternal and aristocratic concern looks more like the difference of right against right and compels Trollope to lead her to the recognition of how and why she is wrong. Her conservatism, even as she is brought to acknowledge Lucy's worth (ch. 35), and her attachment to her son (ch. 34) make that recognition all the more difficult to attain, and Trollope is not slow to exploit the opportunities, especially in interviews between her and Lucy, which this situation presents.

Lufton himself, rather like Chiltern in the Palliser novels, though less markedly, is gradually improved by his association with Lucy. Trollope was aware that Lufton might not be thought worthy of Lucy (ch. 21), but he insists that he is a credible young man who will settle down, not unlike many others 'worthy of the excellent wives that ultimately fall to their lot'. (ch. 31) He is shown to be possessed of common sense and a certain penetration into character that enables him, in danger though he had been of making a mistake, to notice the great difference between the superficial beauty, Griselda Grantly, and the person of genuine worth, Lucy.

Lady Lufton reads Lucy's character wrongly. Biased as she is by other considerations, she persists almost to the end in thinking her insignificant, despite the evidence of the interviews and the partial conversion that followed them. Lufton is instinctively sure, but in some danger of allowing himself to be led into error. Lucy herself is clear-sighted about the whole matter. Indeed, it is this quality which makes her all too aware of the difficulties that lie in the path of her love. It determines her initial reserve towards Lufton (ch. 11). and results in her justifiably angry resentment at his mother's attempts to head her off. (ch. 13) At the same time Lucy cannot help regretting her own resoluteness, a regret that Trollope brings out, in telling detail, in the uncharacteristic flash of temper which leads her to whip the pony when she thinks that Lufton may yet marry Griselda. (ch. 21) She tries to persuade herself that he would repent of his love for her and even that she herself might not really love him. (ch. 26) She is as resolute in confronting Lady Lufton's criticism of the link with her son as she had been in refusing the son himself (ch. 35), and she insists to him that any marriage can only be with his mother's agreement. Trollope had more scope within a richer situation for Lucy than he had for Mary Thorne. He made the most of it.

It was only at the insistence of the publishers, Chapman & Hall, that Trollope consented to include *The Small House at Allington* (1864) in the first collected series of Barsetshire novels. Certainly it does not have much to do with the clerical affairs of the county, but then nor has *Doctor Thorne*. Like its predecessor, *Framley Parsonage*, it was serialised in the *Cornhill* – in the winter of 1862-3. As in that novel, Trollope is quick to adopt an anti-heroic, or perhaps more accurately a non-heroic, line – 'Whatever of the magnificent may be produced will be diluted and apportioned out in very moderate quantities' (ch. 2); and, as in that novel again, we find the corrupting and destructive influences of the capital invading the countryside. The plot is slight and the novel is long. Lily Dale falls in love with Adolphus Crosbie. Attracted by rank and the other trappings of the aristocratic aura, he deserts her for Lady Alexandrina de Courcy, to his ultimate sorrow, for the marriage quickly breaks down. Meanwhile, to balance Crosbie, a man from the city without family or connections, there is Johnny Eames, the local boy, immature beside his experienced rival, who also loves Lily, but in vain. She resolves to be an old maid.

The *Saturday Review*'s critic saw Trollope as doing 'what Miss Austen did, only that he does it in the modern style, with far more detail and far more analysis of character, although, perhaps, with less of lightness of touch and gentle pervading wit'. (14 May 1864, XVII, p. 595) Mr Robert Polhemus has pursued the comparison more deeply in his critique of this novel. He compares Lily with Emma Woodhouse, saying of the latter:

> The moral center and the social ideals of her world *do* coincide and her love for Knightley is ultimately a rational emotion.... Lily Dale lives more precariously.... The society itself is changing.... The characters are unsure about their values.... Her stubborn, unhappy love counteracts her fear of nothingness.... Love in *Emma* is a force for integration in the world; in *The Small House* it is an

idealistic means of escape from a disappointing world.
(Polhemus, 1968, pp. 93-4)

Enlightening though this is, it surely goes too far in taking the wish for the deed, and, moreover, one suspects it is our wish rather than Trollope's. Society was changing, the classes were mingling, the poorer genteel like Lily were vulnerable, the Dales were insecure and indeed about to give up their tenure of the *small* house, but does the novel so explicitly demonstrate her 'fear of nothingness'?

That this is our wish rather than Trollope's, he makes clear when he writes 'in the love with which she has been greeted I have hardly joined with much enthusiasm, feeling that she is somewhat of a French prig'. (*Autobiography*, ch. 10) In a letter to Miss E. B. Rowe he put the case more descriptively by saying that his aim was 'to show that a girl under such circumstances should bear the effects of her own imprudence, & not rid herself of her sorrow too easily'. (*Letters*, No. 234) In the novel itself Trollope views the question not in terms of obligation but of observed experience: 'Love does not follow worth, and is not given to excellence; – nor is it destroyed by ill-usage, nor killed by blows and mutilation.' (ch. 31)

The compulsion was psychological, and here is the supreme merit of the book. As the *Spectator* put it, the appeal of the characters lies 'in the hold they get or fail to get over other characters, and in the hold they yield to other characters over them' (9 April 1864, XXXVII, p. 421), what the writer calls the 'moral "hooks and eyes" of life'. Thus Lily, apparently conceived by Trollope as more endearing (ch. 2) than he thought she eventually was, gives herself with characteristic whole-heartedness to Crosbie, gives herself in her innocence, is prepared to sacrifice herself by releasing him when he complains of likely financial straits, and, when he does desert her, with the same wholeheartedness does forgive, does resolve not to hate, indeed to love him always. She is innocent but strong.

Crosbie is neither. Trollope is careful to suggest that he is incapable of passion. Just when Lily has declared 'Oh, my love! . . . My love! my love!', he is described as making 'a firm resolution that no consideration of worldly welfare should ever induce him to break his engagement'. (ch. 9) The very mention of the possibility is ominous of the likelihood. She is in his hands, he the victim of the all-too-certain allurements of the de Courcys, and the nearer he approaches them, the more vehement he is in assertion of his love for Lily. The relationship is summed up thus: 'He still hardly understood the depth of her character. He was not himself deep enough to comprehend it all. But yet he was awed by her great love.' (ch. 15) When he marries Lady Alexandrina, both of them, as with unconscious irony he recognises in his letter to Mrs Dale (ch. 30), have got what they deserved. From the first he acknowledges to himself his mistake and that he has lost immeasurably by his decision (cf. chs 35, 38). The quieter, smoother course of the love of Bell Dale and Doctor Crofts brings a harmonious counterpoint to the discord of the main story. That musical figure may be extended to Johnny Eames, for his immaturity is a mere tinkle beside the profound note of Lily's 'great love'. *The Small House at Allington* is too long and too slow, it lacks Jane Austen's incisive and economical grasp of character and event as well as her wit and irony, but it does demonstrate in Lily, *pace* some of her creator's own comments, that 'love's not Time's fool' nor 'alters when it alteration finds'.

The Last Chronicle of Barset (1867) completed what the *Examiner* (20 July 1867) called 'the best set of "sequels" in our literature'. With this book Trollope produced what he has been far from alone in regarding as the best novel he ever wrote. (*Autobiography*, ch. 15) In it he gathered together several strands from earlier volumes, so that practically everybody who has mattered in Barsetshire is there – from the first of them, Mr Harding, to those who had appeared more recently such as Johnny Eames and the others in *The Small House at Allington*. Whether it be his best or not, *The Last Chronicle* is, with only *The Way We Live Now* to approach it, Trollope's most ambitious novel. As a result, some, like Bradford Booth, for example, have complained of its lack of organisation. On the other hand, Polhemus finds those parts that have been most criticised such as the introduction of new characters into the London life of the novel to represent the intrusion into Barsetshire of 'a utilitarian culture which obliterates regional differences and minimises man's spiritual nature'. (1968, p. 132) This may, however, be to sophisticate the situation somewhat. Johnny Eames is in this London life and he is affected by it; there is the 'game of love-making' in which he participates, playing frivolously and altogether unworthily with Madelina Demolines until we reach the melodrama-cum-farce of the climax when her mother bursts in and she and her daughter attempt to coerce him into marriage, an attempt which he ingeniously foils by opening the window and bidding a passing policeman wait until he had escaped from the house. (ch. 80) This London relationship does invade Barset with Madelina Demolines's anonymous notes to Lily Dale. (ch. 59) In addition, one cannot help but notice the skill of Trollope's disposition in the contrast between the juxtaposed episodes of Johnny's escape and the death-scene of good old Mr Harding. (chs 80-1) Nevertheless, this is to argue for a relationship between the London scenes and Barset that Trollope does not seem to be quite so deliberately enforcing, not even indeed so much as he had done earlier. London, incidentally, is not all bad: there is, for instance, the very helpful lawyer, Mr Toogood, who comes down to Barsetshire to help Crawley.

Trollope, as elsewhere, seems in *The Last Chronicle* to be reaching forward as well as back. His London is a ruthless, heartless world of money and show. It usurps his interest and, to some extent, does make for the lack of organisation of which Booth complained. Dobbs Broughton's wealth is unreal, though ostentatious. Behind him is Mrs van Siever, and she uses his partner, Musselboro. Broughton is driven to drink and eventually to shooting himself. His wife, trivial and bored, flirts with the artist, Conway Dalrymple, and he paints Clara, the van Siever daughter, in his composition 'Jael and Sisera'. The choice of subject is apt, for men die slain, at least symbolically, in the houses of their so-called friends in London. The false romanticism which surrounds the creation of this ghastly picture is itself shattered by Mrs van Siever's incursion into the artist's extempore studio in the Broughton household, and with it the picture is shattered, too, slashed by Dalrymple's own penknife. It all reads like a trial run for *The Way We Live Now*. As Johnny Eames puts it, 'There is a sort of persons going now, – and one meets them out here and there every day of one's life, – who are downright Brummagem to the ear and to the touch and to the sight.' (ch. 24)

All this contrasts with, but especially in the second half it also dissipates somewhat, the intensity of the main plot. This latter is conceived in the most utterly simple terms – how did Crawley, the impoverished curate of Hogglestock, obtain and use a stolen cheque for twenty pounds? Trollope himself came later to question how 'even such a man as Mr Crawley could have forgotten how he got it,' (*Autobiography*, ch. 15) but I do not think that many readers are troubled by this problem of credibility. It was a touch of genius on the novelist's part to develop the character who had so impressively made an altogether too brief appearance in *Framley Parsonage*. There

71

we read of Crawley as 'a stern, unpleasant man . . . morose, silent and dogged. He had always at his heart a feeling that he and his had been ill-used'. (ch. 1) We commiserate with his sufferings, we can understand his despair, we admire his courage, but yet he is not, in the last resort, tragic, because of his pride and egotism. In his independence he rejects assistance, but that independence is essentially selfish and stupid. He attracts our pity, but his wife, ministering lovingly and treated often with a brutal disregard for her feelings, attracts it more. He is conscious of his once high potential and even now he envies Arabin's superior achievement. Our sympathies are always modified. In his poverty he recalls St Paul's similar condition and his stripes, imprisonment and dangers, but, Trollope adds and thus detracts from our pity, 'Mr Crawley, – so he told himself, – could have encountered all that without flinching'. (ch. 12) His courage and independence can soar above his situation, as when he routs Mrs Proudie, who interrupts his interview with the bishop, with the words 'Peace, woman' (ch. 18), but typically he relishes that victory to himself on his way home. At the nadir of his experiences we are moved by that strong mind reduced in illness to phases of incoherence in his conversation with Grace. (ch. 41) Trollope is, as ever, careful to prepare the ground, to tell us that even his wife was baffled by him, that 'she knew that he was almost a saint, and yet almost a castaway through vanity and hatred of those above him'. (ibid.) The master-stroke, however, lies in what follows: 'But she did not know that he knew all this of himself also.' The novelist insists on Crawley's self-regarding nature:

> He pitied himself with a commiseration that was sickly in spite of its truth. It was the fault of the man that he was imbued too strongly with self-consciousness. He could do a great thing or two. He could keep up his courage in positions which would wash all the courage out of most men. He could tell the truth though truth should ruin him. He could sacrifice all that he had to duty. He could do justice though the heaven should fall. But he could not forget to pay a tribute to himself for the greatness of his own actions. (ch. 61)

It is not surprising therefore that he could compare himself with Samson, 'Eyeless in Gaza, at the mill with slaves'. (ch. 62) Such self-consciousness may lead us to withhold some of our sympathy, but it also serves, by the degree to which it enables him to recognise himself, to make Crawley's suffering even greater. Could such a man ever be happy or, for that matter, tragic? Trollope has a meaningful parenthesis in his dismissal of Crawley, now vicar of St Ewold's, 'quiet . . . , and, as I think, contented'. (ch. 84)

The gathering of the strands in this novel involves also the dismissal of the Proudies and the Grantlys. Mrs Proudie fights her last battles. She is beaten by Crawley and her interference at the interview with Dr Tempest produces one of Trollope's saddest scenes. The bishop plucks up courage to tell her she has disgraced him and to lament that he may never be able to show his face again: 'How happy could he be if it were only possible for him to go away, and become even a curate in a parish, without his wife! Would there ever come to him a time of freedom? Would she ever die?' (ch. 47) He rejects her attempt at reconciliation: 'When a man's heart is broken, he cannot forget it.' (ibid.) That feeling persists, for in what is to be their final interview he sadly wishes that she would leave him. In the aftermath of her sudden death Trollope does not disguise the bishop's realisation that he is free at last, but with it there is also 'the dreariness of his loneliness'. (ch. 47) Pathos of a different kind is reserved for Mr Harding's quietus, the completion of a life full of gentleness and kindness, with his daughters at his bedside. 'They buried him in the cathedral which he had loved so well, and in which nearly all the work of his life had been done . . . The chronicler may say that that city never knew a sweeter gentleman or a better Christian.' (ch. 81)

Archdeacon Grantly remains, but changed. Throughout this novel he is harassed by his son's attachment to Grace Crawley. With his characteristic belief in the effectiveness of the weapons of worldly power he threatens disinheritance, but with equally characteristic humanity he cannot sustain his opposition to Grace when once he has met her. Prejudiced and impulsive he remains, but he can neither maintain his wrath nor withhold his generosity. As with Plantagenet Palliser, Trollope came to admire the archdeacon and to realise that even his prejudices enshrined traditional values worthy of respect and retention. The differing financial standing of the clergy, of a Crawley and a Grantly, is something that the contrasts in the book enforce. The archdeacon can speak of a certain standard of life as being that by which 'the people around him expected a gentleman to live'. (ch. 22) None the less, at the end he can put the word in a different context when to Crawley, apologising for his inability to provide Grace with a dowry, he replies: 'We stand . . . on the only perfect level on which such men can meet each other. We are both gentlemen.' (ch. 83)

Trollope bids farewell to Barset with obvious regret: 'To me Barset has been a real county, and its city a real city . . . and the voices of the people are known to my ears.' (ch. 84) He did, however, have one word more, a late, slight and little-known word in the tale of *The Two Heroines of Plumplington* (1882). Plumplington, we are told, is the second town of Barsetshire and the two heroines are Emily Greenmantle and Polly Peppercorn, who are respectively in love with Philip Hughes and Jack Hollycombe, each to her father's sorrow and opposition. The parallel histories proceed to parallel and happy ends. The link with Barset is as slight as the tale, but there is over all a cheerfulness and vitality that makes this late piece attractive reading. It was written in the last year of its creator's life. One can imagine that he was pleased to return, even though so fleetingly, to the county which he added to the map of England.

5

The Semi-Political Novels

(*Ralph the Heir; Can You Forgive Her?; The Eustace Diamonds; Phineas Finn; Phineas Redux; The Prime Minister; The Duke's Children*)

There are those who would criticise my title, but Trollope would have approved. He called the six novels now usually grouped together as the Palliser series (from the name of their most important recurrent character) 'semi-political tales'. (*Autobiography*, ch. 17) To these I add *Ralph the Heir*, which contains the fictional account of his own experiences as Liberal candidate at Beverley in 1868. I am aware of the criticism that was put both most strongly and most succinctly by Leopold Amery, himself a consummate politician, when he wrote of 'Trollope's sketches of a political world with the politics left out'. (Introduction to *The Prime Minister*, Oxford, 1952, p. xi) This view allows too little for Trollope's own conscious purposes as a novelist. He knew what he liked, but he also knew what his audience wanted: 'If I write politics for my own sake, I must put in love and intrigue, social incidents, with perhaps a dash of sport for the benefit of my readers.' (*Autobiography*, ch. 17) We need to remember also what he said in *The Last Chronicle of Barset* about not being concerned with the professional lives of the clergy: the same might well apply to his politicians. There may be little of Parliament in these novels, though that can hardly be said of some of them. It does not mean that there is little of politics.

Trollope believed that 'to sit in the British Parliament should be the highest object of ambition to every educated Englishman'. (ibid., ch. 16) He wrote this after his own sad experience at Beverley, and he had said it before. In *Can You Forgive Her?* he spoke of the entrance to the House of Commons as 'the only gate before which I have ever stood filled with envy'. (ch. 45) Such ambition may have heightened his feelings for, perhaps exaggerated his impression of, the politics he saw more closely than on the floor of the House where he never went. The primary political figures

75

may seem a little remote; some we only hear about, whilst the one we know best, Palliser, is by temperament rather cold and reluctant in his calling. The vividness of Trollope's political world is found in two settings – his elections and what I may call the social world of politics, in London clubs like the Reform and in the great Whig country houses during the Indian summer of their ascendancy.

Of his semi-political tales Trollope wrote: 'As I was debarred from expressing my opinions in the House of Commons, I took this method of declaring myself.' (*Autobiography*, ch. 17) His solitary attempt at election is a rather sordid story. He went to Beverley as a last-minute, carpet-bagging candidate with no illusions. His agent told him: 'Oh, no! . . . You won't get in . . . You will spend £1,000, and lose the election. Then you will petition, and spend another £1,000. You will throw out the elected members. There will be a commission and the borough will be disfranchised.' (ibid., ch. 16) It was a remarkably accurate forecast, and the event proved to be the culmination of an unsavoury electoral history which included some earlier disqualifications of members. The situation in 1868 was complicated by the accession under the Reform Act of the previous year of a large number of new voters (many of them no doubt hungry for the spoils of electoral bribery) combined with stringent new provisions against such corrupt practice.

Trollope stood as a Liberal, but what kind of a Liberal was he? He described himself as an 'advanced conservative Liberal'. (*Autobiography*, ch. 16) He was not a Conservative because he could not accept the Tories' belief in divinely prescribed inequality. (*The Prime Minister*, ch. 68) Instead, he advocated what he described as 'a tendency towards equality' (*Autobiography*, ch. 16), a kind of freedom slowly broadening down or *festina lente*. In this he believed that he was co-operating with history, seeing, as he thought, a diminution of inequality all around him.

The mid-nineteenth century and onwards was a critical time for Liberalism, despite the fact that in one guise or another it was in government for most of the period. In the face of persistent public pressure for reform those before cried 'Forward' and those behind cried, if not 'Back', at least 'Steady'. These latter were the old Whigs, men like Trollope's Duke of St Bungay, the 'Establishment' of that age. 'Its personnel', writes Donald Southgate, 'was aristocratic. Its influence was based essentially on oligarchy.' (1962, p. 77) Its great figures were Palmerston and Russell. On the other wing of the Liberal party and with whom Trollope had little sympathy were the Radicals, brash new free-trade manufacturer M.P.s like John Bright, on whom it appears that the character of Turnbull was based. St Bungay would not, like Sidney Smith's Mrs Partington, attempt to oppose the Atlantic Ocean; he would not resist, but he would try to postpone, the inevitable. (*The Prime Minister*, ch. 68) Trollope himself would

> be generous in our concession. . . . The coach must be allowed to run down the hill. Indeed, unless the coach goes on running, no journey will be made. But let us have the drag on both wheels. And we must remember that coaches running down hill without drags are apt to come to serious misfortune. (*Phineas Finn*, ch. 35)

Trollope's fellow Liberal at Beverley was Marmaduke Constable Maxwell, son of a local landowner, and their opponents were the retiring member and chairman of the Beverley Iron and Waggon Company, Sir Henry Edwards, and Captain E. H. Kennard. The main national issue was the disestablishment of the Irish Church and a subsidiary local issue was Edwards's alleged support for the attempt in the previous year to deprive the constituency of one of its two members. Trollope also picked out in his election address the education of the people as 'the question which will press upon Parliament'. He may have been recalling Robert Lowe here with his famous remark after the 1867 Act: 'Now we must educate our masters.' He was certainly anticipating Forster's Education Act of 1870. The campaign itself was boisterous and full of mutual recrimination, but it was nothing as compared with the election day itself. This and the rest of the story can be told in words which I have written elsewhere.

> The two Beverley newspapers, the Liberal *Recorder* and the Conservative *Guardian* produced, to say the least, somewhat conflicting reports. The latter for instance reported that the Conservative candidates were 'enthusiastically received', the former that they 'could not be heard'. On a show of hands the Liberals were declared elected, but the Conservatives demanded a poll. After which the Mayor 'complimented the electors on the orderly conduct which had prevailed, remarking that they were an example to the electors of England'. Trollope has something to say about just such a remark at the end of the hustings speeches in *Ralph the Heir*. On polling day the Liberals led till about 11 when, to quote

the *Recorder*, 'it was apparent that the Tories had begun their old practice of bribery'. There was a raid on the Conservative committee room, described by the *Hull News* (21 November 1868) thus:- 'A band of the Liberals, headed by Mr Daniel Boyes, forced an entrance – and took possession of a money-bag and some documents', but by the *Beverley Guardian* (21 November 1868) as:- 'A party of roughs . . . forced their way up the stairs of Mr. Thomas Clowes, saddler. . . . Knocking aside a man or two who were stationed on the landings, they broke into a room where two clerks were engaged in ticking off the voter's list and after abusing them, causing one to bleed severely, and ransacking the room, they proceeded, we understand, to break into a private lodging room.' The result was:-

Sir Henry Edwards	(Con.)	1132
E. H. Kennard	(Con.)	986
Hon. M. C. Maxwell	(Lib.)	895
A. Trollope	(Lib.)	740

The declaration produced a riot, but again there is a nice variation in the rival newspapers' reports, the *Recorder* stating that Edwards and Kennard 'had only just time to escape by a back street when the crowd rushed round to meet them' while the *Guardian* preferred to state that, 'finding it impossible to obtain a hearing, [they] withdrew with their friends'.

Inevitably there was a petition. It was heard by Baron Martin on 9 March 1869. He uncovered evidence of extensive bribery at the municipal elections held a fortnight before the parliamentary contest, most of it by a local draper, Wreghitt, who acted as Edwards' agent and who over a period of years had rigged the control of 'Walker's gift', a local charity with considerable funds at its disposal. Declaring that 'the place [was] a mass of corruption from beginning to end . . . It seems to be a town which is unfit to send members to Parliament', Martin reported the election null and void, but exonerated the candidates because no bribery could be traced directly to them. The half had not been told. A commission of enquiry arrived. It discovered that before 1867 there were only 300 'straight' voters out of an electorate of 1,000 and its report lists over 600 who either bribed or were bribed. As *The Times* put it, 'in 1854 there really was a pure election, but it was quite an accident' (quoted in *Beverley Recorder*, 26 February

1870). Edwards' systematic management of the borough was exposed; Trollope, Maxwell and their agent were cleared; and Beverley was disfranchised. (Pollard, 1968, pp. 8-9)

ecause it arose directly from the election and because it is not part f the series with which this chapter is principally concerned, I shall ke *Ralph the Heir* out of chronological order. Trollope wrote of in the *Autobiography* (ch. 19):

I have always thought it to be one of the worst novels I have written, and almost to have justified that dictum that a novelist after fifty should not write love-stories. It was in part a political novel; and that part which appertains to politics, and which recounts the electioneering experiences of the candidates at Percycross is well enough. Percycross and Beverley were, of course, one and the same place.

ike so many of Trollope's novels, *Ralph the Heir* has a weak hero. hackeray has his Pendennis and his George Osborne as well as his lenry Esmond. 'But for one Henry Esmond there are fifty Ralph lewtons, – five hundred and fifty of them.' (ch. 56) This comes om a passage late in the book, remarkable for its obtrusiveness. rollope there declares that 'No man or woman with a cons- ence ... can go on from year to year spinning stories without the esire of teaching' and ends his remarks thus: 'The faults of a Ralph lewton, and not the vices of a Varney or a Barry Lyndon, are the ils against which men should in these days be taught to guard lemselves. ... Such is the writer's apology for his very indifferent ero, Ralph the Heir.' That reads much like an *ex post facto* attempt justify what in fictional terms as well as moral is a dreary eation. It might, however, have been worse if Ralph had been so sistently terrible a warning as Trollope's words suggest he was leant to be.

As the author himself remarks in the *Autobiography*, Ralph is lore lively than his namesake who is not the heir. Together these vo provide a contrast rather like that between Roger Carbury and is cousin Sir Felix in *The Way We Live Now*, but, unsatisfactory lough that is in some ways, the juxtaposition of the two Ralphs more so; it is too simple and too pointed. Ralph, not the heir ind Trollope makes things awkward for himself by giving them oth the same name), natural son of the Squire of Newton, is ladowy and impossibly good. His cousin is credibly, but all too

obviously, worthless. What power Trollope gets out of th
character is not in what is recorded about him but in the reflection
that arise from this behaviour in a man of his position.

A spendthrift, deep in debt, Ralph the heir is, in the eyes of
women, 'handsome, well to do, of good address, and clever
(ch. 32) He declares his affection for Clarissa Underwood, but i
the course of his history is involved with Polly Neefit and aspire
to the hand of Mary Bonner. When he is in need of money, h
borrows from his breeches-maker, Neefit, who conceives the idea c
an advantageous marriage for his daughter. She, however, prefer
the boot-maker and Radical politician, Ontario Moggs. It is her
that Trollope examines the implication of class and money. Neef
is a social climber, whose aim is to find some 'gentleman' to marr
Polly and to whom he would give all his money, 'knowing as h
did so that the gentleman would probably never speak to hir
again'. (ch. 5) Ralph's contemplation of himself as that gentlema
is as follows: 'Fancy old Neefit for one's father-in-law! Everybod
is doing it now; but I don't think I'd do it for ten times the money
but he continues, 'The fact is, one has got to get used to thes
things, and I am not used to it yet.' (ibid.) Neefit's whol
behaviour is mercenary, lacking in social delicacy and tact. Th
comment from Newton Priory is: 'You wouldn't be glad to se
some shopkeeper's daughter calling herself Mrs Newton of New
ton. . . . The chances are that a shopkeeper's daughter will not be a
educated lady.' (ch. 14) Polly Neefit was indeed, 'good-humoured
somewhat given to frank coquetry and certainly fond of youn
men'. (ch. 5) She contrasts markedly with the Underwoo
daughters and Mary Bonner, who combines beauty, intelligence an
character. When Ralph offers marriage to Mary, she rejects hin
and so too, with proper poetic justice, does Clarissa when h
ultimately returns to her. After a comically pathetic persecution b
Neefit, he finally settles for Augusta Eardham, who, in the languag
of the clubs, 'has been running ten years, and been hawked abou
like a second-class racehorse'. (ch. 56) He has his reward, but hi
history is of obligations ill regarded, of social dangers all too nearl
embraced, of superficiality that makes him unfitted for the rank h
is called upon to occupy.

Ralph is vague enough, but the other characters of the main plo
and especially Clarissa Underwood and Mary Bonner, are vague
still. It is not surprising that Trollope confined his praise to th
political story. I have often wondered whether this was somethin

f an after-thought. It does not appear until chapter 20, where we
re told that 'the readers of this story have not as yet been troubled
on this head, there having been no connection between that great
matter and the small matters with which our tale has concerned
tself'. It brings an immediate feeling of vitality into the novel.

The character through whom the experience of the election is
onveyed is the dignified Conservative ex-Solicitor-General, Sir
Thomas Underwood. His fellow-Conservative is Griffenbottom, the
retiring member and his Liberal opponents Westmacott and On-
ario Moggs. Together they represent a fair cross-section of society.
Westmacott is the former member and gentleman. It is the other
two who attract attention. Griffenbottom is based on Trollope's
own opponent at Beverley, Sir Henry Edwards. Sir Thomas regards
him with extreme distaste.

> He could boast neither birth, nor talent, nor wit, – nor,
> indeed, wealth in the ordinary sense of the word.... It had
> all gone in procuring him a seat in Parliament.... Life
> without Parliament would be [misery] to him.... He
> rubbed against the shoulders of great men, and occasionally
> stood upon their staircases. (ch. 25)

The canvassing that Underwood finds so distasteful Griffenbottom
glories in. By little touches and short speeches Trollope conveys the
man's bluff, hearty manner and his complete disregard for any of
the views that his electorate might hesitatingly utter. It demonstrates what Trollope had described in his appearance, the 'assured
impudence about him that nothing could quell or diminish'. It is
soon obvious that, with a man like him, an agent like Trigger and
voters like Pile, Sir Thomas's insistence on purity and no bribery has
little chance of being regarded, much less of being upheld. There is
the inevitable petition against the election of Griffenbottom and Sir
Thomas. The latter is more and more nauseated by the cynical way
in which the business is managed. It even reaches the point where
Trigger suggests that Sir Thomas should resign his seat to allow a
place for the Liberals and the dropping of the petition. The end of
it all is the disfranchisement of Percycross, with Griffenbottom
exposed but still jauntily resilient. By contrast, Sir Thomas, whose
money had been spent against his will, acknowledges that his plea
for purity had failed. He is hooted out of the place for his pains.

Griffenbottom is a social-climbing businessman. Ontario Moggs
is a determinedly Radical businessman, who to the consternation

and mystification of his father, urges the rights of labour. Trollope caricatures him as an aspirant to realms beyond his reach. His name itself is vaguely funny, the Christian name coming from a Canadian godfather. His tub-thumping activities at the 'Cheshire Cheese' whilst seen as sincere enough, are endowed with an air of burlesque whilst Moggs's high hopes of the election campaign are but the bathetic prelude to the reality, conveyed with devastating power by Trollope in his description of the meeting of the candidates when Moggs 'bowed and attempted to make a little speech; but nobody in one army or the other seemed to care much for poor Ontario (ch. 25) The inference here as in the inheritance of Newton is the same. At that place the tenants recognised the right of the real squire, Ralph the heir, reprehensible though much of his behaviour was and commendable though that of his cousin might be. At Percycross – and in Parliament – there was a place for the Underwoods and the Westmacotts. By contrast, Griffenbotton epitomises Trollope's disgust at some who could get into Parliament (see especially ch. 40), whilst Moggs merely personifies the pretentious in the dimensions of farce. That determined young lady, Polly Neefit, saw the several-faceted appropriateness of an engagement between herself and Ontario Moggs. (ch. 48)

Two of the Palliser series had preceded *Ralph the Heir* (1871). The first was *Can You Forgive Her?* (1864), the second *Phineas Finn* (1869). The latter was the more definitely political. In preparation for it Trollope had pursued a course of political reading and attendance at the House of Commons before the book's serial appearance in *Saint Paul's Magazine* in October 1867. This same preparatory work did much to stimulate Trollope's own appearance at Beverley in 1868. It is well – and easy – to distinguish the extent of political interest in the several Palliser novels, much the greatest in the two Finn novels and in *The Prime Minister,* less so in *The Duke's Children,* least in *Can You Forgive Her?* and *The Eustace Diamonds.*

 Can You Forgive Her?, with its three plots in parallel, is more tautly organised than many of Trollope's novels. This may be because he used this book to translate into novel form his unsuccessful play, *The Noble Jilt.* Each of the plots concerns a woman's choice between rival suitors, the one worthy, the other much less so. Alice Vavasor is torn between the claims of John Grey 'the worthy man' and her cousin George, 'the wild man' (as chapters 3 and are entitled). In making her decision she has before her the example of Glencora who, or, more accurately, for whom was, preferred the sincere, loving, but unimaginative Plantagenet Palliser at the expense of the handsome, reckless, attractive Burgo Fitzgerald. The third affair between Alice's unlikely aunt, the vulgar Mrs Greenow, and Mr Cheesacre and Captain Bellfield provides some comic relief, but is of no intrinsic importance in the novel.

Can You Forgive Her? is Trollope's first deep study of the marital relationship that in its varied aspects became a recurrent concern of his work. In *Ralph the Heir* he wonders about the ill-considered union – 'It takes years to make a friendship; but a marriage may be settled in a week, – in an hour,' but yet, he argues, 'It is a fair question whether they do not answer better than those which have less of chance. . . . There are some leaps which you must take in the dark if you mean to jump at all.' (ch. 56) In *Can You Forgive Her?* he utters sentiments not dissimilar:

> I am not sure, however, that marriage may not be pondered over too much; nor do I feel certain that the leisurely repentance does not as often follow the leisurely marriages as it does the rapid ones. . . . I do not know that a woman can assure to herself, by her own prudence and taste, a good husband any more than she can add two cubits to her stature; but husbands have been made to be decently good, – and wives, too, for the most part, in our country, – so that the thing does not require quite so much thinking as some people say. (ch. 11)

But what is a 'good husband' without love? That was Lady Glencora's problem. We recall Thackeray's virulent denunciation of the marriage market when she says:

> We talk with such horror of the French people giving their daughters in marriage, just as they might sell a house or a field, but we do exactly the same ourselves. When they all come upon you in earnest, how are you to stand against them? (ch. 22)

In an outspoken declaration after her marriage that shocked some of Trollope's contemporaries, Glencora declares her continuing love for Burgo. In brilliant variations on the meanings of falseness she first considers the claims of her guides that Burgo would ill-use and desert her and concludes: 'It is better to have a false husband than to be a false wife.' Alice misinterprets this as meditated infidelity, to which Glencora vehemently retorts:

> Tempt me to be false! Why, child, it has been false
> throughout. . . . By law I am his wife; but the laws are liars!
> I am not his wife. . . . When I went to him at the altar, I
> knew that I did not love the man that was to be my husband.
> But him, – Burgo, – I love him with all my heart and soul. I
> could stoop at his feet and clean his shoes for him, and think
> it no disgrace! (ch. 27)

It is possible to understand why Henry James thought that this novel should have been Glencora's tragedy rather than Alice's, and it is certainly no surprise that the former becomes a continuing and developing character in Trollope's saga.

Nevertheless, it is Alice about whom the title's question is asked, and her irresolution, vacillation and change of purpose puzzle even Glencora. This is hardly surprising since her problem was so clear-cut. Glencora counsels Alice to withdraw even at the altar 'if you did not love him'. When Alice replies, 'But I did love him,' she can only respond with 'Then I don't understand it.' Trollope summarises Alice's situation at the beginning. She loved John Grey 'and she loved him only. But she had once loved her cousin . . . and was tormented by a feeling that she had had a more full delight in that love than in this other that had sprung up subsequently.' (ch. 3) A later chapter (35) sums it all up in its title: 'Passion versus Prudence.' John Grey, she thinks, is too good for her; he is certainly too dull for her. The irony is that, as George Vavasor grows worse and indeed as her own inclination declines, she feels greater obligation to give herself to him. Appropriately in the melancholy wildness of a Christmas afternoon on Swindale Fell she contemplates marriage to George in a mood of weary resignation:

> She was beginning to think that love . . . did not matter. Of
> what use was it, and to what had it led? What had love done
> for her friend Glencora? What had love done for her? Had she
> not loved John Grey, and had she not felt that with all her
> love life with him would have been distasteful to her? It
> would have been impossible for her to marry a man whom
> personally she disliked; – but she liked her cousin George, –
> well enough, as she said to herself almost indifferently. (ch. 31)

How well those final words epitomise her whole malaise! She does not go long before she has to realise that 'she had been mad when she had told herself, whilst walking over the Westmorland fells, that after all she might as well marry her cousin'. (ch. 37) She perceives with horror that she would be doing precisely what Glencora had done.

Unlike Glencora, she did not love 'the wild man', however much she might be prepared to help him, because, as later in the book Trollope makes clear, whatever parallels there might be in their paths, the natures of the two girls were essentially different:

> Love with [Glencora] had in it a gleam of poetry, a spice of fun, a touch of self-devotion, something even of hero-worship; but with it all there was a dash of devilry, and an aptitude almost for wickedness. She knew Burgo Fitzgerald to be a scapegrace, and she liked him the better on that account. She despised her husband because he had no vices.... In all that she might have done, there would have been no thoughtfulness . . .
>
> But Alice's love had been altogether of another kind. . . . It was too thoughtful. I will not say that there was no poetry in it, but I will say that it lacked romance. There was certainly in it neither fun nor wickedness; nor was there, I fear, so large a proportion of hero-worship as there always should be in a girl's heart when she gives it away. But there was in it an amount of self-devotion which none of those near to her had hitherto understood. (ch. 69)

In her thinking overmuch Alice made the same mistake as Glencora, of giving herself to one man when she loved another. John Grey, 'imperious in his tranquillity', forgives her. He takes up a word we have heard earlier: 'I know that you will say nothing to me that is false. Through it all you have spoken no word of falsehood.' (ch. 74) Even when her faith appeared unfaithful, she was really being falsely true.

It is surprising that Henry James should have preferred Glencora's history to that of Alice with its greater complexities. What is remarkable in the former's is the passion and frankness that are themselves so much of the character of the woman herself. There is the powerful scene at breakfast with her husband when her frustration breaks its bounds:

> I do love Burgo Fitzgerald. I do! I do! I do!... I do not love you; - not as women love their husbands when they do love

them. But, before God, my first wish is to free you from the misfortune that I have brought upon you.... How I wish I could die! Plantagenet, I would kill myself if I dared. (ch. 48)

Trollope slips in her regrets at her childlessness. As Robert Polhemus has noted (1968, p. 110), Glencora's neurotic violence is something that a post-Freudian generation may well associate more readily with her sense of sexual failure than did Trollope's own. To her outburst Plantagenet replies by assuring her of his love and deciding to give up his political career at a critical moment. Trollope's psychological mastery is again revealed by a single unobtrusive sentence: 'He was killing her by his goodness.'

That scene is a turning-point in their relationship. As he recalls it, Plantagenet remembers that Glencora had promised that

she would do her best for him. Then something of an idea of love came across his heart, and he acknowledged that he had married without loving or without requiring love.... But now, – now he loved her. (ch. 59)

He could not give her 'the little daily assurance of her supremacy in the man's feelings, the constant touch of love, half accidental, half contrived, ... the softness of an occasional kiss given here and there when chance might bring them together', (ch. 24) as Burgo could. Even when things were better, he could not share her excitement in the action of the swimmers. (ch. 69) Yet, different though they were and could not help but remain, their baby becomes the seal of their happiness together. (ch. 79)

Vavasor and Palliser (and John Grey also, but in his case it is of no importance) are involved in politics. Vavasor is a precursor of Phineas Finn, the man without means seeking a foothold in the House of Commons. With Alice's money he fights an election for the Chelsea Districts with the cry 'Vavasor and the River Bank'. The whole episode is notable only for the unscrupulousness of his agent Scruby and the publican Grimes, whose favours and influence are blatantly on offer to the highest bidder. Scruby, who invents the cry, knows the work of embanking will never be done, 'But you can always promise it at the hustings and can always demand it in the House.' (ch. 44)

Trollope is not, however, in this novel primarily concerned, politically, with elections. Nor indeed does he deal much with the proceedings of the House of Commons, though there are two brief scenes – the opening of the debate on the Queen's Speech (ch. 42) and what is presumably an adjournment debate (ch. 45) which contain some nice touches such as Trollope's reflection on the mock-anger of parliamentary Opposition and the pathos of Lord Middlesex's strenuously prepared and well-informed speech on Church reform delivered to an emptying assembly and finally cut short by the House being counted out for lack of a quorum. Middlesex, Trollope conjectures, must have contrasted his ill success with the differing reception accorded to Farringcourt earlier, and, says Trollope, must have contrasted also his own uprightness of character with the other's worthlessness.

Eloquence is little and integrity is much. Trollope's main concern is therefore with the character of politicians and their attitudes towards their work. 'The George Vavasors, the Calder Joneses, and the Botts are admitted [to the House of Commons]. Dishonesty, ignorance, and vulgarity do not close the gate . . . [but] the best of [England's] Commoners do find their way there.' (ch. 45) Trollope goes on to say: 'From thence flow the waters of the world's progress, – the fullest fountain of advancing civilisation.' With such a high view of the House, Trollope must be concerned to show from what such quality derives. The twenty-fourth chapter gives us cameos of 'Three Politicians'. One is Bott, Lancashire textile manufacturer, Radical M.P., social aspirant, one of the 'men who get into such houses as Matching Priory and whose presence there is a mystery to many'. By contrast, there is the Duke of St Bungay, 'Knight of the Garter, a Lord Lieutenant of his county', with long ministerial experience, – 'a walking miracle of the wisdom of common sense. He never lost his temper. He never made mistakes . . . . He was never reckless in politics, and never cowardly. . . . All the world respected him'; but St Bungay is the veteran statesman, practising Horace's 'Nil admirari', perhaps taking things just a little too easily.

The third man, Palliser, is the ideal:

One of those politicians in possessing whom England has perhaps more reason to be proud than of any other of her resources ... born in the purple, ... already very rich, surrounded by all the temptations of luxury and pleasure; and yet he devoted himself to work with the grinding energy of a young penniless barrister. He was not a brilliant man, and understood well that such was the case. ... He was listened to as a laborious man, who was in earnest in what he did,

who got up his facts with accuracy, and who, dull though he
be, was worthy of confidence.... He had taught himself to
believe that oratory, as oratory, was a sin against that honesty
in politics by which he strove to guide himself.... He was
an upright thin, laborious man; who by his parts alone could
have served no political party materially, but whose parts were
sufficient to make his education, integrity and industry useful
in the highest degree. It is the trust which such men inspire
that makes them so serviceable.

Trollope begins the next paragraph with the words: 'If he was
dull as a statesman, he was more dull in private life, and it may
be imagined that such a woman as his wife would find some
difficulty in making his society the source of her happiness.' We
have seen some of the consequences of this, but one other was
Palliser's willingness to sacrifice the opportunity of the much-
coveted Chancellorship of the Exchequer because he had agreed to
take Glencora abroad at a time when their marriage was under
stress. This is of a piece with the nobility, the cold nobility it must
be said, which he shows throughout. Palliser, in whatever sphere he
finds himself, recognises his duty and pursues his course without
flinching. That Trollope followed his career in novel after novel is
not surprising; nor, given his creator's great and obvious sympathy,
is his belief that 'taking him altogether . . . Palliser stands more
firmly on the ground than any other personage I have created'.
(*Autobiography*, ch. 10)

Palliser is developed through the rest of the series, though in one
novel, *The Eustace Diamonds* (1873), he has little part. If Palliser
represents all that is best in the English aristocracy, we find in Lizzie
Eustace and her entourage all that is worst. *The Eustace Diamonds*
is one of the best-constructed of Trollope's novels, full of narrative
intricacy and suspense, from which he might well have made a
better play than either of those he attempted – *Did He Steal It?* from
The Last Chronicle of Barset and *The Noble Jilt*, later transformed
into *Can You Forgive Her?*. Making fun at his own expense,
Trollope amusingly tears this latter play to pieces in describing an
alleged production of it in *The Eustace Diamonds*. (ch. 52) There is
also a similarly self-ridiculing passage in *Can You Forgive Her?* (ch.
17) in the character of the 'sporting literary gentleman', Pollock.
    The main thread of the story concerns the fate of the Eustace

diamonds, which, Lizzie claims, had been given to her by her late husband and which, the family lawyer insists, belong to the family as an heirloom and are therefore inalienable. They are, however, stolen – or at least thought to have been stolen – in Carlisle, and then, after Lizzie's pretence of their loss, they are actually stolen in London and never recovered. The treasure on which Lizzie had set such store and which she was prepared to go to such lengths to retain becomes the useless diamonds. This aspect of the tale is concerned with Lizzie's machinations and duplicity and with the police enquiries, the subsequent trial and its revelation of the part Lizzie had played.

She also has her love-affairs – her unenthusiastic engagement to Lord Fawn, his obvious discomfort in an association with someone rapidly becoming so notorious; her attempts to inveigle her cousin Frank Greystock, an impecunious Member of Parliament, into a relationship with her, despite her awareness of his engagement to Lucy Morris; and her ultimate alliance with Emilius, a popular preacher and suspected 'renegade' Jew. Trollope is repeatedly scathing about this man, and he is always so within Lizzie's own perspective: 'It was nothing against him in her judgment that he was a greasy, fawning, pawing, creeping, black-browned rascal', (ch. 66) and, as he proposes to her,

> While he was making his speech she almost liked his squint. She certainly liked the grease and nastiness. Presuming, as she naturally did, that something of what he said was false, she liked the lies. There was a dash of poetry about him; and poetry, as she thought, was not compatible with humdrum truth. (ch. 73)

When at the end he returns to his suit in high-flown language, we are told: 'She liked lies thinking them to be more beautiful than truth.' (ch. 79)

Her whole life is a lie, but there is nothing mean about it. After the committal proceedings, her brother-in-law acknowledges her impudently independent attitude with the words: 'She is a very great woman' – and 'Lizzie Eustace returned home to Hertford Street in triumph.' (ch. 72) She adds to this triumph by her withdrawal to Scotland and refusal to appear at the trial itself. This, however, is but the culmination of a supremely managed career, in which each breath-taking effrontery follows quickly on the heels of its forerunner. The chief of them is the deliberate, ruthless way in

89

which she conducts the interview with Frank Greystock, when she dismisses the idea that Lucy Morris in her poverty can possibly make a suitable wife for him and promptly suggests herself instead. He dashes off, frightened. (ch. 62) Then with consummate villainy she tries to persuade Lucy to agree that it is she (Lizzie) whom Frank loves! (ch. 64)

It is evil of heroic proportions and Trollope insists on the gap between ordinary human behaviour and Lizzie's constant assumption of roles. Before Lucy arrives for the interview, Lizzie 'studied the part she was to play with all possible care'. The image of the actress runs through the book. One of the earliest of these references mentions how Lizzie might easily have succeeded as such, 'And her voice would have suited the stage . . . flexible and capable of much pretence at feeling', a flexibility that, significantly, 'could raise it to a pitch of indignant wrath befitting a Lady Macbeth'. Acting is a part of those lies that she found more beautiful than truth – 'The guiding motive of her conduct was the desire to make things seem to be other than they were. To be always acting a part rather than living her own life was to her everything' (ch. 19), and again 'There was no reality about her, and the want of it was strangely plain to most unobservant eyes. But give her a part to play that required exaggerated strong action, and she hardly ever failed.' (ch. 61)

The quotation about her voice occurs in the context of her reading poetry aloud, but poetry for her is something essentially artificial, divorced from reality. We have noted that it is linked with Emilius's lying proposal. Her 'rock-bound shore' where 'the real rocks were not very rocky' is 'a place appropriate for solitude and Shelley' – and Shelley is *Queen Mab!* Trollope implies that reader and poet are well matched in their exaggerated attitudes:

> 'How wonderful is Death! Death, – and his brother Sleep!'
> Then she half-closed the volume, and thought that she enjoyed
> the idea Death, – and his brother Sleep! She did not know
> why they would be more wonderful than Action, or Life, or
> Thought; – but the words were of a nature which would
> enable her to remember them, and they would be good for
> quoting. (ch. 21)

He pursues the quotation:

> 'Sudden arose Ianthe's soul; it stood all-beautiful in naked

purity.' The name of Ianthe suited her exactly. And the antithesis conveyed to her mind by naked purity struck her strongly, and she determined to learn the passage by heart. Eight or nine lines were printed separately, like a stanza, and the labour would not be great, and the task, when done, would be complete. 'Instinct with inexpressible beauty and grace. Each stain of earthliness Had passed away, it reassumed Its native dignity, and stood Immortal amid ruin'. Which was instinct with beauty, - the stain or the soul, she did not stop to inquire, and may be excused for not understanding.

Shelley's ambiguity is suited to Lizzie, though, suggests Trollope, there is in 'naked purity' a clarity only too vivid. Purity - and Lizzie! The ambiguity as to whether stain or soul was instinct with beauty is even more pointed. Elsewhere, and not surprisingly, Lizzie exclaims: 'I like Launcelot better than Arthur.' (ch. 19)

Lizzie's retinue has for its main figures Lord George de Bruce Carruthers, of doubtful nobility in more ways than one, and his female counterpart, Mrs Carbuncle. They provide Lizzie with a supporting chorus of raffishness and adventure. She considers the possibility of an alliance with Lord George, whom she imagines as Byron's Corsair. She is, however, engaged to the conventional - and fearful - Lord Fawn. What a contrast! And it is not simply the bad and the good, for Trollope extracts considerable humour from the terrified ditherings of Fawn, seeking to extricate himself from his attachment as Lizzie's notoriety increases. If this association represents naïvete entangled with cunning, that of Mrs Carbuncle's niece, Lucinda, with the effete young aristocrat, Sir Griffin Tewett, consists of frigidity involved with superficiality. Tewett has no real feelings but is propelled by a mixture of his own fantasies and Mrs Carbuncle's coercion into an engagement with Lucinda, which she does not want. She finds him physically repulsive and, finally and spectacularly, she repudiates her unwilling commitment on the very morning that she is to be married. This minor action of the novel derives its power from Lucinda's candour which yet at the same time is mixed with and derives from other less reputable qualities, a certain cynicism and a definite sexual abnormality.

By contrast with these there is Lucy Morris. Of her and Lizzie Trollope says: 'Lucy with her simplicity was stronger than was she with her craft.' (ch. 21) As with so many of Trollope's heroines, the decisiveness of her delineation is affected by the need to emphasise her reticence. She is a governess to the Fawn family, and as such maintains a dignity, independence and charm without any of that carping note that comes, for instance, in the Brontës' characters from the same station in life. Moreover, as in her confrontation with Lizzie over Frank, she can show sufficient resolution and courage, when all the odds seem against her, to discomfit her opponent.

Indeed, the resolution possessed by both these combatants contrasts with the lack of it in Frank Greystock, and the passage quoted above goes on to consider his dual nature, 'in whose breast not only is evil always fighting against good, – but to whom evil is sometimes horribly, hideously evil, but is sometimes also not hideous at all'. (ch. 18) Greystock's course in relation to Lizzie moves counter to that of Lord Fawn (they are political enemies also). He is attracted towards her, aided, of course, by her endeavours; he is 'Our hero ... falling lamentably short in his heroism.' (ch. 60) His history is a study in half-hearted, but yet ultimately successful, resistance to temptation. He and Lucy finally marry, but nothing is said of his future. Unlike Phineas Finn's fate, with whatever convenience that may appear to be settled, Greystock's does not resolve the problem that Trollope succinctly put: 'We feel that truth to his sweetheart is the first duty of man. I am afraid that it is not the advice we give to our sons.' (ch. 76)

In the *Autobiography* Trollope says of the *Phineas* novels that 'they are, in fact, but one novel'. He also says:

> As I fully intended to bring my hero again into the world, I was wrong to marry him to a simple pretty Irish girl,' who could only be felt as an encumbrance on such return. When he did return I had no alternative but to kill the simple pretty Irish girl, which was an unpleasant and awkward necessity. (ch. 17)

Fortunately, the greater incidence of mortality in childbirth during the nineteenth century gave Trollope a greater bonus of verisimilitude than he could obtain now. Of course, he was wrong to marry Finn as he did. He was wrong too, I am pretty sure, in his *ex post facto* belief that he intended to bring Finn back into the world. Such a suggestion hardly goes convincingly with his confession that he had not even made any provision as to what to do with him at the end of *Phineas Finn*. And such improvisation went on, apparently, even with such a much more intricately organised novel as *The Eustace Diamonds*. (ibid., ch. 19)

Of this novel he wrote: 'I doubt whether I had written anything so successful ... since *The Small House at Allington*', but immediately makes a significant distinction: 'I had written what was much better, – as, for instance, *Phineas Finn*.' Despite its ending, most readers would agree. As a story *The Eustace Diamonds* is the more accomplished achievement, but for the realisation of a world, the interaction of characters, the reaction of character within ethos, it would be difficult indeed to better the Finn novels. Indeed, striking events seem to be out of accord with the tone of these novels. One may believe Kennedy's insanely jealous attack on Finn, but the latter's earlier rescue of his attacker when he is beset by garrotters is practically superfluous, whilst the accusation and trial of Finn for the murder of his odious fellow-politician, Bonteen, is not only difficult to believe but also tediously drawn-out. Nor do we feel that anything is gained in the way of character-development or the like by this episode.

The novel derives its strength from Phineas Finn himself in two ways – first, in his personal relationships with the several women in the tale, and second, as he acts as the focus through which the world of London society and politics is projected. Though he falls for nearly every woman in sight, we find it difficult to see why they should fall for him. 'There were many questions about himself which [Finn] usually answered by telling himself that it was his fate to walk over volcanoes.' (ch. 4) In this sentence Trollope tells us more than he perhaps intended. Those volcanoes include the relationships with Lady Laura Standish (later Kennedy) as well as other minor, but active, craters involving Violet Effingham, Madame Goesler and Mary Flood Jones. Indeed, Trollope faces his own discomfort with the last when he honestly contrasts her success with Finn's chance of marrying Madame Goesler, 'the most beautiful women he had ever seen, the most witty, and in many respects the most charming', whereas Mary lacked 'the spirit of Lady Laura, or the bright wit of Violet Effingham, or the beauty of Madame Goesler'. (ch. 74) Finn was an adventurer in politics and he was prepared to be an adventurer in love. He accepted Mary with 'many regrets'.

The only defence of this acceptance could be, as with others of Trollope's weak heroes, that circumstances alter inclinations. Some support for this comes from Phineas's self-persuasion about Violet

93

Effingham after his attraction to Laura Standish: 'He told himself with oaths that he had never loved any one but Violet Effingham.' (ch. 53) He tells himself that he had been merely a boy when he loved Lady Laura (ch. 39); he is not beyond thinking of her, however, after he has lost Violet. (ch. 56) At the same time, despite this degree of calculation in him, he can yet refuse Madame Goesler's money which would give him the independence he requires for his political career, and he can impulsively propose to Mary. In *Phineas Redux* the field is left clear for Phineas's marriage to Madame Goesler, a character whom Trollope skilfully develops in her relationship with the aged and dying Duke of Omnium, giving her a generosity and serenity of spirit that makes her one of his most attractive creations.

There is indeed a pattern among the women of the Finn novels which places Madame Goesler between such turbulent fellows as Laura Standish and Glencora Palliser. The latter we have seen before and shall see again more fully in *The Prime Minister*. The former is one of the triumphs of the Finn novels, attracted from the first to Phineas, giving away her fortune to pay her brother's debts and then, marriage to Finn being out of the question, sacrificing herself to the wealthy but gloomily Calvinistic Scottish 'laird', Robert Kennedy. His melancholia, which leads to jealous fantasy and ultimate violence, makes him fit to stand in kind, if not extent, beside Louis Trevelyan (*He Knew He Was Right*). His self-righteousness gives him an inflexibility and irrationality that prevents the development of any fruitful relationship, but Trollope also shows the cumulative effect of living in proximity to him. Weeping tears both of anger and frustrated affection when Phineas has told her of his love for Violet, Laura is surprised by Kennedy. She thwarts his well-meant approach, the consequence both of her own agitation and the state no doubt into which their relationship had entered. The reader cannot forget, either, that the man she had loved has just left before the man she has married entered:

> 'Oh, – is that you?' . . . .
> 'Yes, – it is I. Is anything wrong?'
> 'Very much is wrong.'
> 'What is it, Laura?'
> 'You cannot help me.'
> 'If you are in trouble you should tell me what it is,
> and leave it to me to try to help you.'

'Nonsense!' she said, shaking her head.
'Laura, that is uncourteous, – not to say undutiful also.'
'I suppose it was, – both. I beg your pardon, but I
could not help it.'
'Laura, you should help such words to me.'
'There are moments, Robert, when even a married woman
must be herself rather than her husband's wife. It is so,
though you cannot understand it.'
'I certainly do not understand it.'
'You cannot make a woman subject to you as a dog is so.'
(ch. 39)

he has ruined her life, and that ruined life, estranged from her
husband, living abroad with her invalid father, is told in all its
weary pathos in *Phineas Redux*. Trollope sums it all up with
admirable conciseness and justice after Kennedy's death:

Though she had felt him to be a tyrant and herself to be
a thrall ... yet she had known through it all that the fault
had been hers, and not his. He only did that which she
should have expected when she married him; – but she had
done none of that which he was entitled to expect from her.
The real fault, the deceit, the fraud, – the sin had been with
her, – and she knew it. Her life had been destroyed, – but not
by him. (ch. 70)

In the Laura-Kennedy story Trollope brings out, in his
characteristic minor key, the human tragedy that, though life is
what we make it, our creation does not always match our intention, and that even noble sacrifice may turn out to be both
mistaken and unbearable.

In a world where manners usually successfully control spirit,
Laura Standish is an exception, and so is her brother, Lord Chiltern,
successful suitor for Violet Effingham and over whom, with all too
little provocation, he fights a duel with Phineas Finn. Strongly built,
with short-clipped red hair and a red beard, he looks and is
ferocious. In contrast with the deferential drawing-room manner of
so many of Trollope's young men (and presumably that was the
accepted mode of the time), Chiltern wastes no words but simply
asks Violet to be his wife and then seizes her and kisses her
violently, forehead, cheeks, lips, hands, all. (ch. 52) In *Phineas
Redux* his ferocity is concentrated into the role for which his wife

very accurately says he was born, that of Master of Hounds, and hi
activity consists chiefly in a running battle against the Duke o
Omnium's agent, who shows no concern to preserve foxes. Chil
tern's fitness for the role is confirmed in Trollope's description of it

> It is essential that a Master of Hounds should be somewhat
> feared by the men who ride with him. . . . He should be a
> man with whom other men will not care to argue; an
> irrational, cut and thrust, unscrupulous, but yet distinctly
> honest man. . . . He should be savage and yet good-humoured;
> severe and yet forbearing; truculent and pleasant all in the
> same moment. He should exercise unflinching authority. . . .
> His speech should be short, incisive, always to the point, but
> never founded on argument, His rules are based on no reason,
> and will never bear discussion . . . . He must so train his heart
> as to feel for the fox a mingled tenderness and cruelty which i
> inexplicable to ordinary men and women. (ch. 7)

The hunting man, as Trollope was, will recognise the likeness. It i
dedication of this kind that contributes so much to the humour o
Chiltern's interview with Palliser, as the latter, whilst conceding hi
landowner's duty to preserve, yet manifests his own indifferenc
and, to the horror-stricken Chiltern, his belief that foxes will b
gradually exterminated. (ch. 46)

Let us turn, however, to what matters most in the Finn novels
the politics. We have the elections as we have them elsewhere
There are Finn's successive representations of Irish Loughshane, th
pocket-borough of Loughton and the bribery-beset Tankerville, bu
it is the conduct of politics at the centre, in Parliament, tha
occupies Trollope here. Amery, we know, felt that the picture wa
not real enough. In a sense, the question is not for him and his lik
to judge, for though the realist must always try to convince th
expert, his primary task is to convince the outsider of the realism
of his scene – and surely none will doubt that Trollope has done
this. Amery complains that the politics are left out; to have pu
more of them in might have made the novels seem altogether too
specialised. Curiously enough, Trollope himself seems to have felt
that there was too much politics, that *Phineas Finn* was not 'a
brilliant success' because the general reader 'could not care much for
a hero who spent so much of his time either in the House o
Commons or in a public office. But', he went on, 'the men who
would have lived with Phineas Finn read the book.' (*Autobiography*

ch. 17) Has the atmosphere of politics changed so very much between his day and ours? Is it now really more intense and more professional?

Certainly it is a world that we both recognise, and recognise to be different. The fortunes of a Private Member's bill (*Phineas Redux*, ch. 73), the treatment of a maiden speech (*Phineas Finn*, ch. 26) or the reply to the address (*Phineas Redux*, ch. 8) are surely much the same and prompt the same reflections. And so too must be much of the mock-fury of opposition (*Phineas Finn*, ch. 9), the need for a 'thick skin' (*Phineas Redux*, ch. 33) and even the way in which groupings are affected by the willingness or otherwise of individuals to work together. (*Phineas Finn*, ch. 9) Where it is different is in the issues and the environment. Decimal coinage, which so engrosses Palliser and would, apparently, occupy a session of parliamentary time, is only symbolic of much that seems trivial, but we need to realise both the more limited degree to which it was thought that legislation should interfere with men's lives as compared with today and the different emphasis that was placed on the several areas of the national life. Thus the disestablishment of the Church of England, again to us perhaps an issue of little, if any, importance, was of the highest significance then. 'The Church in danger' was a rallying-call that never failed. Thus, also, Trollope's considerable skill in making his Tory Daubeny, like Disraeli with the 1867 Reform Act, arrogate to himself the very measure that belonged, by fundamental belief, to the Liberals.

This action reminds us, however, that Trollope was dealing with political issues of universal significance, whatever the time or place in which they arise. Must political principles remain ever inviolate? Can they do so in the face of new pressures? What is the relationship of government and the various sectional groups within the nation? Can expediency be justified? Is there such a thing as political inevitability? What is the obligation of a member to his party? Trollope ponders all these questions in the setting of politics as he knew it in his time. He distinguishes the participants, some of them of little significance, men such as the dull and mediocre Tory Browborough, the cynical, careless Laurence Fitzgibbon, the popularity-seeking Radical Turnbull, and Barrington Erle, totally devoted to party loyalty, come what may. These men are seen against the background of the time – the setting of London clubs such as the actual Reform and Brooks' and the fictional Universe, the backstairs influence of women (cf. *Phineas Redux*, ch. 37), the rising power of the populace, much of it beginning to be expressed through the Trade Unions (*Phineas Finn*, ch. 7) and the probably exaggerated importance of the kind of gutter-press journalism represented by Quintus Slide and the *People's Banner*.

These latter remind us that not least of Trollope's concerns, and so characteristic of the very period in which he was writing *Phineas Finn*, was the changing direction and balance of political power. For none was this more critical and in none was it more interesting than the great Whig families. We are told early on that 'the St Bungay people, and the Mildmay people, and the Brentford people had all some sort of connection with the Palliser people' (ch. 5): and later 'it was almost a rule of political life that all leading Whigs should be uncles, brothers-in-law, or cousins to each other'. (*Phineas Redux*, ch. 13) By contrast with the Tories under Daubeny, 'they still entertain a pride in their Cabinets, have, at any rate, not as yet submitted themselves to a conjuror. The Charles James Fox element of liberality still holds its own, and the fragrance of Cavendish is essential.' (ibid., ch. 40) But change is inevitable. They must accept a Gresham even if they prefer a Duke; 'there must be Bonteens', but 'a constant, gentle pressure against the door would tend to keep down the number of the Bonteens'. (ibid.) Thus Trollope summarises the Whig reaction to the infiltration of Liberalism.

In its miscellany of adherents the Liberal Party necessarily included the advocates of electoral reform, and it is to the most thoughtful of his politicians, Monk, that Trollope gives a long letter on the subject in which he argues that the House of Commons should be 'like the people whom it represents'. He would not give power to 'a bare numerical majority of the people', but he acknowledged the claims of a people that is 'thoughtful, educated and industrious'. (*Phineas Finn*, ch. 35) It is this same man who leads Phineas to espouse the cause of Irish tenant-right and thus to resign from government. In so doing, yet another problem is posed, namely, the differing relationship of minister and private member to the people. Monk seems to argue for a necessary opposition between people and government (ibid., ch. 65), but, as Turnbull illustrates, 'the people's minister' is irresponsible:

> Having nothing to construct, he could always deal with
> generalities. Being free from responsibility, he was not called
> upon either to study details or to master even great facts. It
> was his business to inveigh against existing evils. ... It was

his work to cut down forest-trees, and he had nothing to
do with the subsequent cultivation of the land.
(ibid., ch. 18)

Turnbull has no problems. Finn has. As Madame Goesler puts it,
'there is such a difference between life and theory'. (ch. 40) That
difference, when he feels impelled to espouse Irish tenant-right, leads
Finn out of politics. His sense of insecurity is repeatedly linked with
his considering the possibilities of marriage with a wealthy woman.
Even when he has done that at the end of *Phineas Redux*, he cannot
forget the past. Asked whether public life is 'altogether a mistake',
he replies:

> For a poor man I think that it is, in this country. A man of
> fortune may be independent; and because he has the power of
> independence those who are higher than he will not expect
> him to be subservient. A man who takes to parliamentary
> office for a living may live by it, but he will have but a dog's
> life of it. (ch. 79)

This sums up what the reader has been conscious of all along,
namely, the contrast between the ease and confidence, the sense just
of being were they belong, which marks the Whig nobility, and the
precariousness of life for a man like Finn.

In *The Prime Minister* (1876) there is another example of a man
aspiring beyond his means, but now he is portrayed unsympathe-
tically. Such rancour informs Trollope's description that at Lopez's
highest moment of success, his marriage, whilst acknowledging his
genuine love for his aristocratic bride, Emily Wharton, the novelist
writes: 'He was a self-seeking adventurer, who did not know
honesty from dishonesty when he saw them together.' (ch. 24) He
is an upstart, as Emily's father notes, with 'no relatives, no family,
no belongings' (ch. 5), or John Fletcher less elegantly, 'a greasy
black foreigner'. (ch. 16) The reader of *The Way We Live Now* –
and *The Prime Minister* followed this novel – recognises the type, the
man without origins, without profession, who lives by speculation
and the fraudulent involvement of others in his speculation,
the man who seeks respectability by opportunist incursion into
established society through marriage and Parliament. By contrast
with Melmotte in *The Way We Live Now*, Lopez operates on a

smaller scale, but quite as devastatingly. Trollope allows us to see the effects of his activities even on his gullible fellow-speculator, Sexty Parker, or rather on that man's family as they are shown in his wife's pathetic visit to the Whartons after Lopez's death. The Parkers, however, serve another purpose, namely, to illustrate the way in which Lopez brings Emily with her fine breeding into defiling contact with them when, at his insistence, the two couples share a holiday at Dovercourt. Parker's familiarity and colloquial register which Trollope catches so perfectly with its references to 'a dooced nice little place', a 'bit of fish', 'glass of cham.' and 'sherry wine' (chs 45-6) is the measure of Emily's degradation.

In *The Prime Minister* Trollope presses home the effects of this social contamination in that area of English life which he most admired for its purity and standard of values, the landed gentry, for although Emily herself is the daughter of a London barrister, he is the brother of one Herefordshire squire, and her unsuccessful suitor is the son of another. Contrasted pairs of young men form a recurrent phenomenon in the structure of Trollope's novels. John Grey (the surname is appropriate) and George Vavasor were rivals for the hand of Alice in *Can You Forgive Her?* There are marked and deliberate differences between Tregear and Silverbridge in *The Duke's Children*, but nowhere is the opposition apparently so intentional and so full of meaning as between Arthur Fletcher and Ferdinand Lopez, the one the epitome of nobility and traditional values, the other self-seeking, unscrupulous, defrauding his partner, deceiving his father-in-law, oppressing his wife. Emily's disillusionment and sorrow is the product of realising that she had not married a gentleman. Preferring her own doctrine of a 'beau ideal . . . graced, first with intelligence, then with affection, and lastly with ambition', she gave herself to Lopez, scorning 'gentle blood and gentle nurture' which she found, 'could exist without intellect, without heart, and very moderate culture'; but she ignored that essential moral characteristic, the 'love of honest, courageous truth'. (ch. 31) Lopez deceives his wife, swears at her, bullies her. By contrast, Arthur Fletcher (the Christian name reminds us of the chivalry of the Round Table, 'the courage, and constancy, and loyalty of the knights of those days' (ibid.)), even after being rejected, always has regard to her feelings, writing to her when he finds that he is to be opposed in an election by Lopez and visiting her before the necessitated emigration. On both occasions he is made the object of Lopez's violence for his pains. This sustained concentration on Lopez's behaviour as an individual and its effects on others is even more bitter an attack on the 'new men' than was the portrayal of Melmotte. His villainy is all the more evident by contrast with the traditional values embodied in Fletcher. There is only one good thing to say about Lopez; by his suicide, it can be said of him, as it was of Cawdor in *Macbeth*, 'nothing in his life became him like the leaving it'. It is, however, so much out of character that it is hard to believe that Lopez, no matter how desperate, would have had the resolution to do it. To suggest, as does Polhemus (1968, p. 204), that this is a society where dog eats dog and Lopez is in some ways an admirable *unus contra mundum*, against 'the Wharton clan [who] look upon themselves as *the elect*' seems to me to be reading a different book from the one that Trollope wrote.

What the novelist is increasingly concerned with, both here and in *The Duke's Children*, is the friction in personal relationships within the hothouse of domesticity. Not only do Lopez and Emily, Emily and her father, and even Everett and Wharton, show this, but so also do Palliser and Lady Glencora. Even as Palliser reaches the zenith of his career, we find Glencora more ambitious than ever, scornful of his modest assumption of power, and more interfering. Trollope skilfully modulates the tension and the tenderness, and at high moments the reader realises that the degree of the one is conversely related to that of the other. Thus, for example, the ecstasy of her embrace when Palliser tells Glencora he is to be Prime Minister (ch. 6) or the way in which their conversation moves from sharpness to sympathy:

> 'The Darby and Joan kind of thing is what I like.'
> 'Only Darby is to be in office all day, and in Parliament all night – and Joan is to stay at home.'
> '. . . You are doing the best you can to further what you think to be my interests.'
> 'I am,' said the Duchess.
> 'I love you the better for it, day by day.' This so surprised her, that as she took him by the arm, her eyes were filled with tears. (ch. 18)

It is her mistaken and independent public actions that cause most of the trouble, and particularly her interference in the Silverbridge election by her clandestine support for Lopez. Other women, notably Lady Laura Standish, had interfered in politics. At a time when Women's Rights and Mill's advocacy of them were much in evidence, Trollope, through Palliser, makes two things clear, the extent of feminine power and the confines of its proper sphere:

> Ruat caelum, fiat – proper subordination from his wife in regard to public matters! No wife had a fuller allowance of privilege, or more complete power in her hands, as to things fit for women's management. . . 'Justitia' to him was not compatible with feminine interference in his own special work. (ch. 32)

That special work was the carrying on of the Queen's government in the difficult circumstances of a coalition. It is one of Trollope's master-strokes in the first place to have made Palliser his Prime Minister. Might one not have expected and been more easily pleased by somebody obviously more exuberant and more energetic? Trollope himself considers this point in a conversation about Palliser:

> 'He has not the obduracy of Lord Brock, nor the ineffable manner of Mr Mildmay, nor the brilliant intellect of Mr Gresham.'
> 'Nor the picturesque imagination of Mr Daubeny.'

Apparently Palmerston, Russell, Gladstone and Disraeli; but Trollope goes on:

> 'Nor his audacity,' said Mr Rattler. 'But he has peculiar gifts of his own. . . He is a just, unambitious, intelligent man.' (ch. 38)

Later the Duke of St Bungay lists the necessary gifts:

> He should be clever but need not be a genius; he should be conscientious but by no means straitlaced; he should be cautious, but never timid, bold but never venturesome; he should have a good digestion, genial manners, and, above all, a thick skin. (ch. 41)

Palliser lacked the last, and that is why he was always a reluctant Prime Minister. He does not aspire, he seeks no spectacular programme, he is unwilling to compromise his integrity. Hence the split with the ambitious Sir Orlando Drought over the proposal for new battleships, hence also the decision which brings down the government when to the chagrin and anger of his Conservative colleague, Lord Drummond, he gives a vacant Garter Knighthood not to a political ally but to Lord Earlybird, a man of local philanthropic activity, who could in no sense be regarded as the recipient of reward for services rendered.

Trollope was describing a condition of political flux, an old world dying and a new one struggling into what promised to be a violent infancy. St Bungay and Brock were of the old world with 'no belief in perpetuating [England's] greatness by any grand improvements. Let things take their way naturally'. (ch. 11) Palliser chafed because nothing had been done. The new world was coming in the somewhat ridiculous guise of the young radical, good-for-nothing brother of Emily Wharton who

> believed of himself that he had gone rather deep into politics. . . . He had the great question of labour, and all that refers to unions, strikes, and lock-outs quite at his fingers' ends. . . . He was quite clear on questions of finance, and saw to a 't' how progress should be made towards communism, so that no violence should disturb that progress.

The best comment on this young man is Trollope's own epilogue to this account: 'In the meantime he could never contrive to pay his tailor's bill regularly out of the allowance of £400 a year which his father made him, and was always dreaming of the comforts of a handsome income.' (ch. 2)

Amid labour unrest and the presumptuous popular aspirations from which we have suffered ever since, the views of the two main historic parties about equality could not be ignored. Trollope expresses them appropriately through his most thoughtful politician, Palliser. The context is that of yet another extension of the franchise. The stresses within Liberalism itself are apparent – with the old Whig Duke of St Bungay for further postponement and Mr Monk urgent for action. Palliser recognises the Conservative belief in hierarchy and paternalism but thinks it impossible because men are not good enough to practise the necessary benevolence, whereas the Liberal believes in lessening the distance between men. That, says Phineas Finn, means equality, and the Duke acknowledges that such 'would be a heaven if we could attain it', and hence the need to 'march on to some nearer approach to equality; though the thing itself [in] its perfection is unattainable'. (ch. 68) The Duke of Omnium would leave the Tories behind, but he was not willing to travel to the terminus. Was this, in the words of the *Autobiography*, being an 'advanced conservative liberal'? The passage from which this phrase comes is concerned with the problems of social relationships, of the pain in feeling inferiority and the pain too in feeling superiority – 'unless when it has been won by their own efforts'. Trollope adds:

> We do not understand the operations of Almighty wisdom,
> and are therefore unable to tell the causes of the terrible
> inequalities that we see. . . . Make all men equal to-day,
> and God has so created them that they shall all be unequal
> to-morrow. (ch. 16)

Liberal and Conservative share these beliefs, but in Trollope's view the former was more willing to ameliorate the condition of the lower orders in society. He believes, that is, in 'a tendency towards equality' in a society where the Liberal acts as a mild accelerator and the Conservative as a necessary brake.

In the final novel of the series, *The Duke's Children* (1880), Omnium's eldest son, Silverbridge, admittedly an immature, if not indeed a silly, young man, has forsaken the family's traditional Liberalism on the grounds that 'we've got to protect our position as well as we can against the Radicals and Communists'. He quite readily acknowledges that a man's political opinions must be so formed as to protect 'his own and his class. The people will look after themselves, and we must look after ourselves. We are so few and they are so many, that we shall have quite enough to do.' (ch. 7) He saw more clearly than his father the way that things were moving, but by the end of the novel, out of no more than filial loyalty, he is considering a reversion to Liberalism. In this move, however, one must allow for Silverbridge's dislike of the unsympathetic Tory leader, Sir Timothy Beeswax, a man who, though 'industrious, patient, clear-sighted, intelligent, courageous, and determined' (ch. 21), was yet nothing more than a parliamentary opportunist; like Daubeny before him, with 'all the art of a great conjuror'; a fluent speaker, glib, skilled in repartee (ch. 26); disliked, yet regarded as indispensable. (ibid.) *The Duke's Children* represents a Tory interlude: at the end the Liberals are back in office.

It is not, however, the politics, but the personal relations which provide the principal interest in this novel, as the title itself indicates. That title also reminds us that Trollope is once again facing, as he does so often in his last novels and as he did in his own life, the problems of what would now be called the 'generation-gap'. Palliser has to handle his problem without the help of his wife, for Lady Glencora's death is reported at the beginning of the novel. Here, too, as in his political life, Palliser as father, always somewhat remote, undemonstrative and out of touch with his children, is at once unusual and eminently suitable for Trollope to exploit in the role he has to play. Each of the three children causes him heartache – Silverbridge, with his expulsion from Oxford and his involvement on the Turf, culminating through his association with fraudulent characters in a loss of £70,000; Lady Mary, with her imprudent and unrelenting attachment to the impoverished Tory, Tregear, a man, however, noble and upright; Gerald, repeating on a smaller scale the misdemeanours of his elder brother.

The relationship of Lady Mary and Tregear finds Palliser not only in the difficult position of a widower trying to advise a daughter, but also having to try to counteract the activities of his late wife. Lady Glencora's schemes have pursued Palliser even beyond her grave (ch. 2), so much so, he believes, that Trollope can write of him: 'Now, in that very excess of tenderness which her death had occasioned, he was driven to accuse her of a great sin against himself, in that she had kept from him her knowledge of this affair.' (ch. 5) To this wounded tenderness and to his sense of lonely responsibility for his daughter are added two other things – first, his belief in rank (ch. 50) and, second, his comparison of his daughter's position with what had been her mother's *vis-à-vis* himself, by which he believed 'she would have reconciled herself at last to her new life'. (ibid.) In this latter consideration he blatantly ignores the difference in character between Tregear and Burgo Fitzgerald and, how pathetically, he either ignores too or else had never appreciated that Glencora's reconciliation to her marriage was, and remained, in many ways resignation rather than accep-tance.

The Duke is pathetic – 'In every way he had been thwarted', we read later (ch. 71). Yet Trollope always mingles sympathy with clear-sighted candour. The Duke's moral concern for his sons, the need to 'make them see the foolishness of folly, the ugliness of what is mean, the squalor and dirt of ignoble pursuits' (ch. 65), does not, for a long time, extend to noticing the difference in Tregear, even though in his reflections on the latter's letter about the obstacles placed against his relationship with Mary he has to modify his impulsive first reactions. Trollope notes the movement of feeling succinctly:

> Not only was the letter arrogant; – but the fact that he should dare to write any letter on such a subject was proof of most unpardonable arrogance. The Duke walked about the room thinking of it till he was almost in a passion. Then he read the letter again and was gradually pervaded by a feeling of its manliness. Its arrogance remained, but with its arrogance there was a certain boldness which induced respect. (ch. 50)

In many ways the Duke is the most important character in the Lady Mary-Tregear narrative. Trollope compels us to sustain our admiration for this man who was above all things fair. The last sentences of the novel take us back to the letter incident. They are a handsome resolution of the Duke's sense of conflicting attitudes in Tregear's missive: 'What surprised me most was that he should have looked so high. There seemed so little to justify it. But now I will accept as courage what I before regarded as arrogance.' They are also a handsome recognition of which mattered most in the two things the Duke valued so highly – the moral quality before the social position. It is altogether appropriate that this character, of whom his creator thought so well, should leave us on such a note.

By contrast both with Tregear and his father, Silverbridge is a wastrel – sent down from Oxford, associating with such dubious characters as Major Tifto, losing heavily on the Turf, causing his brother to be sent down from Cambridge, and even in his supposedly serious avocations deserting his father's politics and giving others the chance to embarrass his father. Not surprisingly he is a member of the Beargarden Club, first seen in all its squalor in *The Way We Live Now* and still sporting among its members such barely admirable characters as Nidderdale and Dolly Longestaffe. Trollope is once again reinforcing his bleak opinion of the younger aristocracy.

The 'right people' formed a close-knit circle:

> It is a point of conscience among the – perhaps not ten thousand, but say one thousand of bluest blood – that everybody should know who everybody is. . . . It is a knowledge which the possession of the blue blood itself produces. (ch. 35)

Tregear may not be part of that group, but Silverbridge's own ultimate attachment was to make even more severe inroads on such concepts of social exclusiveness. There is a passage in chapter 30 charged with ironies, implicit criticisms and sardonic expectations. It is one of those rare occasions when Silverbridge considers his father's worries and problems. He decides that the greatest of these was Tregear's attachment to Lady Mary and that Tregear must 'be got out of the way'. This, after deciding that his own extravagance had not caused the Duke any incurable wounds! This, after acknowledging that he had told his father that he intended to please him by marrying Lady Mabel Grex, but then deciding that it was hard that 'this intention of marriage should stand in the way of having a good time with Miss Boncassen for a few weeks'! Marriage, he concludes, 'clipped a fellow's wings', but at the same time 'it meant complete independence in money matters'. (ch. 30) As we might almost have guessed from this passage in which he is proposing to relieve his father of the worries of one unacceptable alliance, marriage also meant for Silverbridge, the American, Isobel Boncassen. So much for blue blood and the best families, as she herself honestly enough recognises in speaking of her paternal grandfather, founder of her family's wealth, who came as a labourer from Holland (ch. 40). We note the prospective irony in the Duke's proud statement: 'There is no greater mistake than to suppose that inferiority of birth is a barrier to success in this country.' He was speaking about public life; Isobel wondered why it should not apply in such private affairs as marriage.

Trollope treats Silverbridge better than he deserved and one is left wondering why anyone so intelligent as Isobel Boncassen could have married him – and why anyone equally intelligent, like Lady Mabel Grex, could have sorrowed at not doing so. Lady Mabel is probably, in strict psychological terms, the most interesting creation in the novel. She was in love with Frank Tregear, but their respective poverty led them to agree to part. She witnesses the growth of his relationship with Lady Mary with mingled restraint and jealousy. She attracts Silverbridge, but he is to her nothing more than 'a rather foolish, but very, very sweet-tempered young man'. (ch. 20) She thinks of her possible ultimate position as Duchess of Omnium, but because of her fundamental honesty, perhaps also because of her ineradicable affection for Tregear, she cannot help herself. She scorns Silverbridge's advances, making him appear more foolish than he really is. It is only when Isobel Boncassen appears as a serious challenger that she rouses herself, but all too late. (ch. 59) Subsequently, as he compares the two girls, Silverbridge notes the spontaneity of Isobel as against 'Lady Mabel with all her grace, with all her beauty, with all her talent, . . . a creature of efforts' (ch. 68) – efforts, in fact, doomed to futility. Lady Mabel is a complicated character, not always knowing or doing what she herself wants, and for this reason one of Trollope's most fascinating minor characters. After her final quarrel with Frank she retires, an embittered woman, to the dark, decaying country house at Grex. Such is the end of one who might have been either Mrs Frank Tregear or the Duchess of Omnium. Her shadow is not absent from the wedding celebrations that conclude the novel.

6

Other Longer Novels, 1858-70

(*The Three Clerks; The Bertrams; Orley Farm; The Claverings; He Knew He Was Right; The Vicar of Bullhampton*)

Professor Gordon Ray in an appendix to his article 'Trollope at Full Length' (1967-8, pp. 313-39) listed the novels and included details of the number of words and the 'units' which Trollope allotted to each, the 'unit' being 70,000 words, as contained in each volume of his first great success and first serialised novel, *Framley Parsonage*. Some fourteen of the larger novels written before *The Way We Live Now* (1875) have been considered in earlier chapters. The rest are dealt with here, and the shorter novels (i.e. those consisting of less than three units), with the exception of *The Struggles of Brown, Jones and Robinson,* in the next chapter.

The first of the remaining longer novels, *The Three Clerks,* appeared in 1875 after *Barchester Towers* and before *Doctor Thorne*. Indeed, this pattern of a longer novel on another subject punctuating the Barsetshire series continues with *The Bertrams* (1859) preceding *Framley Parsonage,* and *Orley Farm* (1862) *The Small House at Allington*. Subsequent opinion has not concurred with either that of Trollope himself or of contemporary reviewers who generally found *The Three Clerks* a better novel than its two Barsetshire predecessors. The *Spectator,* for instance, declared that it had 'more of story, with stronger individual interest, as well as greater depth.' (XXX, 12 December 1857) It certainly possesses a neatly arranged plot in the relationship of the three clerks with the three Woodward sisters, the first of those many charming young English girls who were to become stock-figures, but none the less attractive for that, in novel after novel that followed. It contains also some good-humoured analysis and criticism of the civil service, drawn from the author's own experience, and from this comes also something of the history of one of the clerks, Charley Tudor. Charley's career also forms a neat balance with that of another of the clerks, his cousin Alaric – a contrast of amiable lack of application with ruthless ambition that eventually overreaches itself through the assistance of Undy Scott, one of Trollope's most convincing and repulsive villains. Nevertheless, *The Three Clerks* is marred by the introduction of characters who do not contribute sufficiently to the tale as a whole, whatever their individual and incidental value. Such are Clementina Golightly, whose wealth makes her a possible wife for Charley and solution for his financial embarrassments, and the Neverbend sisters. Even worse as an intrusion is the story *in extenso* of 'Crinoline and Macassar', one of Charley's early literary efforts.

This reminds us how extensively autobiographical parts at least of *The Three Clerks* are. Two incidents are clearly paralleled in Charley's history and that of Trollope himself, as he tells it in the *Autobiography*. There we learn of the novelist's encounters, 'a most heart-rending but a most intimate acquaintance', with a moneylender who for £4 in cash and a tailor's bill for £12 extracted no less than £200. Jabesh McRuen, like Trollope's moneylender, of Mecklenburgh Square, gave Charley £4 on a cheque for £15 (ch. 19) and bade his debtor, as does his later re-creation, Clarkson in *Phineas Finn*, to 'be punctual'. Trollope's own moneylender used to visit him daily at the Post Office 'and come and stand behind my chair, whispering to me always the same words: "Now I wish you would be punctual. If you only would be punctual.... "' (*Autobiography*, ch. 3) Another of Trollope's visitors prompted another incident. In the novel Charley Tudor rashly promises marriage to the barmaid, Norah Geraghty, and her landlady invades the Internal Navigation Office to confront him with the question: 'And, Mr Tudor, what are you a-going to do about that poor girl there?' (ch. 27) Trollope's own experience, though not so degrading, was no less embarrassing. He disclaims any blame for the episode in which

> a young woman down in the country had taken into her head
> that she would like to marry me.... The invitation had
> come from her, and I had lacked the pluck to give it a
> decided negative.... At last the mother appeared at the Post
> Office.... She followed the man in, and walking up the
> centre of the room, addressed me in a loud voice: 'Anthony

Trollope, when are you going to marry my daughter?'
(*Autobiography*, ch. 3)

One also recalls Johnny Eames's involvement with Amelia Roper. Trollope ends his account in the *Autobiography* with masterly understatement: 'These little incidents were all against me in the office.'

The formula of the Palliser novels, some public affairs and some love judiciously intermingled, is found more explicitly in *The Three Clerks* than in any of its predecessors. The contrast in tone is also more marked than in many of Trollope's other novels. For one thing, the romantic interest is less complicated than in the Palliser group; for another, the public affairs are considered less sympathetically and are more obviously a matter of satire. Trollope was proud of the Post Office and his part in it, proud indeed of the Civil Service as a whole: 'There is no profession by which a man can earn his bread in these realms, admitting of a brighter honesty, of a nobler purpose or of an action more manly and independent.'(Parrish, 1938, p. 6) Nothing, however, could have been calculated to produce conflict more certainly than the collision of his own boisterously prejudiced temperament and the regulated character of the service itself. Not that he objected to its conservatism; indeed, he opposed what he regarded as a fundamentally disastrous change from appointment by nomination and promotion by seniority to selection based on merit and examination. His conflicts arose largely because he identified what he did not like with the people concerned with it, developed an animosity to the people and thereby magnified the degree of his distaste for the original innovation.

In *The Three Clerks* the subject of his dislike is competitive examination and the character associated with it, Sir Gregory Hardlines, a caricature of Sir Charles Trevelyan, the advocate of reformed entry procedures to the Civil Service. Sir Gregory is seen as a man glorying in his own vision – 'What if the Civil Service, through his instrumentality, should become the nucleus of the best intellectual diligence in the country!' (ch. 6), a vision which, Trollope is quick to tell us, leads to his own promotion to Chief Commissioner at the Board of Civil Service Examination with a salary of £2,000 a year, a K.C.B. and a present of £1,000. Ambition is gratified; and for his successor there must be a competition. Alaric Tudor succeeds and ambition wins again. To Trollope,

111

however, this was the door into the jungle. Old stabilities wer
being put to flight. Competition might be acceptable for 'youn
men at college. But it is a fearful thing for a married man with
family, who has long looked forward to rise to a certain income b
the worth of his general conduct and by the value of his seniority
Moreover, in an age of increasing standards in education 'th
prodigy of 1857, who is now destroying all the hopes of the ma
who was well enough in 1855, will be a dunce to the tyro of 1860
(ibid.) Trollope goes further in his exposure of what he regards a
ill-considered zeal for reform. Throughout the novel the tw
government offices, the Weights and Measures initially under Si
Gregory and the Internal Navigation under Mr Oldeschole, ar
contrasted with each other, the one efficient and go-ahead, th
other leisurely and somewhat ramshackle. (And how much mor
convincing these are than Dickens's Circumlocution Office in th
contemporary *Little Dorrit!*) At the end we have Oldeschole bein
interrogated by Sir Gregory's henchman, 'a personification o
conscious official zeal':

> 'And now, Mr Oldeschole, if you have had leisure to consider
> the question more fully, perhaps you can define to us what is
> the – hum – hm – the use – hm – hm – the exact use of the
> Internal Navigation Office?' . . . .
> What a question was this to ask of a man who had spent
> all his life in the Internal Navigation Office! O reader, should
> it chance that thou art a clergyman, imagine what it would be
> to thee, wert thou asked what is the exact use of the Church
> of England. (ch. 45)

Ultimately, however, it is something other than Trollope's direc
comment or his satire that has the most telling effect. It is th
history of Alaric Tudor himself, the successful man of the worl
who defeats his colleague Harry Norman in both business and love
The attitude of Trollope's characters towards money and it
acquisition is always an important guide to their author's judgmen
of them. Whereas Charley Tudor in his happy-go-lucky fashio
falls into the hands of McRuen for the supply of his daily needs
Alaric calculates and arranges. As so often in this comparativel
early novel, Trollope is more explicit than he felt he needed to b
later:

> [Alaric began] to perceive that money was a thing not to be
> judged of by the ordinary rules which govern a man's conduct

In other matters it behoves a gentleman to be open,
above-board, liberal and true ... but in the acquirement and
use of money – that is, its use with the object of acquiring
more, its use in the usurer's sense – his practice should be
exactly the reverse; he should be close, secret, exacting, given to
concealment, not over-troubled by scruples.... (ch. 17)

This code, with the assistance of Undy Scott, speculator M.P., leads
him first to accept and then fraudulently to misuse a trusteeship, the
outcome of which is trial, imprisonment and emigration,
expediency triumphing over principle but meeting, inevitably, its
just reward. (cf. ch. 29) The end is saved only by Alaric's wife,
Gertrude, in her passionate faithfulness and her dignity even in the
depths of disgrace.

As Alaric's ambition successfully soars, Charley's fortunes at best
languish and at worst decline. After the money-lending and the
Norah Geraghty episodes our attention is switched away from
Charley until we return to his love for the youngest Woodward
sister, Kate, a love opposed by her mother in view of Charley's
manifest ne'er-do-well behaviour. Kate falls into a decline and in
'A Parting Interview' (ch. 42) the reader is led to expect her
approaching death. Much of this scene derives from the novelist's
recollection of his own sister, but, unlike her, Kate does not die.
Trollope said that he could not find in his heart to let her. The
author's tenderness is of a piece with the two characters themselves,
Charley and Kate.

If Kate is tender and Charley careless, Gertrude dignified and
Alaric ambitious, the third couple, Harry Norman (do Norman
and Tudor represent different types of character deriving from
Trollope's view of history?) and Linda represent a happy mean of
common sense and balanced affection. Not, let it be said, Trollope's
ideal, for at the end he still asserts that Gertrude in her deep sorrow
felt that she had married the right man, whilst there is no doubt
that his own preference lay with Charley and Kate. Alaric and
Gertrude, he conceded, 'Perhaps may be called the hero and the
heroine of our tale', but he himself would not have it so, claiming
to do his work without any such appendages to his story'. What
follows is what matters. It sums up this tale, and many of his tales,
of mingled virtue and vice, strength and weakness, purpose and lack
of it: 'Heroism there may be, and he hopes there is – more or less
of it there should be in a true picture of most characters; but heroes

113

and heroines, as so called, are not commonly met with in our daily walks of life.' (ch. 47) There is no ideal as such.

There is a quite remarkable extraneous outburst in *The Three Clerks* (ch. 29) against Sir Robert Peel as 'worshipper of expediency', the triple traitor to his principles and those of his party over Catholic Emancipation, Parliamentary Reform and the Repeal of the Corn Laws. This animosity to Tory chameleonism is carried over to *The Bertrams* (1859) which is set in the pre-Corn Law Repeal era:

> No reform, no innovation ... stinks so foully in the nostrils of an English Tory politician as to be absolutely irreconcilable to him.... Let the people want what they will, Jew senators, cheap corn, vote by ballot, no property qualification, or anything else, the Tories will carry it for them if the Whigs cannot. (ch. 16)

Harcourt, the opportunist political debutant – appropriately Trollope would have said – joins the Tories. Another concern of *The Three Clerks* which re-appears in *The Bertrams,* indeed in the opening chapter, is Trollope's distaste for competitive examinations. The title is 'Vae victis!' and the insistent metaphor is that of skimming the milk, a process which, Trollope hints, may be educationally unwise, but which is far more deleterious in its 'cruelty of spirit.... Success is the only test of merit.... To deserve only is not meritorious.' Therein lies the distinction between George Bertram and Arthur Wilkinson.

There, however, the likeness between the two novels ends. *The Bertrams* is altogether a more sombre book, tracing the sad history of George Bertram and Caroline Waddington, 'a Juno rather than a Venus' (ch. 9), a girl whose ideas of marriage include not only love but also status. George Bertram senior, financial monomaniac uncle of George and grandfather of Caroline, would provide the means towards that status if they were to marry, but the very promise is its own blight. The engagement drags on, growing ever cooler, the marriage is postponed by Caroline, the relationship is finally broken off by Bertram when he finds that she has been discussing it with Harcourt. Trollope suffuses the whole chronicle with a sense of quietly inexorable inevitability. In the overlap before Caroline's break with Bertram and her subsequent engagement to Harcourt, Trollope in a mere four paragraphs skilfully touches on the latter's developing interest in Caroline as 'an affianced bride' and 'probably the heiress of one of the wealthiest men in the city of London'. (ch. 19) Moving from an abortive engagement to a loveless marriage, Caroline resembles Thackeray's young women, a sacrifice on the marriage-market, but with this difference – they are the victims of parental decision, she of her own. Even before they marry, she manifests a dullness that is quite deadening. To Harcourt's enquiry as to her happiness we have replies such as these:

> 'Happy! oh yes – I am happy. I don't believe, you know, in a great deal of very ecstatic happiness. I never did'. . . .
> 'Passionate love, I take it, rarely lasts long, and is very troublesome while it does last'. . . .
> 'I have loved once, and no good has come of it. It was contrary to my nature to do so – to love in that mad passionate self-sacrificing manner. But yet I did. I think I may say with certainty that I never shall be so foolish again.'
> (ch. 28)

In many respects Harcourt is an unsatisfactory character, over-simplified and even with tendencies to the melodramatic. It is, however, when he might have toppled over irrevocably into this category that he becomes most impressive in his role of jealous husband. Caroline always obeys him absolutely – and coldly. Thwarted by her inability to get more money from her grandfather to meet his pressing needs, jealous of George Bertram, Harcourt becomes a domestic tyrant, even forbidding Caroline to dance, an activity at once trivial but sexually significant. (ch. 34) Trollope powerfully reinforces Caroline's pathetic situation by counter-pointing her own and George's mutual regrets and forgiveness for the failure of their relationship against Harcourt's ever increasing jealousy. This is all focussed crucially in the domestic row or 'Matrimonial Dialogue' (ch. 36), where Caroline frankly describes what was meant to be her final meeting with Bertram and confesses her continuing love for him, at which Harcourt calls her a 'brazen-faced harlot'. Caroline neatly turns the tables on him by accepting the description but not in the way he intends it, not as Bertram's lover but as his unloving wife. She therefore leaves him. He loses the solicitor-generalship to which his meteoric political career had elevated him. His creditors foregather when it is known that he will not benefit under old Bertram's will. Alone amid the all too recent splendours of his Eaton Square house, he drinks off glass after glass of brandy, 'his whole mind ... out of tune'; he goes

115

round the Square three times and returns to the dark house, the room 'very gloomy with its red embossed paper and dark ruby curtains'. He remembers, illogically, the time he asked Caroline when they looked at the house before their marriage, 'how many festive guests might sit at their ease in that room'. He wanders aimlessly upstairs and dresses to go out to dinner, and then he sits and 'One resource he did see.' Patient purposefulness now takes over, he awaits the onset of night when the house is still and the servants are a-bed – and he shoots himself. (ch. 46)

The novel tells of George Bertram's career as well as of his love. At the outset he is the academic victor with life's endless possibilities before him; 'The law, the church, letters, art, and politics all enticed him' (ch. 2), but not the City, which his uncle might have wished. His earliest choice is the Church and his pilgrimage to Jerusalem may be said to symbolise this spiritual quest, but, as Trollope makes clear, the reality of Palestine does not always match the ideal. The varying status of the several different churches within the Church of the Holy Sepulchre, the ridiculous physical antics necessary to enter the *sanctum sanctorum,* the careless inattention of the celebrant at the Greek Mass, all serve to emphasise the difference between ideal and actual, whilst for Bertram himself the altogether too unquestioning faith of the two young Greeks (ch. 6), he recognises is something that can never be his. This is not enough to deprive him of his resolve: what is is much less noble. 'His high and holy purpose [was] blown to the winds by a few words from a pair of ruby lips, by one glance of scorn from a pair of bright eyes' (ch 11); Caroline had bidden him 'not bury [him]self in a country parsonage'. (ch. 10)

Bertram is persuaded towards the Bar by Harcourt, who deals brusquely with what he calls the former's 'Quixotic' hesitations about defending those considered guilty, 'a doctrine of puritanism – or purism, which is worse. All this moonshine.' (ch. 12) Later, however, Bertram decides that 'a man should be known either as a politician or as an author'. (ch. 19) The politician of this novel we know: the author, Bertram, is the writer, amongst other things, of political pamphlets and infidel essays. The pilgrimage to Jerusalem at the beginning is matched by the journey to Cairo at the end, the association with Caroline by a vulgar flirtation with an Indian Army widow on the voyage back; all this after his 'final' dismissal from Caroline. George's is a sombre history of hope and promise unfulfilled. In what they think is their final meeting he and

116

Caroline speak of themselves as 'two children who have quarrelled over their plaything, and broken it in pieces. ... No sounds are any longer sweet. There is no music now', and, as he leaves her, Trollope compares him to Othello: 'He had thrown his pearl away; a pearl richer than all his tribe.' (ch. 35) They do, in fact, marry, but it is a fruitless marriage and a muted happiness: 'Their house is childless, and very, very quiet, but they are not unhappy.' Trollope closes the book simply with two questions, bidding us recall 'the plan of life which Caroline Waddington had formed in the boldness of her heart ... the aspirations of George Bertram, as he sat upon the Mount of Olives.' The sombreness of *The Bertrams* lies in its account of what life does to us, whatever we may plan to do with it, a sombreness all the greater because life only does what by our own actions we enable it to do to us.

The Bertrams has always, even in its creator's lifetime, been one of its author's least popular stories. Trollope thought the story was 'more than ordinarily bad'. (*Autobiography*, ch. 7) So far as the three main characters are concerned, I think he was wrong. Contemporary reviews were in disagreement with each other. The *Examiner* thought the plot-construction excellent, The *Athenaeum* found it thin. Among modern critics Booth considers the plot ponderous (Booth, 1958, p. 116) and Polhemus dismisses the subplots as illogical. (Polhemus, 1968, p. 63) The consensus of these judgments is surely indicative: the contributory and subsidiary interests of the novel are inadequate. We would not willingly lose some of the characters such as the irrepressible spinster Miss Todd, eccentric, unpredictable, lively and comic; but the financial monomania of old Bertram is not sufficiently developed to make him impressive enough in his own right, whilst there is enough of it to make us feel uncomfortably in need of more. His brother, George's father, Sir Lionel, the wandering diplomat of fortune, is an interesting, if also limited, study of a type. The love-story of Arthur Wilkinson and Adela Gauntlet, meant presumably to show the troubles of two more ordinary people than George and Caroline, is never full enough in itself to provide much interest and is forgotten for long stretches of the novel. Trollope's Oriental travels gave him the material which figures so largely at the beginning and end of the novel, but one could wish that he had spared us most of it as he tells us he has spared us a projected extended account of Malta. It is interesting enough, but it does get in the way of the story. Trollope himself queried the quality of the love-scenes: he might have better spared much else than these. In essence, *The Bertrams* is about flawed people making flawed decisions, of a descent from high ideals to sordid realities, from which there could be only a limited recovery. That essence is worth having, despite all the impedimenta surrounding it.

Orley Farm received a very favourable reception on its appearance in 1862 and Trollope records that those of his friends competent to pass an opinion told him that it was the best book he had written. (*Autobiography*, ch. 9) He himself thought the plot his best despite its unravelling itself too soon, and the characters also he thought were good. He concluded: 'I am fond of *Orley Farm*.' Most later readers have shared his opinion, though one so eminent and judicious as Michael Sadleir has attributed to the novel grave faults as a result of its mode of publication. Victorian novels were peculiarly susceptible to the ills that afflict the lengthy work; and length was considered essential in several kinds of publication. If it was not the need to fill out three volumes (as with *The Bertrams*), it might be the related necessity of sustaining interest through serialisation (which Trollope first tried with *Orley Farm*'s immediate precursor, *Framley Parsonage*, in the *Cornhill*) or in monthly parts, the mode adopted with *Orley Farm*. As a result, says Sadleir, 'the tale is episodic; it switches abruptly from grave to gay, from one set of characters to another'. (Sadleir, 1961, p. 388)

In scope and range, *Orley Farm* was Trollope's most ambitious project to date, and one could certainly imagine a slimmer and neater story. It would have been possible to have omitted the chapters dealing with the commercial travellers, but, as Trollope says, 'Mr Moulder carves his turkey admirably, and Mr Kantwise sells his tables and chairs with spirit.' (*Autobiography*, ch. 9) It might have been possible to drop the middle-aged jealousy of Mrs Furnival about what she supposes to be her husband's attraction to Lady Mason. Felix Graham's educating the working-class girl, Mary Snow, to fit her to be his wife is difficult to credit (though one recalls the parallel achievement of Sabine Baring-Gould at almost exactly this time in real life). To have cut out any of these, however, would have been to narrow and to harm the novel by loss of either humour or, more important, psychological interest. Moreover, Trollope relates all the characters from such various social strata in a form that justifies the claims he makes for his plot and which does not suggest much straining of credulity.

Nevertheless, there are superfluities – including, for Bradford Booth, 'the economy of Groby Park, the legal reformations of Von Bauhr, or the marital hesitancies of John Kenneby' (Booth, 1957, p. 147), to name no more.

At the centre of the tale, unassailed by any of the peripheries, stands the powerful agony of Lady Mason, misled in her youth into forging an addendum to her husband's will, giving Orley Farm to her own infant son and thus alienating it from the rightful heir, her step-son, Joseph Mason of Groby. Provoked by the revengeful desires of Dockwrath, a local solicitor, who has been dispossessed of his tenancy of two fields belonging to the farm and who discovers certain helpful documents, the case is re-opened and Lady Mason is charged with perjury at the original trial two decades before when Joseph Mason had contested the will originally. She is supported by her neighbour, Sir Peregrine Orme, the very embodiment of the English gentleman, who goes so far as to propose marriage to her. She eventually has to confess her guilt and, though she is, in·fact, acquitted at the trial (thus giving Trollope the opportunity to raise questions relating to law and justice and the ethics of the legal profession), her real punishment lies in the knowledge of her offence amongst those like Sir Peregrine and her son whose respect she dearly wanted to retain. This was an era of melodrama, from which we nowadays remember only such things as Wilkie Collins's *The Woman in White* and Maria Braddon's *Lady Audley's Secret*. Trollope's tale exists on a different plane from these, concerned not with sensational, exaggerated action and surprise – that was why he was wrong to criticise his plot – but with the psychological consequences of small incidents, the lifelong anxiety that lies behind the critical resurgence of the original crime, the collapse of what is, after all, the real Lady Mason when that long-forgotten *hamartia* returns to exact its grim retribution. The very gap in time is itself part of the pathos.

Lady Mason has puzzled the critics by the difference between what she is and what she did. Booth says that she 'was never intended to be evil, but there is an evident change after her guilt is established that cannot be accounted for solely in terms of the deepening of her nature'. (Booth, 1958, p. 195) He attributes the change to Trollope's self-confessed 'kindlier view in the later stages of his acquaintance with her'. This may be true, but the fact is that Lady Mason neither was intended to be nor was simply evil. She is paying for that deliberate but hastily conceived and hastily executed

119

deed of so long ago. That deed, as Trollope emphasises, was the result of overpowering maternal impulse. The title of the chapter even goes so far as to make the scriptural comparison: 'What Rebekah did for her Son'. (ch. 60) Lady Mason's confession to Mrs Orme describes an unloved childhood in a materialistic environment; she continues: 'But then came my baby, and all the world was altered for me. What could I do for the only thing that I had ever called my own?' This is surely enough to dismiss one misguided view, namely, that Lady Mason must have been made by twenty years' concealment into a hardened hypocrite with 'a resolution, a courage, prepared nerves, a daring spirit, a readiness to run risk and encounter disaster'. (*National Review*, January 1863, p. 34) It is enough also to make us understand Trollope's sympathy which, he admitted, grew upon him 'till [he] learned to forgive her and to feel that [he] too could have regarded her as a friend'. (ch. 79) The sympathy exists, not in spite of what she has done, but for the price she had to pay at so delayed a date at the hands of people so unworthy as Joseph Mason and Dockwrath for a deed which, though wrong, had the tenderest and most demanding of human relationships behind it. She obeyed the instincts of natural justice, which, she believed, transcended the rights of man-made law.

Over twenty years Lady Mason had grown into a position of respect and intimacy with Sir Peregrine Orme. What her situation does to this relationship has been mentioned above. At the beginning of *Orley Farm* Trollope is careful to point the contrast in social standing between the Ormes and the Masons. Sir Peregrine is the English gentleman:

> To those who were manifestly his inferiors he was affable, to his recognised equals he was courteous, to women he was almost always gentle; – but to men who claimed an equality he would not acknowledge, he could make himself particularly disagreeable. . . . Sir Peregrine was very resolute in ignoring all claims made by wealth alone. Even property in land could not in his eyes create a gentleman. A gentleman, according to his ideas, should at any rate have greatgrandfathers capable of being traced in the world's history. (ch. 2)

Sir Joseph Mason was a London merchant and Lady Mason the daughter of one of his bankrupt business-associates. The contrast is maintained in the young men Lucius Mason and Peregrine junior, the one precociously and altogether too self-confidently taking to scientific agriculture, the other getting himself rusticated. 'Fruit that grows ripe the quickest is not the sweetest' says Trollope, referring to his hatred of 'competitive struggles' and with scornful irony contemplating 'what a life it would give to the education of the country in general, if any lad from seventeen to twenty-one could go in for a vacant dukedom'. (ch. 3)

The accusations against Lady Mason only make Sir Peregrine – 'generous, quick-tempered, and opinionated' – all the more definitely take her side. The proposal scene is in some ways a repetition of her original misdeed. She had found someone to love, and at last someone to love her. She knew what she ought to do, she knew the danger in which she was placing him and would not willingly have done so, but her emotions overcame her will. Trollope puts it very succinctly: 'She was one whose feelings were sometimes too many for her, and whose feelings on this occasion had been much too many for her.' (ch. 35) It is ironically this moment, the one which should presage the highest happiness that, in fact, precipitates the crisis. She is driven to acknowledge her guilt to Sir Peregrine (ch. 44), and in so doing to crystallise his dilemma – 'In what way so act that he might best assist her without compromising that high sense of right and wrong which in him was a second nature.' (ch. 45) This generous man is thence constrained by the rigour of his own values. He has pity for Lady Mason, but, unlike his daughter-in-law, he cannot show it. His situation, however, is more complex than this: 'The criminal was one who had declared her crime in order to protect him, and whom therefore he was still bound in honour to protect.' (ch. 53) At the end, still loving her, he recognises that they yet must part. Their farewell is one of the most dignified and moving scenes in the whole of Trollope's work. (ch. 79)

If it is in this relationship that we find the most concentrated expression of the private issues of the novel, it is in the treatment of the law that we meet the public issues. Bradford Booth has reminded us that 'there are eleven jury trials in Trollope's novels, and, additionally, the interpretation of the law is a basic plot-concern in *The Warden, Doctor Thorne, Is He Popenjoy?, Cousin Henry*, and, especially, *Mr Scarborough's Family* (Booth, 1957, p. 155), but in none of these is the law so prominent as in *Orley Farm*. Some lawyers have criticised the accuracy of Trollope's account. Foremost amongst these was Sir Francis Newbolt (*Nineteenth Century*, February 1924) in an essay unsurpassed for its pedantic and totally unimaginative examination of Trollope in terms of technical legal realism, though others (e.g. C. F. Robinson's 'Trollope's Jury Trials', *Nineteenth-Century Fiction*, VI (1952)) have reached a more favourable view. Trollope was unable with the law to steer so far from its professional side as he managed to do with the Church, but the question surely must be not whether his descriptions are technically correct in the eyes of the expert but whether they are imaginatively convincing to the ordinarily well-informed reader.

Trollope exploits the differences of character and attitude between his various legal luminaries in both the development of his tale and the presentation of his own point of view. The young idealist, Felix Graham, is doubtful about some of the methods employed, especially by Chaffanbrass, and it is clear that Trollope shares these doubts. Between Graham and Chaffanbrass is Furnival, who has his scruples, but who none the less applies himself to his task. His cross-examination of Kenneby is relentless and thorough, but fair. By contrast, Chaffanbrass interrogates Bridget Bolster in a 'sharp, angry, disagreeable voice', harasses and threatens her and, failing to shake her evidence, concludes by innuendoes against her character. (ch. 71) Graham feels like interrupting him, and at the end Chaffanbrass dismisses him with the words: 'You are too great for this kind of work I take it. If I were you, I would keep out of it for the future.' The young idealist, be it said, has managed, fairly untroubled, to get rid of the girl he was educating to be his wife when he falls in love with Madeline Staveley; but, nevertheless, one must acknowledge that Graham's qualms are underlined by the authorial comment. At the end of Furnival's speech (ch. 72), Trollope marvels at the lawyer's self-congratulation in having done his best for his client whom he knows to be guilty against witnesses he had attacked and yet knew to be honest. Similarly, he likens the 'honesty' of Chaffanbrass to that of the Irish assassin in Tipperary who had never failed his clients in twelve years. (ch. 75) Trollope's lawyer-critics are surely right in claiming that all this shows a somewhat naïve understanding of the whole system of advocacy. Beyond that and within the economy of the tale itself the reader is left with his own problem, arising from his unwillingness to accept that the rightful sentence of the law can be a proper representation of justice. Twenty years of self-accusation have done far more than the law itself required. Anthony Cockshut (p. 168) does well to draw our attention to the sentence describing Lady Mason's first sight of Joseph after those two decades: 'Her own countenance did not quail; but his eyes gradually fell down.' (ch. 64) As Cockshut adds, 'Guilt and long-suffering have brought understanding to one; the consciousness of being defrauded has hardened the other.'

The love-stories of the novel need not detain us long. There is plentiful irony in the sentence: 'I intend that Madeline Staveley shall, to many of my readers, be the most interesting personage in this story' (ch. 19), and more in what follows. After refusing young Peregrine Orme she accepts Felix Graham. The more vivacious and unpredictable Sophia Furnival attracts both Augustus Staveley and Lucius Mason, but marries neither. Trollope is more interested in the sexual relationships of the older people, for, apart from that of Lady Mason with Sir Peregrine, there is a tentative and persisting friendship between her and Mr Furnival, productive, most of all, of his wife's jealousy. Polhemus has pointed out that 'Trollope's portrait of Furnival and his story of Orme's love for a younger woman coincide with his first meetings and intimacy with Kate Field whom he seems to have come to love in more than a fatherly way.' (Polhemus, 1968, p. 83, n. 24) The Furnivals' relationship reveals the oft-observed phenomenon of the wife's inability socially to match the professional success of her husband, and the consequent nostalgia for the scenes and struggles of their earlier married life, and likewise the husband's weariness and wandering interests. The young-love-interest apart (and, significantly, Trollope does not mention this in the *Autobiography* among the successes of the novel), *Orley Farm* is a major achievement and fully deserving of the praise that has been lavished upon it.

The next major novel to consider here is *The Claverings* (1867), the last Trollope wrote for the *Cornhill Magazine*. He himself felt that its 'chief merit' was the 'genuine fun of some of the scenes' (*Autobiography*, ch. 11), those involving Boodle, Archie Clavering and Sophie Gordeloup. Boodle is of a type with some early Thackeray characters, an amiable, ineffectual, non-vicious precursor of someone like Tifto in *The Duke's Children*, a representative of the peripheral retinue of the aristocratic world. He and Archie Clavering are funny, the latter a brilliant example of the dim-witted scion of an upper-class family, needing to marry money but without even the slightest ability to conceal his intentions. Sophie Gordeloup (the name is itself a warning), however, belongs to a different order of creation. She is of the *demi-monde*, a malign parasite, battening upon Julia Ongar.

Trollope was surely wrong to see this fun as the book's chief merit. In fact, *The Claverings* is in many ways a sombre story. It leaves the impression that what happens is not really what the author might have liked to happen. It even contains, *rara avis* indeed for Trollope, a sympathetically portrayed Evangelical parson. Saul's love for Fanny Clavering, the daughter of his rector, is opposed by her parents. Much is made of his aspiration and the contrast between his poverty (see, for instance, the description of his lodging – ch. 34) and the Claverings' status. Of this latter we are told that

> There is a class of country clergymen in England, of whom Mr Clavering was one, and his son-in-law, Mr Fielding, another, which is so closely allied to the squirearchy as to possess a double identity. Such clergymen are not only clergymen, but they are country gentlemen also. Mr Clavering regarded clergymen of his class ... as being, I may say, very much higher than all others without reference to any money question. When meeting his brother rectors and vicars, he had quite a different tone in addressing them, – as they might belong to his class, or to another. There was no offence in this. The clerical country gentlemen understood it all as though there were some secret sign or shibboleth between them; but the outsiders had no complaint to make of arrogance, and did not feel themselves aggrieved. They hardly knew that there was an inner clerical familiarity to which they were not admitted. (ch. 33)

Some might claim to detect an implicit criticism here. I do not think there is. It is just remarkably accurate observation, and the phenomenon itself a reflection of the subtle distinctions underlying and reinforcing the well-defined Victorian social hierarchy. Saul, the 'enthusiast', is an intruder, but by the end of the novel when Mr Clavering succeeds his nephew as squire, he has been impressed enough by Saul to prefer him to the rectory of Clavering and to agree to the marriage. He cannot understand his daughter's taste, 'she has never been used to men like Mr Saul'; but he acknowledges that Saul is a gentleman, even though, as his son Harry puts it, 'he isn't quite one of our sort' (ch. 48) – and the old rector fears that there will be no more cakes and ale in the parish.

Perhaps Trollope is saying that, alas, the world is changing. Certainly this seems an important facet of the main story about the rival attractions of Julia Ongar and Florence Burton for Harry Clavering. Julia belongs to the right set, sister to Lady Clavering, wife of Harry's cousin, Sir Hugh; Florence is one of the many children of a junior partner in a civil engineering firm. It is not he, but his son Theodore, 'the man who dusted his boots with his handkerchief', as Trollope describes him in a chapter-title (26), who represents the family most prominently. Civil engineering was not quite outside the pale of gentlemanly occupations (see *The Vicar of Bullhampton*, ch. 9) and Harry indeed is articled to that profession, but he is always seen to be socially superior in the Burton environment. The Burtons are prosaic, 'worthy', respectable people, essentially *bourgeois* (see, for example, the discussion of Harry by the Burton parents - ch. 4), and Florence is 'a nice girl, clever, well-minded, high-principled and full of spirit'. (ibid.) We have to take Trollope's description largely on trust, though we do see her display a certain nobility in the stresses of Harry's possible reneging on the engagement. (ch. 32) Her ultimate success, however, has more to do with her sister-in-law's persistence (even to visiting Julia Ongar - ch. 37) and his mother's influence than with her own attractions. The whole passage in which Harry confirms his attachment to her is sickly with sentimentality. He is ill, Florence returns her love-trinkets, his mother maunders over them and begins the interview with a question that is really a statement, even a command: 'This dear girl - to me she is inexpressibly dear - is to be your wife?' (ch. 41) One can see both the mother's moral concern for upright dealing and her loyalty to the 'good' representative of her sex, but when Trollope writes that 'Mr Clavering was good enough, great enough, true enough, clever enough to know that Harry's love for Florence should be sustained and his fancy for Lady Ongar overcome' (ibid.) (note the significant difference between 'love' and 'fancy'), one admires the novelist's submission to the canons of Victorian morality more than his allegiance to psychological veracity. Robert Polhemus does not exaggerate when he says that 'the book ends in shallow dishonesty'. (Polhemus, 1968, p. 118)

Harry succumbs to the combined assault upon him. Like so many of Thackeray's young men, he is weak, and this result is not surprising. Trollope indeed feels that Harry's weakness is responsible for the weakness of the book itself. (*Autobiography*, ch. 11) In this he is surely wrong, for out of his weakness arises the central dilemma and the convincing psychological phenomenon of a young man in love with two women at once, each with some qualities different but attractive. A comparison with *Mansfield Park* is not inapt. Harry is a weaker Edmund, Florence a fainter Fanny and Julia Ongar a nobler Mary Crawford.

Julia has made one terrible mistake in refusing to marry a poor man (Harry) and accepting a rich and decadent one (Lord Ongar) instead. Even after Ongar's death there can be no restoration for her. Partly it is one of life's little ironies that Harry has engaged himself just before she is free again, but mainly it is again Victorian moral insistence that is at work. To adopt the chapter title (ch. 41) describing Harry's reconciliation with Florence, this sheep would not be allowed to return to the fold. The only incongruity in the image is that Julia was no sheep. With all her strength she concentrates, after the horrors of her brief marriage, on regaining Harry's love. The sixteenth chapter is a masterpiece of self-analysis. Distinguishing carefully between her own sardonic experience and a totally cynical view of life, 'she had learned to laugh at romance, but still she believed in love'. Others like Archie Clavering and Count Pateroff are seeking her, but she wants only Harry. He in his turn is attracted and drifts back towards her. The crisis is a stormy scene in which he acknowledges a belief that 'one love blighted might be mended by another' (ch. 25) and declares that he will not marry Florence. Julia insists that he must and he retorts by asking her to marry him. It is one of the most convincing episodes of the book, and we are convinced that love like that could not be gainsaid. When therefore later, in the interview with Cecilia, Julia says somewhat cattily of Florence: 'Men are not always fond of perfection. The angels may be too angelic for this world' (ch. 37), we recognise the emotional consistency with the previous scene. The dialogue at the end between Julia and Florence in which the former speaks so generously has an air of conventional politeness about it. At least, one hopes that Trollope did not want to fill it with much more than this. In the earlier interview with Cecilia we are told that 'the man for whom all this was to be done was not worth the passion' and that we may believe; 'but the passion, nevertheless, was there, and the woman was honest in what she was saying'. (ch. 37) Had her creator been equally honest, Julia Ongar would have succeeded in her passion and *The Claverings* would have been a better novel.

He Knew He Was Right (1869) must always be considered among Trollope's three or four best novels. Near-madness had already occupied him in *The Last Chronicle of Barset* and actual insanity appears contemporaneously in Robert Kennedy of the Finn novels. The history of Louis Trevelyan is a progress from jealousy through obsession to paranoia. It is a long novel, far too long and far too obviously so. Whereas *The Last Chronicle of Barset* maintains its interest because its minor plots are the continuation of histories with which we are already familiar and *The Bertrams* keeps its consistency and even pace because no one part stands out with excessive prominence from the rest, the unevenness of *He Knew He Was Right* is at times exasperating. There are no less than four subsidiary love-stories and none of them nor all of them together matches the intensity of the Trevelyan history. Nora Rowley, sister to Emily Trevelyan, rejects the heir to an English peerage and he then marries the niece of an American ambassador (giving Trollope opportunity for some mild satire on the Americans). She favours Trevelyan's erstwhile friend, the journalist Hugh Stanbury. His sister, Dorothy, is likewise in a love-triangle, preferring Brooks Burgess, who may thus lose his place as her aunt's intended legatee, to the parson Gibson, who in his turn is at the centre of a marriage-comedy involving the two sisters Arabella and Camilla French, first committed to the one and then to the other. These latter interests, involving Dorothy and the French sisters, are set in Exeter, where the scenes are dominated by Dorothy's redoubtable aunt, one of Trollope's minor masterpieces of characterisation, an ogre with a heart of gold. Aunt Jemima is of that group which constitutes county society within a small town; 'a district apology was made if she was asked to drink tea with people who were simply "town"; ... county persons ... were greeted by her, and greeted her, on terms of equality.' (ch. 7) She might have been at home in Cranford, provided that she had due recognition of her superior position. She is worth all the younger-generation romantic appurtenances of the novel.

Of the main story the *Spectator* wrote:

> There is real genius in the conception of breaking a husband's heart and ruining his mind on so meagre a basis of fact as this, – using as the materials a proud, hard, wilful woman, with no trace of even the superficial flirt in her, and an elderly man of no real power of fascination, but a certain vanity which makes him feel pleasure in the reputation of wickedness. (12 June 1869, XLII, p. 706)

Colonel Osborne, old enough to be, and indeed friend of, Emily's
father, is indeed an 'ancient Lothario', whose visits to her are not
accidental and, though innocent enough, can easily be twisted by a
suspicious mind, especially when that suspicious mind receives its
report through the observation and comment of such a despicable
character as the private detective Bozzle. Trollope does full justice
to both these minor characters. When in his final appearance
Osborne blusters and objects to being told 'that it's my fault that
I have caused all the trouble, because, when I happened to be in
Devonshire, I went to see your daughter', the author quietly adds
about the excuse Osborne chose to take him there: 'We must do the
Colonel the justice of supposing that he had by this time taught
himself to believe that the church porch at Cockchaffington had
been the motive cause of his journey into Devonshire.' (ch. 64)
Trollope is even less charitable to Bozzle, showing him despicable in
word and deed, in ascription of motive and interpretation of action.
Through his association with him Louis Trevelyan is overwhelmed
by 'a crushing feeling of ignominy, shame, moral dirt, and utter
degradation'. (ch. 27) As Trevelyan recognises – aptly, in Venice,
Bozzle plays Iago to his own Othello.

Like Othello, 'Trevelyan would have preferred before all the
prizes of the world to have had proof brought home to him exactly
opposite to that which he demanded.' (ch. 45) The question we ask
is whether he would have believed the proof, had it been forthcoming. We have to remember the book's title. The following
passage sums up the situation:

> He could not submit to acknowledge to himself the possibility
> of error on his own part. . . . He had never hitherto believed
> that she had been false to her vow, and had sinned against him
> irredeemably; but he had thought that in her regard for
> another man she had slighted him; and, so thinking, he had
> subjected her to a severity of rebuke which no high-spirited
> woman could have borne. His wife had not tried to bear it. . . .
> Then had come his resolution that she should submit, or part
> from him. (ch. 38)

Bozzle, Trevelyan's one confidant, builds on Emily's actions to
make his employer believe worse than this. Compelled to live apart
from her husband, she is in part victim of circumstance (with
Colonel Osborne's visits), in part tactless, stubborn and disobedient.

In the *Autobiography* Trollope confessed that he fell completely short of his intention in *He Knew He Was Right*:

> It was my purpose to create sympathy for the unfortunate man who, while endeavouring to do his duty to all around him, should be led constantly astray by his unwillingness to submit his own judgment to the opinion of others. The man is made to be unfortunate enough, and the evil which he does is apparent ... but the sympathy has not been created yet. I look upon the story as being nearly altogether bad. (ch. 17)

One may dismiss his final opinion, but it is interesting to note that the perceptive *Spectator* review referred to above detected something wrong and identified it with Emily:

> The conception with which, as we believe, Mr Trollope clearly set out, of Mrs Trevelyan – the conception of a self-willed, haughty, steely woman, whose little feeling for her husband and easily wounded self-love were even more the cause ·of the whole tragedy than her husband's conceit and weakness, melts away into something which it is impossible to define.

This is right as far as it goes and it would have been right to the limit – if Trevelyan had remained sane. It would then have been merely a matter of justice between the protagonists. We might still have felt repulsed by Trevelyan's assertion of marital superiority, but that would be the influence merely of the difference in *mores* between the present and a century ago. This indeed is the feeling that sometimes emerges at the beginning of the story. Yet there is no doubting Trevelyan's concern, even at so late a date as when, because of Colonel Osborne's visit, Emily is compelled by her hosts to leave her exile at Nuncombe Putney in Devon. His confusion of feeling, however, is increasing, as Trollope makes clear by printing a letter offering conditions to Emily and then commenting on it, mentioning Trevelyan's belief in his own generosity and in his right to her gratitude, whilst utterly failing to recognise 'the force of the language that he used when he told her that her conduct was disgraceful'. (ch. 27) That confusion is reinforced, as in the Othello reference and the repeated mentions of Trevelyan's deteriorating physical health and appearance. (chs 59, 62, 67, 91, 92) His treatment of their child is likewise a measure of his condition. After threatening Emily, he eventually arranges for young Louey's abduction from his mother. He at first staunchly retains him (this in itself reinforces our sympathy for the mother – as well as for the bemused child) and then later, in Italy, the boy is shown as 'cowed and overcome ... by the terrible melancholy of his whole life'. (ch. 79) As Trevelyan worsens, he agrees to surrender the child, but then there is an outburst before he allows him to be taken away. The surrender is the mark of his final despair. All else has gone except his obsession. Emily 'confessed' to him in Italy, and when in his last moments, caring for him in his last illness, she claims that she has always been true, he returns to the accusation by asserting that she must have lied at Casalunga. There is a confused and inconclusive – and, for that reason, convincing – reconciliation in a kiss of her hand before he dies. It is sufficient for Emily, but 'she never explained to human ears ... the manner in which it was given'. In this the main plot Trollope is quick to reach the central conflict between two people, each determined to have his or her own way. Thereafter he builds up the tension and in the psychological history of Trevelyan reveals the ebb and flow between reason and emotion with the turbulence of the latter relentlessly gaining ever new strength towards that obsessive condition which culminates in self-destruction. In his ultimate paranoia Trevelyan, in the words of Henry James, 'alone, haggard, suspicious, unshaven, undressed, living in a desolate villa on a hill-top near Siena and returning doggedly to his fancied wrong ... is a picture worthy of Balzac.' (James, 1957, pp. 110-11) In this creation of obstinacy, gloom and madness Trollope obviously did better than he knew.

Because Emily was probably meant not to be so sympathetic as she turns out to be, it is interesting to consider whether Trollope meant there to be greater than incidental significance in the various references to feminism which the book contains. Among the first such references is a not surprisingly unsympathetic one from the ultra-conservative Miss Stanbury who associates divorce bills and women's rights with 'a woman [who] has been married a year or two [beginning] to think whether she mayn't have more fun for her money by living apart from her husband'. (ch. 15) Later, the American minister, Spalding, refers approvingly to John Stuart Mill's championship of the cause of female equality and gets a stinging reply from Mr Glascock, about which Trollope expresses no disagreement: 'I don't read what he writes myself.... Can he manage that men shall have half the babies?' (ch. 55) It is Wallachia Petrie (is the name meant to be ridiculous?) who campaigns most fervently for women's rights. Possibly deriving something from Kate Field, she is shown as arid, humourless and over-earnest. She has all the stock American antagonisms in full profusion; 'She hated rank, she hated riches; she hated monarchy.' Some American feminists, Trollope concedes, 'have noble aspirations, good intellects, much energy, and ... are by no means unworthy of friendship', but, he adds, 'the hope in regard to all such ... is that they will be cured at last by a husband and half-a-dozen children.' He advised Kate Field to find a husband (*Letters*, No. 449), but for Wallachia Petrie 'there was not, perhaps much ground for such hope'. (ch. 77)

To return to my conjecture at the beginning of the previous paragraph, there is a conversation early enough in the novel between Trevelyan and Glascock that we should note. The latter refers to American women as clever and pretty, upon which Trevelyan remarks: 'They are so hard. They want the weakness that a woman ought to have.' Glascock replies: 'We prefer women to rule us by seeming to yield.' All this might refer to Emily, but the dialogue ends with Glascock's reference to the different tactics of American men and his *faux pas:* 'You very rarely hear of an American being separated from his wife.' (ch. 37) The various views on feminism, to which Trollope was to return less sympathetically in *Is He Popenjoy?*, are here an illustration of several ways of being wrong; but one feels that Trollope would have preferred to err with Glascock or Trevelyan rather than with Wallachie Petrie. 'The Miss Petries of the world have this advantage ... that they are never convinced of error.' (ch. 77) She knew she was right. Her over-confidence was an intellectual aberration; Emily's was an emotional defiance; Trevelyan's was a paranoiac obsession. Our sympathies may lie with Emily. They only fail towards Louis, in the sense that Trollope thought they did, because he is beyond sympathy. His fate is a matter of more than simple feeling; it is tragic, not just pathetic.

The Vicar of Bullhampton (1869) is really three stories and there is little, if any, connection between them. The vicar and his wife provide the only link there is. There is the customary love-interest, the contention between the vicar and Lord Trowbridge, and the story of Carry Brattle. The first of these concerns the rival claims of Harry Gilmore and Walter Marrable for the hand of Mary Lowther, friend of Mrs Fenwick, the vicar's wife, and a frequent guest at the vicarage. By contrast with most of Trollope's other triangles, in this one Mary is confronted with a choice not between bad and good (of whatever variety these might be) but between good and good. Gilmore is a persistent suitor and 'a man with a good heart, and a pure mind, generous, desirous of being just ... good-looking, though, perhaps, somewhat ordinary in appearance' (ch. 1), but Marrable is the man Mary loves. Not uncommonly in Trollope, there are financial obstacles in the way and, again not uncommonly, these are fortuitously and fortunately removed in time, but not before Mary has agreed to an engagement with Gilmore. The dilemma of decision is not a difficult one, because the force of her love for Marrable is too strong for anything else, but the whole of this story lacks immediacy. In particular, we never realise the pressures, if there are any, within Mary. But then Trollope himself said in the *Autobiography*: 'As I have myself forgotten what the heroine does and says ... I cannot expect that any one else should remember her.' (ch. 18)

He does not even mention the second narrative thread, the opposition of parson and peer which leads to the latter's permitting the construction of a Dissenting tabernacle outside the vicarage gates. The controversy took its origin in Fenwick's defence of young Sam Brattle, who was suspected of murdering one of Lord Trowbridge's tenant-farmers. Trollope rightly describes the vicar as good but imprudent. Fenwick is a man who will defend to the utmost what he believes to be right, but he also has a certain ironically eirenical streak in him. Thus the Dissenting pastor, 'Mr Puddleham had not been quite happy in his mind amidst the ease and amiable relations which Mr Fenwick enforced upon him' (*The Vicar of Bullhampton*, ch. 35), and in just this same spirit Fenwick accepts the building of the chapel. Nevertheless, he can be pugnacious when need be, and he does not fail to be so in answering Lord Trowbridge's assertions about his association with Carry Brattle. The end of it all is the discovery that the land on which the chapel has been built is glebe and the offending building has to be taken down and erected elsewhere. In the latter stages of the story, however, the irony is turned a little on Fenwick himself, for Lord Trowbridge's heir, St George, takes over and, even more eirenical than the vicar, produces a settlement that is sealed by a hitherto hardly credible visit by the Fenwicks to the Trowbridges.

The novel, however, is really about Carry Brattle. Unusually, Trollope wrote a preface to justify her, and most of it he reproduced in the *Autobiography*. She was that thing abhorrent to

Victorian morality, a 'castaway', a fallen woman, and Trollope tells us that the novel 'was written chiefly with the object of exciting not only pity but sympathy for a fallen woman, and of raising a feeling of forgiveness for such in the minds of other women.' *Autobiography*, (ch. 18) Unlike Mrs Gaskell in *Ruth*, Trollope says nothing of her lover and their affair, but simply presents Carry exiled from home and ostracised after the event. When Fenwick finds her, there is a touch of the conventional in Trollope's description of the 'poor, sickly-looking thing [with] beauty obscured by flashes of riotous living and periods of want'. There is a touch also of the sentimental with the recollection of 'the little Carry Brattle of old who had sometimes been so sweetly obedient, and sometimes so wilful, under his hands, whom he had petted, and caressed, and scolded, and loved', but there is some neat psychological realism in the 'disreputable-looking old novel' hastily taken up but not deceiving Fenwick as to the recent departure of someone else who had been there. (*The Vicar of Bullhampton*, ch. 25) The vicar displays both his immense loyalty and his generosity – and his realism, when later

> he would fain have drawn from her some deep and passionate expression of repentance.... But he knew that no such eloquence ... would be forthcoming. And he knew, also, that humble, contrite, and wretched as was the girl now, the nature within her bosom was not changed. (ch. 40)

Escott suggested that Fenwick was Trollope in orders (1913, p. 240), and the description of Carry's despair during her perplexed journey (ch. 42) would reinforce this idea. All Trollope's sympathy is distilled in the account of the girl's wandering without a plan:

> Think of it! To walk forth with, say, ten shillings in your pocket, – so that there need be no instant suffering from want of bread or shelter, – and have no work to do, no friend to see, no place to expect you, no duty to accomplish, no hope to follow, no bosom to which you can draw nigher.

She finishes almost aimlessly in her father's garden.

Her father will not forgive, and she knows it. Trollope is often comic in his creation of the lower classes. Not so with Jacob Brattle, 'a hard-working, sober, honest man. But he was cross-grained, litigious, moody, and tyrannical.... He never forgot, and never wished to forgive.' (ch. 5) If Fenwick is Carry's champion, her father, with the disgrace to his family ever in mind, is her

133

unrelenting antagonist. Beside his deeply offended integrity by an offence brought upon him by her whom he had most deeply loved, Carry's sister-in-law's rejection of her when Fenwick pleads for a refuge for her is just conventional morality: 'Them days and ours isn't the same, Mr Fenwick. . . . And Our Saviour isn't here now to say who is to be a Mary Magdalen and who isn't.' (ch. 41) The distance between Fenwick and Brattle is all the more unbridgeable because the old man is an atheist, to whom the suggestions of repentance and forgiveness can make no appeal. (ch. 63) When eventually he does forgive her, it is a struggle for old Jacob Brattle, and when Carry asks him to call her by her name after he has done so, it is the signal for a long speech and an honest conclusion –

> 'I will bring myself to forgive her. That it won't stick
> here,' and the miller struck his heart. . . . 'I won't be such a
> liar as to say. . . . But there shall never be a word more of it
> out o' my mouth' . . . . but he did not call her by her name.
> (ch. 66)

He did later: such things could come only by stages. And he would later 'bide nigh' her in her ordeal as witness at the murder trial.

As A. O. J. Cockshut has noted, 'Fenwick forgives too easily, or rather half-condones; Brattle can hardly bring himself to forgive at all.' (1955, p. 119) We like the humanity of Fenwick, but it is the integrity of Brattle that we are forced to admire. We are reminded that behind and beneath the residual morality which manifested itself as the respectability of Carry's sister-in-law, itself reminiscent of the Dodson values in *The Mill on the Floss*, there was a deeper morality that those knew best who suffered most. It is easier to take sides for a Maggie Tulliver against the Dodsons than to sympathise with a Carry Brattle and yet not lose sight of the integrity and, in consequence, the suffering of her father. Trollope was generous without ceasing to be just.

7

Shorter Novels, 1863-74

(*Rachel Ray; Miss Mackenzie; The Belton Estate; Nina Balatka; Linda Tressel; Sir Harry Hotspur of Humblethwaite; The Golden Lion of Granpere; Lady Anna; Harry Heathcote of Gangoil*)

In a letter of 1869 Trollope, writing of *The Claverings*, speaks of its length as that of 'a novel in 3 volumes'. (*Letters*, No. 397) In fact, after serialisation in the *Cornhill* it came out in two volumes. Presumably he viewed this with more pleasure than he did the proposal to publish *Sir Harry Hotspur* in two volumes when he insisted on one (and succeeded), and certainly than he did the publisher who 'had a two-volume novel of mine running through a certain magazine, and had it printed complete in three volumes before I knew where I was'. (*Autobiography*, ch. 18) From a look at Appendix A of Professor Ray's article (1967-8), it would seem that this book was *The Belton Estate* and the offending publisher was Chapman & Hall. They took over the bankrupt magazine, the *Fortnightly Review*, of whose Finance Committee Trollope was chairman and in which the novel had first appeared in 1865. They published it in book form before the serialisation was even completed. It may be significant that, apart from *Clergymen of the Church of England* in March 1866, Trollope did not publish with them again until 1873, after his son, Henry, had joined the firm as reader.

The problems in publishing *Rachel Ray* (1863) were different. Trollope was approached by Norman Macleod, one of his friends and editor of the religious periodical *Good Words*, for a serial in which Macleod presumptuously thought Trollope 'could let the *best* side of [his] soul ... better far than ever in Cornhill'. What exactly he meant by this we shall never know, but, considering what Trollope had already said about Evangelicals, it seems strange that, whatever their friendship, Macleod could think him a suitable writer for his pious periodical. We shall also never know in what frame of mind the novelist set out upon his commission, but it

135

almost looks as though he was determined to out-do his mother's unsympathetic *Vicar of Wrexhill,* for one cannot imagine that he was so insensitive that he did not know that he would offend contemporary Evangelical susceptibilities as, to use Macleod's words, he 'cast a gloom over Dorcas Societies, a glory over balls till 4 in the morning'. (quoted in Sadleir, p. 250) As Trollope put it, 'they have tried to serve God and the devil together, and finding that goodness pays best, have thrown over me and the devil ... I am altogether unsuited to the regenerated! It is a pity they did not find it out before.' (To Millais, *Letters,* No. 193) The end of it all was that *Good Words* rejected the tale, Trollope got his money (£500) and published in book form in October.

The story of *Rachel Ray* concerns the opposition of the severely Evangelical sister, Dorothy (the young widow, Mrs Prime) to the romance of her sister Rachel and Luke Rowan. Mrs Prime exaggerates every possible incident against Rachel, and their mother looks on helplessly, wishing to be charitable but anxious not to alienate the affections of either daughter. There is also a subsidiary romance between Dorothy and a repulsively portrayed Evangelical clergyman, Mr Prong. There is an election in which Luke Rowan becomes involved, but the other chief area of interest which includes him is the quarrel with his elder partner in the local brewery and his ultimate assumption of control.

The interest of a love-story in Trollope is often greatest, not in the relationship between the lovers themselves or even in the difficulties they have to encounter, but in the way in which others react to it and attempt to interfere with it. We shall see this several times in the books to be considered in this chapter. In none, however, is it more vividly realised either at close or more distant quarters than in *Rachel Ray.* The love of Rachel and Luke Rowan is a matter of immediate concern to Mrs Prime and Mrs Ray and of continuing interest to the various inhabitants of Baslehurst.

There may have been Evangelicals like Mrs Prime, but the portrait of this sententious, sour, morose woman is, nevertheless, a caricature. Nor is Trollope's pretence of professing his belief in her sincerity as a recurrent preface to damning remarks one that commends itself to the unbiased reader. We must, however, accept her as she is. As such, she represents a narrow, persecuting point of view that results in oppression both of her mother and her sister. She shows herself ready to believe the worst of Rachel on the slenderest of evidence conveyed in the course of gossip. To the mother's defence she retorts with a decision to quit the house. Rachel's spirited response is eventually shared by the mother in a scene where Mrs Prime is rebuked for black looks and hard words. From this scene one of her replies and Trollope's comment must be quoted:

> 'I don't know that there have been any black looks,' said
> Mrs Prime, looking very black as she spoke. (ch. 25)

It shows the level on which Trollope treated her.

The treatment of Mrs Prime's lover, the Evangelical clergyman, Samuel Prong, is, if anything, even less generous, but it is more successful because his role falls within narrower limits. There is less interaction between him and other characters. Apart from some contrast with another parson, Mr Comfort, a manifest 'trimmer' whom Trollope gently satirises, Prong's relationship is exclusively with Mrs Prime. He is described as 'energetic, severe, hardworking, and, I fear, intolerant', proud of preaching the Gospel but convinced that many other clergymen did not, 'careless shepherds, or shepherds' dogs indifferent to the wolf'. Trollope later develops the use of this image in a long passage in which he takes up Rachel's own antipathy to Prong, 'educated at Islington, and ... sometimes he forgot his "h"s'. (ch. 4) The novelist describes Prong's appearance, allowing for certain good characteristics, the 'eyes by no means deficient in light and expression', but noting also the 'small, rather upturned nose ... the mean mouth' and 'about his lips an assumption of character and dignity which his countenance and body generally failed to maintain'. This, however, is but the prelude to a summary of character – 'a devout, good man; not self-indulgent; perhaps not more self-ambitious than becomes a man to be; sincere, hard-working, sufficiently intelligent, true in most things to the instincts of his calling'; all, however, as preliminary to the damning qualification: 'but deficient in one vital qualification for a clergyman of the Church of England; he was not a gentleman'. This prepares us for an important passage in which Trollope says that the mark of a gentleman is recognisable but not definable, a recognition, moreover, not confined simply to those who possess the quality. 'It is caught at a word, it is seen at a glance, it is appreciated unconsciously at a touch by those who have none of it themselves.... Now Mr Prong was not a gentleman.' (ch. 6) So be it; and so effective was Trollope's satire. Mr Prong was not a gentleman, but were none of the Evangelicals gentlemen? Surely the Villiers, the

Barings, the Pelhams, the Waldegraves, all aristocratic families who provided Evangelical bishops, to name no others, must have produced some gentlemen. As a portrait of one kind of sanctimonious clergyman the characterisation of Prong is effective, but so fierce and so single-minded is Trollope that it almost looks as though he was deliberately going out of his way to antagonise his potential Evangelical readers.

Luke Rowan does not escape Trollope's criticism – he is 'conceited, prone to sarcasm, sometimes cynical and perhaps sometimes affected' (ch. 4), but the criticism is always muted, even to qualifying his political radicalism as of a man not accepting the doctrine of equality, but possessing 'a manhood that will own no inferiority to the manhood of another'. (ch. 26) The relationship of Rowan and Rachel is that of two healthy-minded young people in contrast with that of Prong and Mrs Prime, 'governed ... by a sense of duty, rather than by the poor creature-longings of the heart'. This is said in the course of an interview between them, about which Trollope cannot help but comment puckishly: 'How fearfully wicked would Rachel have been in her eyes, had Rachel made an appointment with a young man at some hour and some place in which she might be found alone!' (ch. 9)

The power of public opinion, and especially as it represents the sense of a small community, is one of the novel's greatest strengths. Trollope's sure touch conveys the feeling of intermingled interests and curiosity at every level from the squire Butler Cornbury to the brewery foreman Worts. Little things are exaggerated and quickly spread abroad. An erroneous assertion about a single charge against Luke Rowan speedily becomes 'all over the town that he had left unpaid bills behind him' (ch. 17), and then that he was head over ears in debts. The 'scrutinising eyes' of Miss Pucker, confidante of Mrs Prime and vicious scandal-carrier, see Luke on his way to visit Rachel.

> She carried the tidings up into Baslehurst, and as she repeated
> it to the grocer's daughters and the bakers' wives she shook
> her head with as much apparent satisfaction as though she
> really believed that Rachel oscillated between a ruined name
> and a broken heart. (ch. 28)

Trollope is rarely as crisp as in that last clause, but the passage like many others and like the whole story of Luke's quarrel with Tappitt and of new methods succeeding old inefficiency constitutes part of Trollope's masterly evocation of Baslehurst. We feel that we know the small town as well as Barchester Close, and here is the greater achievement, for to realise Baslehurst meant a wider and more various scenario than the somewhat specialised precincts of the cathedral.

Writing to George Eliot, Trollope said:

> You know that my novels are not sensational. In *Rachel Ray* I have attempted to confine myself absolutely to the commonest details of commonplace life among the most ordinary people. ... I have shorn my fiction of all romance. (*Letters*, No. 207)

In *Miss Mackenzie* (1865) he tried 'to prove that a novel may be produced without any love' (*Autobiography*, ch. 10), but he did not succeed. The heroine is thirty-six and is sought in marriage, for her money, by three suitors – Rubb, a rapacious and unscrupulous business-partner of her brothers; a squint-eyed Evangelical curate in Littlebath, Jeremiah Maguire; and her cousin, John Ball, a widower with nine children who, but for an altered will, would have inherited the wealth that has gone to Miss Mackenzie. Eventually, by discovery of a hitherto unknown document he does inherit, but he also marries her. Most of the reviewers recognised that here was another instance of 'the commonest details of commonplace life among the most ordinary people'. It was their reaction to it that varied. On one side was the *Times* reviewer, speaking of 'pictures which are not dull of dull lives, dull households, dull dinner parties, dull teas and dull prayer-meetings'. (23 August 1865, p. 13) On the other, in his first review of Trollope, the precocious young Henry James complained of the author's lack of imagination by which all the detail was of no avail when the characters whom it should illustrate were so intrinsically dull, nay, worse, stupid in themselves. 'Why should we follow the fortunes of such people? They vulgarise experience and all the other heavenly gifts.' (*Nation*, 13 July 1865, p. 52) But then in another review he had just dismissed *Bleak House*, *Little Dorrit* and *Our Mutual Friend* in a single sentence.

James was unjust, though it is true that he might himself have made much more of Miss Mackenzie. As it is, she is allowed to recall pathetically the romantic verses of her youth and to compare with these the reality of the sordid pursuit by her sordid suitors – Maguire, 'a very strict evangelical clergyman ... somewhat in debt, and with oh! such an eye' or Rubb, the tradesman who wore yellow gloves and was decidedly not a gentleman. 'She tore [her verses] very gently, into the smallest fragments. She tore them again and again, swearing to herself as she did so that there should be an end of all that.' (ch. 15) James ought surely to have liked that touch. Then, too, there is a nobility in her later suffering when she faces life, deprived of all her wealth and still beset by those who have already battened upon her, such as her sister-in-law or those who would do so, such as Rubb and Maguire.

Trollope establishes a gradation among the three suitors. Rubb has already defrauded her of some of her money by offering security that has already been mortgaged elsewhere, but he does in the course of his association with her come to something like real affection for her. Maguire never does, and by his later pursuit and his deceitful assertion of an engagement he places her attachment to John Ball in utmost peril. The scheming of Lady Ball destroys any sympathy the reader may have for John Ball's interest in Margaret Mackenzie, but this is gradually overcome by his utter honesty, so rare a quality in the characters of this novel. He is not without concern for the money and at one stage, just before his final proposal, he vehemently complains about the loss he has suffered in having been denied the inheritance for so long, but his honesty is never in doubt. By it he is able both to win Margaret and to put to rout his mother's hostility.

It remains, however, that none of the characters in *Miss Mackenzie* possesses either sufficient variety or depth to interest the reader at the length to which Trollope takes him, and its successes are incidental rather than integral. In particular, some of the characters at Littlebath, a location taken over from *The Bertrams,* remain memorable. One of these is Miss Todd, 'a stout jolly-looking dame' of decided opinions and no restraints in expressing them (herself taken also from *The Bertrams*), and another is her opposite, Mr Stumfold, a rare instance of a jolly Evangelical in Trollope, a man whose 'chief enemies were card-playing and dancing as regarded the weaker sex, and hunting and horse-racing – to which, indeed, might be added everything under the name of sport – as regarded the stronger', but yet 'he could be very jovial at dinner parties. He could make his little jokes about little pet wickednesses. A glass of wine, in season, he never refused. Picnics he allowed, and the flirtation accompanying them.' (ch. 2) He is more human than his wife and most of their circle. Unfortunately, we see little enough of him and all too much of the severe, self-seeking

Maguire who would 'defy any man or woman to be happy here'. (ch. 4) As a whole, however, *Miss Mackenzie* possesses neither characters interesting in themselves nor, and this is more important, a closely knit community whose values and attitudes supply the backdrop for the action of the principal personages of the kind that we find in *Rachel Ray* and which together serve to make this much the more successful novel of the two.

If *Miss Mackenzie* was an attempt at a novel without love, *The Belton Estate* (1866) is a novel with nothing but love. Trollope himself placed it on the same level as the two novels we have just discussed, considering it 'readable, and contains scenes that are true to life; but it has no peculiar merits, and will add nothing to my reputation as a novelist.... I seem to remember almost less of it than of any book that I have written'. (*Autobiography*, ch. 10) It is a story with but few characters. It was necessary therefore, more than elsewhere, that Trollope should tell us not just what the characters did, but why they did it. The tale concerns the long-delayed choice by Clara Amedroz of the right man, Will Belton, and her rejection of the wrong one, Captain Frederick Aylmer. To this must be added the fact that Will is heir to the estate held by Clara's father and when the latter dies, she must prepare to leave it; whilst she is to receive through Aylmer's agreement a sum by way of interest from the will of her foster-aunt Winterfield. The behaviour of the two men is contrasted markedly here, as in everything, with Will generously wanting her to stay on at Belton Castle and Aylmer merely formally and quite coldly sending her the exact amount due to her. 'But then Aylmer was a cold-blooded man – more like a fish than a man.' (ch. 20) His very proposal of marriage had been but to fulfil his promise to his Aunt Winterfield. He only discovers any real passion when he has also discovered that Belton insists on breaking the entail and leaving Clara in possession of the estate. Aylmer is not only dictated to by his aunt. What is more serious, he is dominated by his mother, and in some of the most effective scenes in the book, depicting Clara's visit to Aylmer Park, we see her insulted by this domestic dictator who makes the lives of all around her, from her husband down to the meanest servant, miserable by her interference and criticism. The climax of the visit occurs with Lady Aylmer's accusing Clara of having a hold over her son, an insolence which Clara fiercely repudiates. (ch. 26) In their final interview, as his renewed interest shows itself,

141

Clara gives Aylmer the *coup-de-grâce* with a reference to the way he 'looked on and saw her treated in his own home, by his own mother'. (ch. 29) His selfishness apart, there is little to Aylmer, but Trollope has succeeded in using his very shadowiness through the more positive qualities of other characters, his mother and Will Belton.

Polhemus has seen Clara's ultimate choice as a decision for progress. (Polhemus, 1968, p. 127) In so far as it is a rejection of negative values (Mrs Winterfield and Aylmer are both associated with Trollope's *bête-noire*, the Evangelicals), this may be true, but Belton belongs to long-established order. He will restore a Belton to Belton, and Clara's father, the old squire, contrasts him with Aylmer in Parliament, which

> used to be something when I was young, but it won't make a
> man a gentleman nowadays. It seems to me that none but
> brewers and tallow-chandlers, and lawyers go into Parliament
> now. Will Belton could go into Parliament if he pleased, but
> he knows better than that. (ch. 15)

Against calculation Belton re-asserts the old values, and with them generosity and spontaneity. Indeed, the spontaneity is sometimes unacceptably impulsive and masterful as when he kisses Clara and immediately realises that he has offended her by doing so. (ch. 22) His meeting with Aylmer at, so appropriately, the Great Northern Hotel at King's Cross is at once dramatic and comic. This meeting of fire and water ends:

> 'You shouldn't let your passion get the better of you in this
> way,' [Clara] said ...
> 'I suppose not,' said [Will].
> 'I can forgive him,' said Captain Aylmer.
> 'D --- your forgiveness,' said Will Belton.... The door
> was shut, and Will Belton was gone. (ch. 24)

This dominant character wins, because he speaks for life and love.

In a minor key there is the contrast between the negative values of the Aylmers and the wisdom and kindliness of Mrs Askerton, Clara's only possible companion and Will Belton's champion. She is an interesting introduction in that, as an Army widow, she had lived with her husband in India three years before they were able to marry. This, of course, makes her in Aylmer eyes quite unsuitable for Clara. They judge her by a code; Will Belton by what she is. Trollope, anticipating Carry Brattle but on a different social evel, cannot exonerate her, but he does show a sensitive under-standing of the effect of her experience upon her and of the way in which she has accommodated herself to living with 'the one sin which she had committed'. (ch. 21) She is not without an oc-casional touch of vulgarity, but overall her wisdom, insight and tact add to the qualities of Belton in establishing the values which the book commemorates.

The next four novels (taking *Sir Harry Hotspur* later and out of order) are all based on a common relationship of characters – the conflict of preferences about lovers between a young girl and her parent, guardian or other elders. Three of these four have a European setting, the exception being *Lady Anna*. *Nina Balatka* (1867) is set in Prague, *Linda Tressel* in Nuremburg and *The Golden Lion of Granpere* in Alsace. The first two of these were published anonymously in 1866 and 1867, and Trollope may have hoped that his choice of a setting and social ambience unusual for him would help to conceal his identity. He claims, rather curiously, that he embarked upon this experiment in order to assume again the role of a beginner and not to profit from the fame of an established reputation which had already meant that 'that which [he] wrote was received with too much favour'. Apart from R. H. Hutton's guessing the authorship, Trollope did not succeed by these works in 'obtain[ing] a second identity'. After these two attempts Blackwood, the publisher, was unwilling to carry on 'and declined a third attempt, though a third such tale was written for him'. (*Autobiography*, ch. 11) This third was *The Golden Lion of Granpere*, written in 1867 but not published until 1872.

The opposition to Nina Balatka's love for Anton Trendellsohn comes not from her father, the impoverished partner of Anton's father, but from her Aunt Zamenoy and family, who among other things object to her marrying a Jew. The Zamenoys not only persecute Nina but also plot to place her under suspicion of withholding from the Trendellsohns a deed due as security for money lent to her father. In addition, Anton is under pressure from his father and his community to marry a Jewess, Rebecca Loth. It will be seen therefore that to the personal and family stresses involved in the relationship are added the racial and religious circumstances. The ruthless persecuting Aunt Zamenoy is repeated in Aunt Staubach of *Linda Tressel* and Lady Lovel of *Lady Anna*. To the burden of this tyrant is added for Nina the extreme and almost incredible poverty, amid which she endeavours to keep herself and her father alive. This helps to contrast the benevolence of the Trendellsohns, who do something to relieve the poverty with the entire absence of such relief on the part of the Zamenoys. To crown her troubles, Nina has to combat Anton's suspicions. Through this relationship we trace the subtlety of Trollope' characterisation of a man with all the tender sensitivity of his persecuted race, one who sincerely loves and will be stubborn against his fellow-Jews for his love, but who at the same time shows how easily his love may be disturbed. It is another characteristic of this group of tales that, with the possible exception of *The Golden Lion of Granpere*, the girl shows herself of much greater moral fibre than her lover. Nowhere does the character of the two, Nina and Anton, come out better than in the scene where his suspicions, kindled and fed by the Zamenoys, lead him to demand that she demonstrate her love by obedience in secretly opening her father's desk to find the deed. (ch. 8) It is found there after old Balatka's death; the Zamenoys have succeeded; Anton deserts her; she contemplates suicide, but the truth is revealed to Anton and she is rescued.

Of this tale and *Linda Tressel* Trollope wrote: 'There was more of romance proper than had been usual with me. And I made an attempt at local colouring. . . . Prague is Prague, and Nuremburg is Nuremburg.' (*Autobiography*, ch. 11) The descriptions of scenes and places are vivid, and in particular one remembers the bridge and the river, the bridge that separates the Jewish and Christian quarters and the river that flows beneath, the bridge over which Anton and Nina pass and re-pass to meet each other, and the river, 'fine, silent, dark' (ch. 15), over which in her own darkest moment Nina meditates suicide. Not least in her consideration at that hour is Nina's recognition that 'the inborn suspicion of [Anton's] nature had broken out in opposition to his love, forcing her to acknowledge that she had been wrong in loving a Jew'. Their love is a bridge, beneath which flows the river of death. The bridge is the symbol of the attempt to transcend conflicting faiths and *mores*, but those who do so do it only with difficulty and only for themselves. Because it can be only for themselves, they, like the lovers in *Linda Tressel*, cannot remain in their native place. 'Early in the following year, while the ground was yet bound with frost . . . a Jew and his wife took their leave of Prague, and started for one of the great cities of the west.' (ch. 16)

: is in one such city, Nuremburg, that *Linda Tressel* (1868) is set.
1 a household oppressive with Calvinism, an intensified European
ersion of Mrs Prime's Evangelicalism in *Rachel Ray*, Aunt Staubach
ndeavours to compel Linda into a marriage with her lodger, the
nattractive, middle-aged town clerk, Peter Steinmarc. The type of
eligious pressure exemplified in *Nina Balatka* is thus replaced by
nother, but whereas the pressure there took the form of differing
aiths of the lovers, here, and more compellingly, it becomes the
xploitation of belief to instil into Linda an obligation to love
nrough a sense of obedience and of the guilt in disobedience. Thus
) Madame Staubach,

> a broken heart and a contrite spirit were pretty much the
> same thing. It was good that hearts should be broken, that all
> the inner humanities of the living being should be, as it were,
> crushed on a wheel and ground into fragments, so that
> nothing should be left capable of receiving pleasure from the
> delights of this world. (ch. 9)

'his imagery of fracture and crushing recurs, and Linda is shown
s accepting this view (ch. 2), such is the success of her aunt's
idoctrination. Again, the imagery is transferred to Steinmarc after
inda has scorned his approaches: 'He thought it would be well that
inda should be crushed. Yes; and he thought also that he might
robably find a means of crushing her.' (ch. 3) It is bad enough
nat Steinmarc should represent for Linda dull, middle-aged re-
bectability, but when he becomes spiteful and vengeful, he has
eached the point of being completely intolerable.

Set over against Steinmarc is the young lover, Ludovic Valcarm,
vely, enthusiastic, but something of a scapegrace, one who visits
er, all unexpecting, at the most unusual times and even by the
10st unlikely means – such as coming in through the rafters! He
; persecuted by Steinmarc and arrested for his misdemeanours.
scaping, he persuades Linda to elope with him to Augsburg, where
ney stay apart and she decides that she will end the association. She
ven agrees to marry Steinmarc, but, with every inner determina-
on not to do so, she escapes to her uncle in Cologne, falls ill on
ne way there and dies.

The men characters are unsatisfactory except as a contrast to each
ther. This is particularly so in the case of Valcarm, whose antics
equire from the reader a justification at times, for which Trollope
as simply not supplied sufficient information. These deficiencies,

however, are amply compensated by the portrayal of the two women. Madame Staubach is an honest tyrant, who believes she is doing what is right, even to the extent of blackmail in a display of religious hysterics, but who yet recognises that, in succeeding and putting Steinmarc in power as master of the house, she would be placing 'a thorn in her own side'. (ch. 9) Linda, better still, shows a resolute and resilient spirit in withstanding the two-fold attack of aunt and would-be lover and at the same time coping with the imprudent activities of Valcarm. Trollope brings out the conflict between her resolve on the one hand and the demands of obedience imposed by her faith, very much in the person of Aunt Staubach, on the other. Denounced as a castaway, pleaded with as a potentially penitent Mary Magdalene, Linda can resist and yet never sufficiently free herself to see that she is any the less true to her faith as a result of the disobedience she must show to the wishes of her aunt. The climax of outside pressures, which comes when she pretends to agree to a marriage, is matched by the stresses within her mind. People think her mad. As elsewhere in other respects, we have to take Trollope too much on trust. It shows in other and greater examples of character under stress, in a Melmotte, for example. The external manifestations are there; the inward tortures, except perhaps of a Crawley or a Trevelyan, are missing.

The religious tensions of *Nina Balatka* and *Linda Tressel* might have been paralleled in *The Golden Lion of Granpere* (1872), where there is a Protestant father and son and a Catholic mother and daughter and a Protestant lover of the daughter. The religious relationships exhibit such a tolerance, in fact, that we see a Catholic *curé* urging the daughter to accept her unwanted Protestant lover in the course of what Booth describes aptly enough as this 'sunny summer idyll of airy inconsequentiality'. (Booth, 1958, p. 68) Marie Bromar, daughter of Madame Voss, is in love with her step-brother George, but her parents, and especially her step-father, would have her marry the linen-draper of Basle, Adrian Urmand. She half commits herself to Urmand because she thinks, wrongly, that George Voss has ceased to be interested in her. One of the most touching aspects of the book lies in those passages in which Michel Voss presses Marie to accept Urmand, touching because he thinks he is doing what is best for her and she, hating the idea, is anxious in her love for him not to cross his purpose. Her ultimate refusal is the signal for the outbreak of his wrath, but this latter is skilfully mingled in this part of the novel with Voss's developing realisation that he would much prefer what Marie herself wants, namely, a union with his son George. The latter part of the story is marked by the increasing discomfiture of Urmand ase realises the futility of his interest, a discomfiture that is often amusing but that also is not without some touches of harshness. This, however, is a tale with no villains, and at the final banquet Urmand forgives and everyone is happy. Lacking the sombre overtones of its two precursors, *The Golden Lion of Granpere* is both lighter and slighter than they, a 'summer idyll' indeed.

Lady Anna (1874) is considerably more substantial than its three predecessors based on the same set of relationships. There is not only the clash between mother and daughter about one young man or the other as an acceptable lover; there are also the questions of the legality of the marriage of the mother, Lady Lovel, and therefore also of the legitimacy of her daughter, Lady Anna, the progressive madness of Lady Lovel in her obsessive desire that Anna should marry her cousin, the new Lord Lovel, and the social problem that arises out of Anna's preference for Daniel Thwaite, a tailor, over the claims of her cousin. With his customary vigorous comment Trollope exclaimed: 'Everybody found fault with me for marrying her to the tailor. What would they have said if I had allowed her to jilt the tailor and marry the good-looking young lord?' (*Autobiography*, ch. 19) He elaborates on this comment in a letter to Lady Wood: 'Of course the girl has to marry her tailor. It is very dreadful, but there was no other way.' (*Letters*, No. 520) He there says that he wished to examine the conflict between truth to troth and truth to lineage 'when, from early cirumstances the one had been given in a manner detrimental to the other' and he determined to make the social discrepancy between the couple as great as possible.

The *Saturday Review* was especially critical: 'There are Radicals in the abstract, but a man must be embittered by some violent present exasperation who can like such disruptions of social order as this.' (9 May 1874, p. 598) It rightly remarked that we do not see anything of Thwaite in the 'posture and surrounding circumstances of his calling' and though, by the accession of his wife's wealth, at the end he does not need his calling, the reader cannot help but feel that Trollope has shied away from some of the embarrassing problems of showing Thwaite in society, even though he has

Thwaite himself recognise the difficulties. (ch. 47) Trollope did not shirk such necessities in his portrayal of Melmotte in the closely contemporary *The Way We Live Now*. The novelist was interested in Radicals at this time, as we see from the portrait of the lively Ontario Moggs in *Ralph the Heir*. Earlier, there had been Luke Rowan in *Rachel Ray*, but he was very much a theoretical Radical. In Thwaite, however, Trollope had the opportunity of showing a committed Radical in a highly stratified society. It cannot be said that he really exploits it. Thwaite 'was ambitious, discontented, sullen and tyrannical. He hated the domination of others, but was prone to domineer himself. He suspected evil of all above him in rank.' (ch. 21) There is no idealism, no fervour of the kind that we find even in the somewhat comic Moggs. It is difficult to see in him the protagonist in a conflict, as his apologist Sir William Patterson puts it, between generosity and valour on the one hand and rank and wealth on the other. In addition, there is more than rank and wealth in Lord Lovel, and there is more also than a handsome manner and appearance; and but for the fact that she was in love, we would find it hard to believe Anna who sees Thwaite as handsomer than Lovel. It is harder still to see him as 'a very man' (ch. 36), for Trollope just has not shown and proven this. In making his task so difficult, not just a tailor but a sullen tailor, he has not succeeded in carrying his reader along with him to sustain and establish a sympathy with Lady Anna, particularly as at an early stage we are told that she not only loved Thwaite but that she also feared him. 'The man had become her master; and even could she have brought herself to be false, she would have lacked the courage to declare her falsehood to the man to whom she had vowed her love.' (ch. 10) In a sense, Trollope has to rest on Anna's troth too much, and Anna herself is not vivid enough. She lacks the spirit, except in this one regard, of a Nina Balatka or a Linda Tressel.

In this one regard, however, she is able to withstand her mother, the one character in whom we see any development. In the early years she is the outcast, the questioned wife of an evil earl, questioned because he had himself thrown doubt on their marriage. Trollope stresses her tenacity and courage. Once recognised, however, she takes her place in society, is acknowledged by the Lovels and looks forward to the union of her daughter and the new peer; this was her reward, a reward to be dashed from her hands, her planning ironically futile, when Anna conveys the news of her engagement to Thwaite. With her ambition thwarted, the qualities which had proved so admirable earlier take a violent turn. The history of Lady Lovel is one of obsession kindling ever-greater hostility. She castigates Anna fiercely (ch. 20), she refuses to let her live with her, she threatens to kill either Thwaite or Anna (ch. 37), in one scene 'the Countess with great violence knocked the [Bible] out of her daughter's grasp, and it was thrown to the other side of the room' (ch. 39), and in another, as the climax of a carefully developed hysteria in the character, she takes a pistol and wounds Thwaite with her shot. At that point the tension within her snaps, and 'she almost forgot now the misery of the last year in the intensity of her desire to escape the disgrace of punishment'. (ch. 44) Whereas Madame Staubach's is a nagging, self-righteous obsession well suited to the comparatively static situation in *Linda Tressel*, Lady Lovel's is violent and unstable and benefits in its turn from the broader canvas and the greater movement of *Lady Anna*. It is near to melodrama without ever becoming so.

Not least responsible for this escape is the setting of the novel within a solidly realised society which, though ranging from earl to tailor, finds its firmest expression in the opposed figures of Sir William Patterson and Parson Lovel, the one defending Anna's choice, the other obedient ultimately to the wishes of Lord Lovel by agreeing to marry Anna and Thwaite but resolute in his hostility, the voices respectively of reason and prejudice. Trollope may indeed have been struggling with reason and prejudice himself. There is something just a little facile about Sir William, and in the last pages of the book he is impelled to pay tribute to the rector as

> an honest, sincere man, unselfish, true to his instincts, genuinely English, charitable, hospitable, a doer of good to those around him. In judging of such a character we find the difficulty of drawing the line between political sagacity and political prejudice. Had he been other than he was, he would probably have been less serviceable in his position. (ch. 48)

Trollope could not rest easy in seeing such a man defeated, a man who was 'true to his instincts, genuinely English'. He was not troubled that Anna had dissipated her mother's hopes, but he was not, could not be altogether happy that she had proved untrue to her lineage. In his last paragraph he half-promised 'the further doings of Mr Daniel Thwaite and his wife Lady Anna'; they never came.

Sir Harry Hotspur of Humblethwaite (1870), despite Trollope's remark that it 'was written on the same plan as *Nina Balatka* and *Linda Tressel* ... and is of the same nature', represents an achievement of an altogether different and superior dimension to both these and, indeed, to any of the other shorter novels. It is, in fact, not strictly on the same plan as the group we have just considered, since the second lover, preferred by the parent, is shadowy and leaves the story early in its development. The emphasis therefore is not on the girl's resistance to an unwanted lover but on her persistence for the one she wants. Furthermore, unlike Lady Anna, Emily Hotspur does not face a choice between truth to troth and to lineage, but the desperate necessity, as she sees it, of being faithful to both. Again, by contrast with the other novels we have discussed, the parent is not simply the persecutor of his daughter. Sir Harry's motives are nobler than those of the others, and the pathos of the situation is reinforced by the conflict within himself, caused by the need to protect his daughter from a worthless suitor. A man with his deep regard for his order would have preferred to accept the heir to his title as his daughter's future husband, and he vacillates more than once about this, but always the moral turpitude of George Hotspur, reinforced by new revelations, precludes acceptance.

Harper's Magazine (October 1871) called *Sir Harry Hotspur* 'the saddest story, and at the same time the simplest' that Trollope had written. Emily, knowing George Hotspur for what he is, will not betray her fidelity; we pity her. Sir Harry, seeing the consequences of a union between them and aware also of certain family advantages in it, nevertheless, has to oppose her desires; we pity him. It is an impossible situation. Emily sums it up when she says: 'I told him ... I would never marry without your leave. ... But I told him also that I would always be true to him.' (ch. 13) Anthony Cockshut calls it perceptively a 'tragedy of the pure in heart'. (1955, p. 127) George Hotspur, his debts paid and an annuity provided by Sir Harry, has no qualms in deserting Emily and quickly marrying the actress, Mrs Morton, who was already his mistress. Emily pines and dies, Sir Harry is left desolate with 'pressing energy left to him for one deed', to leave his estate away from George to his wife's nephew.

Trollope had earlier investigated the theme of love unworthily bestowed in *Can You Forgive Her?*, the love, that is, between Alice and George Vavasor (also, incidentally, in an at least partly

Cumbrian setting), but Alice vacillates, whereas Emily is possessed of a terrifying single-mindedness. Her fidelity is such that George's infidelity does not count with her. 'His untruth would not justify hers. And untruth was impossible to her.' (ch. 17) This is her reiterated reply to every mention of George's unfaithfulness. Convincing as this reaction is, if anything, it leaves us with too simple an impression of her. Trollope does not tell us enough about what she feels, and it is not surprising, though it is not so satisfying either, that the final months of her life are passed so quickly and so uninformatively. The only specific references are to her feeling 'old, worn-out and weary', and on hearing of his marriage and finally recognising that she was to have been merely the means of getting George out of his disreputable difficulties, 'she could not sustain her contempt for herself as she remembered this'. (ch. 24)

George Hotspur forms with George Vavasor and Sir Felix Carbury an infamous trio – 'a gambler, a swindler ... a forger and a card-sharper [who] has lived upon the wages of the woman he has professed to love'. (ch. 16) Above all, in Sir Harry's words, 'he is as false as hell'. (ch. 23) Again and again, Trollope emphasises George's propensity for lies. Even when he is being made the most generous offers, such as the chance of living on the Hotspur estate at Scarrowby, he can glibly promise to give up his London life without having any intention of doing so. Trollope observantly describes it: 'George's face fell – his face being less used to lying than his tongue; but his tongue lied at once.' (ch. 20) The lies are 'gratuitous, unnecessary, and inexpedient'. Trollope even suggests a pathological condition: 'The man has to be taken, lies and all, as a man is taken with a squint, or a harelip, or a bad temper. He has an uphill game to fight, but when once well known, he does not fall into the difficulty of being believed.' (ch. 8) Nobody does believe George Hotspur except – and this is the tragic irony – Emily, whose fidelity was firmest.

Sir Harry is outraged by him. He, a man proud of his family and his order in society, having just lost his only son, is faced with the prospect of this man as his heir and, even worse, his son-in-law. He would not willingly separate the property from the title, but how can he as a man of honour allow it to pass to such a reprobate? Love of his daughter and regard for what he considers the proper behaviour of an English landowner as trustee for his successors are the two activating forces in his conduct. The first chapter emphasises his position as 'a great English commoner' with his responsibilities to the 'House of Humblethwaite', and thereafter, mingled amongst his dialogues with Emily and his encounters with George, there are set-pieces describing the hall, the London house in Bruton Street, meetings with the blacksmith and the bailiff and the like.

The *Saturday Review,* in a strangely partial review of the novel, attacked Trollope's hostility

> to an aristocracy. He has been all along at pains to show that blood and descent and great possessions are no safeguard against the lowest aims and meanest vices. He is much more alive to the dangers of luxurious idleness than to the stimulus to virtuous action which so many people delight to see in high place and its noble opportunities. (10 December 1870, p. 754)

Trollope may have heeded this in his creation of Roger Carbury, though it is unlikely. This quotation is true enough in relation to George Hotspur and to the young men who would come later in *The Way We Live Now,* but Sir Harry represents a different code. It is this which Trollope admires; but he refuses to be as one-eyed as the *Saturday Review.* Indeed, he seems to have anticipated the criticism:

> Noblesse oblige. High position will demand, and will often exact, high work.... And good blood too will have its effect – physical for the most part – and will produce bottom, lasting courage ... but good blood will bring no man back to honesty. The two things together, no doubt, assist in producing the highest order of self-denying man. (ch. 20)

Surely we have to see that, whereas George had only good blood, Sir Harry and Emily had both good blood and honesty. Possessed of these virtues, they had to suffer at the hands of the most unscrupulous dishonesty. Emily's misplaced and tenacious virtue wrought the tragedy of two good people.

Harry Heathcote of Gangoil (1874) was written as a Christmas tale for the *Graphic.* It sprang out of Trollope's own experience of Australia, where he spent fourteen months in 1871 and 1872. In the course of travelling and writing he stayed some five weeks with his younger son, Frederick.

It is a neatly constructed tale, working up to the climax of a bush-fire and then concluding quietly with a Christmas dinner and a proposal of marriage. The events are centred upon and emanate from the character of Heathcote himself, a squatter, master of 120,000 acres and 30,000 sheep, marked by 'what his enemies called pig-headedness, his acquaintances obstinacy, and those who loved him, firmness'. (ch. 1) His prejudices lead him to a dislike of free-selectors, men who purchased land from the Australian government and for which the possessor received no compensation. His especial displeasure is concentrated on his neighbour Medlicot, one such, who runs a sugar-estate of 200 acres. Heathcote's firmness makes enemies, not least among the employees he dismisses. One of these, Nokes, is employed by Medlicot, who refuses, in the absence of what he regards as sufficient evidence, to have him watched. Another is Boscobel, whom Heathcote dismisses for 'ringing' trees and being paid for this when he should have been acting as watchman for which he was also being paid. These two join the neighbouring, down-at-heel and criminal Brownbie family and set fire to Brownbie land in order that the fire may spread to Heathcote's. By means of a scorched-earth exercise in front of the fire, executed on Brownbie land, Heathcote and his workmen stop the fire from spreading. Medlicot, his suspicions of Nokes now aroused, comes to their help. A fight ensues, Medlicot's collar-bone is broken, and the novel ends with his being nursed by Heathcote's sister-in-law, to whom he makes a proposal of marriage.

Trollope firmly establishes the Australian atmosphere – indeed perhaps too deliberately almost to the point of parody in some of the opening speeches with their references to 'nobbles', 'pannikins', 'dampers' and the like. Nevertheless, we derive a vivid impression of a sheep-station, with its main house and surrounding buildings, workmen's huts, wool-store and the rest. More important, we get the sense of vastness, of great distances, say, from the station to the nearest doctor (some thirty miles) or the miles of fencing on the borders of the sheep-run. Above all, there is the sense of helplessness in the face of enemies and climate. Though Heathcote works himself to the point of exhaustion in a situation where a fire would bankrupt him and destroy his whole way of life, there is always the feeling that, no matter what he does, only good fortune will save him.

Trollope is not a Hardy and his purpose is not to emphasise any sense of a malign Fate. He concentrates, therefore, on the personal antagonisms that arise from clash of personality, and especially from the high probability of Heathcote's bringing disaster upon himself.

With this in mind he balances his hero's character against that of someone like Medlicot, 'more rational, more logical and less impulsive' (ch. 4), and at the same time he stresses the harshness of a situation in which 'all that a man has is exposed to the malice of a scoundrel like Nokes'. (ch. 7) To go back to the beginning, pig-headedness or obstinacy it may be – and we may both prefer and recognise the greater empirical wisdom behind Medlicot's capacity for tact and diplomacy – but in the end we have to admire Heathcote's stern adherence to principle:

> 'I'm not going to pick my words because men like Nokes and Boscobel have the power of injuring me. I'm not going to truckle to rascals because I'm afraid of them. I'd sooner be burned out of house and home, and go and work on the wharves in Brisbane than that.'

On this Trollope reports: 'There was a feeling within the hearts of the men that Harry Heathcote was imperious, still they respected him – and they believed him.' (ch. 10) Trollope makes us respect him also.

8

The Final Phase

(*Is He Popenjoy?*; *John Caldigate*; *Cousin Henry*; *Dr Wortle's School*; *Ayala's Angel*; *The Fixed Period*; *Marion Fay*; *Kept in the Dark*; *Mr Scarborough's Family*; *An Old Man's Love*)

We have already looked at some of the novels of Trollope's last years, including *The Landleaguers* which was left unfinished at his death. His later works received a mixed reception, and one detects even in some of the more favourable reviews a note of boredom with the ceaseless flow and the mechanical talent. His popularity was certainly on the wane and it plummeted after his death. None of his novels suffered more than the last ones, and it is only since Mr Cockshut's book in 1955 that we have come to see that, mixed in quality though they are, these final products of Trollope's pen include some of the best work he ever wrote.

Is He Popenjoy? (1878) includes in its ridiculous title one of the themes of the novel – the question of the legitimacy of the Marquis of Brotherton's son, fruit of his mysterious union with an Italian woman. By none is this legitimacy more doubted than by Dean Lovelace, the Dean of Brotherton and father of Mary, who is married to the Marquis's younger brother, Lord George Germain. The marital history of this latter couple follows a chequered course, punctuated by the flirtations of Jack de Baron with Mary and of Lord George with Mrs Adelaide Houghton, de Baron's sister. A minor interest is provided by a debased replica of Wallachia Petrie (*He Knew He Was Right*), Baroness Banmann, another champion of women's rights.

A sordid note pervades this novel. One is used to Trollope's worldly clergymen, but the Dean outdoes them all. He is a self-made man. He had 'preached himself into fame ... holding opinions which, if not peculiar, were at any rate advanced', and he was 'urbanity itself' (ch. 1); in fact, altogether a fashionable priest. There is not much urbanity, more fervour bordering on frenzy, in his investigations of the possible bastardy of the Marquis's offspring in the hope that his own grandson may succeed to the title in due course. It is on another matter, however, that this fervour bursts out in physical action, the Marquis's allegation that the Dean's daughter is a whore. Against all the Marquis's expectations ('The normal dean is a goodly, sleek, bookish man, who would hardly strike a blow under any provocation' – ch. 41), the Dean seizes him by the cravat, hauls him about the room and finally hurls him into the fire-grate. It is no more than the Marquis deserves, however surprising it may be and degrading to the Dean, for the Marquis is quite simply mad (Ruth ap Roberts (1971, p. 158) thinks that there are enough hints for us to conclude that he is syphilitic, a reasonable supposition), a fiendish figure, delighting in making life as uncomfortable as possible for all around him.

Had he possessed his brother's spirit, Lord George Germain might have been another Louis Trevelyan in his jealousy, but as it is, he is simply a prig. Mary is thrust among his sisters and he would have her live like them, despite their being staid and uninteresting. (ch. 5) In London he tries to circumscribe his wife's activities, especially in relation to Jack de Baron, though at the same time he is carrying on an affair that is far more serious, but not actually immoral, with Adelaide Houghton. (ch. 20) A prig in his situation exhibits both the accusations of conscience and the urge to self-justification. With the concentration and economy that he so often brings to his crises Trollope sums it all up thus, with Mrs Houghton speaking:

> 'I cannot wear him in my heart. Nor, George, do I believe that you in your heart can ever wear Mary Lovelace!' But he did, only that he thought that he had space there for two. (ch. 30)

Trollope goes on to refer to this second love as adding to the 'excitements' of Lord George's life. Then in comes Houghton, and Lord George trembles to consider what it would have seemed a minute earlier with Adelaide at his knees. To deflate the whole situation, relationship and Lord George's position, Trollope tells us that Houghton has come back, on his way to have his hair cut, for a glass of sherry!

Lord George is a half-reluctant and incompetent debauchee. After receiving a letter from Adelaide he goes, determined to break off the relationship, and *en route* finds that he has given Mary the letter in mistake for one from her father! Though actuated both by expediency and principle to break off his affair, he is still unable to see Mary's activities in even the least generous light. 'There was that feeling of Caesar's wife strong within his bosom, which he could, perhaps, have more fully explained to her but for that unfortunate letter from Mrs Houghton.' (ch. 34) His jealousy bursts forth in physical action when he strides into a room where Mary is one of a dance-set partnering Jack de Baron, seizes her and takes her away.

Lord George and Jack de Baron are opposites in temperament.

> There are men whose very eyes glance business, whose every word imports care.... And then there are men who are always playfellows with their friends ... who come across one like sunbeams, and who, even when tears are falling, produce the tints of a rainbow. (ch. 12)

Jack de Baron's affair with Mary is symbolised by the dancing; it is a light, insignificant matter, but it is also a contrast to his frustrated relationship with Guss Mildmay, an association doomed by lack of money. For this same reason Adelaide de Baron had taken Houghton when she could not have Lord George. If money does this to love, it does things just as bad to other ideals. Trollope has little enough to admire in the women's rights cause as it is personified by Baroness Banmann and Dr Olivia Q. Fleabody (note the names). The Baroness's address is an uproarious caricature (ch. 17), but her end is absconding with a thousand pounds of other people's money. (ch. 60)

Altogether, *Is He Popenjoy?* is a sad, at times sordid, book with its materialist Dean and his expedient morality, its debased Marquis, Lord George as oppressive husband and cowardly lover, the Brotherton family down-at-heel in their dilapidated house, the charlatanry of women's rights, the sirens and matchmakers, and the empty love-making and general triviality of a futile society.

Those critics who have given any attention at all to *John Caldigate* (1879) have usually found it long-winded and repetitive. This is true, and it is sad that it is so, for it contains a strong, coherent plot and, especially in Mrs Bolton and her daughter Hester, some powerful characters. John Caldigate, son of a Cambridgeshire squire, is the object of affection both of his cousin Julia Babington and his friend's sister, Maria Shand. Neither, however, is destined to succeed, for he is in love with Hester Bolton, whom he eventually marries on his return as a wealthy man from the Australian

157

goldfields. In Australia he has been involved with Euphemia Smith, an actress, whom he had met on the voyage out. She, with his erstwhile partner Crinkett, returns home and tries to blackmail Caldigate into paying a huge sum of money, in part because the mining venture he had left to them had fallen on hard times. For this reason he agrees to pay, but only after the blackmailers have alleged a marriage to Mrs Smith in Australia. Thus a charge of bigamy arises from his marriage to Hester. Caldigate is convicted, but the arrival home of Dick Shand and the activities of Bagwax, a Post Office clerk, who proves that a vital piece of evidence, a postmark, was false, secure his pardon. Before his trial Hester has herself been lured and temporarily imprisoned in her parents' house as a result of her mother's implacable hostility to Caldigate. Unlike many of Trollope's earlier novels, this does depend on suspense. Sometimes this is expressed with vivid immediacy as, for instance, in the foreboding presence of Crinkett at the christening of John and Hester's baby. More often, however, it rests on the withheld and delayed revelation of the next stage in the narrative. To some extent this may explain the tracts of narrative where we have little to sustain us beyond our expectation. The *Times* reviewer neatly described it as 'a good novel expanded into a dull one' (8 August 1879).

The Australian scenes derive from Trollope's visits there in 1871-2 and 1875. He depicts the rigours and roughness of life on the goldfields by a fine attention to detail – the need to travel light and the consequent effect on personal hygiene, the harsh conditions of working and the subsequent inordinate recourse to drink, the vast differences of fortune between those who struck and those who did not, and, above all, the impossibility of trusting one's fellow-men beyond, at any rate, one's mate – and, good as Mick Maggott is in some respects, not even him too much. It is no surprise therefore that out of this shifting and unstable society should come the threat to Caldigate's happiness amid the serene certainties of English country society. 'Yes; – [Nobble] was different from Trinity College, different from Babington.' (ch. 9) Caldigate does not return unstained, for the infatuation with Euphemia Smith, to which Trollope gives so much attention on the voyage out, led to her becoming his mistress, a fact confirmed only after the birth of his heir when the ex-mistress appears on the scene claiming to be Euphemia Caldigate.

With the exception of this episode, John Caldigate, by contrast with his partner Dick Shand, who degenerated and went off to the bush as a shepherd, returns home a stronger character than when he left, a fact revealed in the nobility with which he faces the accusation brought against him. Nevertheless, with his characteristically certain appreciation both of circumstance and behaviour, Trollope shows how motive is inevitably affected by situation. Thus he remarks that Caldigate would have felt 'for the satisfaction of his own honour' that the money should be refunded, 'But nevertheless he was aware that he had been driven to do it now ... by an undercurrent of hope that these enemies would think it best for themselves to go as soon as they had his money in their hands.' But that is not all. Trollope shrewdly adds first: 'He might succeed in making others believe that he had not attempted to purchase their absence; but he could not make himself believe it', and then: 'Even though a jury should not convict him, there was so much in his Australian life which would not bear the searching light of cross-examination! The same may probably be said of most of us.' (ch. 40) Trollope's psychological observation may not be complex, but it is sure and realistic, as that last short sentence in the quotation reminds us.

In Hester there are no mixed motives, but only an abiding and unswerving loyalty to her husband. She is yet another of Trollope's women of set purpose and firm determination. In a moving scene she declares her ability to bear anything whilst Caldigate is with her and is frank with her. His word that she is his wife is alone sufficient, let the world think what it will. (ch. 29 – cf. chs 41, 44) That world, however, is a world of violence. We recall *He Knew He Was Right* as we observe the dark passions and dire actions. When Mrs Bolton imprisons her daughter, with Caldigate outside banging on the door and Hester in the hall almost in hysterical convulsions and with her baby in her arms, Trollope does not underplay the physical commotion.

Against Hester's will is pitted that of her mother, one of the most impressive characters Trollope ever created. She dominates her husband and would, with her sense of her own rightness, dominate all others. She is another in the roll-call of Trollope's Evangelicals, but she belongs to a different order of creation from the rest. She opposes all who 'live in opposition to the Gospel' (ch. 21), and hence she opposes Caldigate. She does so, because she loves Hester, but, as the novelist comments, 'Love on the part of a mother may be as injurious as cruelty, if the mother be both tyrannical and superstitious.' (ch. 19) That sentence summarises the relationship. In a telling passage (ch. 18) Trollope compares Mrs Bolton's attitudes to the severest discipline of Roman Catholic nunneries, and hence we are not surprised by the lengths to which she is prepared to go in her mistaken notions of protecting her daughter.

Where she differs from, and where Trollope goes deeper than in his treatment of, many others of his Evangelicals is in her fervent devotion to her principles and his recognition of it.

> Mrs Bolton believed every word that she said. There was no touch of hypocrisy about her.... She knew she was right. She knew at least that were she to act otherwise there would be upon her conscience the weight of sin.

That third sentence is notable. Trollope goes on to stress the rationalisation that had taken place – and of which she was unaware: 'She did not know that the convictions on which she rested with such confidence had come in truth from her injured pride.' He puts her in the context of the fanatics of all ages: 'When we read of those who have massacred and tortured their opponents in religion ... how shall we dare to say that they should be punished for their fidelity?' (ch. 22) Mrs Bolton, we are then told, spent much of the afternoon 'wrestling for her child in prayer'. It is of a piece with her character that she cannot believe the evidence which exonerates Caldigate and that she is brought only to a tardy, reluctant and not very convincing reconciliation with her daughter. She had, indeed, hoped to cherish Hester and her grandson, homeless and helpless through a bigamous union, as part of her revenge against the members of her family, her husband and step-sons, who had permitted the marriage against her advice. That scheme frustrated, 'with the force of human disappointment heavy upon her, her heart was now hot with human anger, and mutinous with human resolves'. Mrs Bolton belongs to Trollope's gallery of monomaniacs, of whom only Mr Crawley and Louis Trevelyan are better known.

Cousin Henry (1879) is a masterpiece of brevity and it too contains a figure of memorable psychological traits. That figure is the title-character, and the book is, for all practical purposes, about him alone from the point where he inherits his uncle's estate until a month later when he loses it by the discovery of a later will which he had known about all the time. The book has received little critical attention, despite being, as Polhemus calls it, 'one of the strangest and most original works in Victorian fiction'. (Polhemus, 1968, p. 231) His interpretation, however, is undoubtedly perverse when he talks about Henry as 'a harried and doomed victim' and the book as 'Trollope's note from the Victorian underground complaining about the tyranny of bourgeois respectability and oppressively conformist morality.' (ibid., p. 233) What he means by the last phrase is difficult to comprehend, for Henry is a thief in all but name and a liar to compound the felony.

Trollope's language is unmistakable: 'The game he had to play was for Llanfeare' (ch. 3), and for that he was prepared to marry his cousin Isabel, for long the companion of her uncle, the expected and indeed the ultimate inheritor of the estate. She rejects him imperiously, for she is as imperious as Henry is mean. As Isabel remarks of him, 'If you could have seen how his craven spirit cowered beneath my eyes!' (ch. 12) He is too mean for the magnificence of evil, and from the moment of his finding the later and valid will in one of his uncle's books it is remarked 'how wan, how pallid, and how spiritless he had become'. (ch. 5) At every danger his fear reveals itself in his perspiration, and yet he can never bring himself to destroy the threatening document. He perjures himself in the signatures required to prove the will under which he inherits, and in several passages, notable for their questions and short sentences, he shows as much terror when alone as he does in the presence of others. Trollope delineates a mind racked with guilt, even as he shows a will paralysed by its owner's cowardice.

Faced with the need to give evidence in a libel action against the *Carmarthen Herald,* he again meditates destruction of the later will, but immediately fears that he will be seen, accused and sent to prison for destroying it. Even if it did not come to this, 'still there would be the damning guilt on his own soul – a guilt which would admit of no repentance except by giving himself up to the hands of the Law!' (ch. 15) Thus he dithers, all the time being driven steadily more desperate. At his last attempt to do the necessary deed, he faces at its most insistent

> The damning of his own soul! Would it in truth be the giving
> up of his own soul to eternal punishment? God would know
> that he had not meant to steal the property! ... God would
> know how cruelly he had been used. ... He almost taught
> himself to believe that in destroying the will he would be

161

> doing no more than an act of rough justice, and that God
> would certainly condemn no one to eternal punishment for a
> just act. (ch. 20)

This is the anticlimax before the lawyer Apjohn invades the house whilst Henry is at breakfast and finds the will, though not before the latter has fought like a cornered animal.

The forces of right bear down upon Henry. He is suspected and shunned by the local inhabitants, criticised by the local newspaper, and harassed and eventually exposed by his own attorney Apjohn. This might enable some readers to gain what Polhemus describes as 'a subjective and unflattering picture of organised society from the perspective of a social misfit', but I hardly think that Trollope makes or intends to make 'the reader sympathise with the weak and disreputable side of human nature and distrust the supposedly virtuous and respectable side'. (Polhemus, 1968, p. 231) What Trollope himself says, is that

> For the man himself, the reader, it is hoped, will feel some
> compassion. . . . It was hardly unnatural that the idea of
> retaliation should present itself to him. . . . At the last his
> conscience saved him. . . . Much was due to him in that he
> had not destroyed the will. (ch. 23)

But Isabel was both virtuous and respectable, not just supposedly so, and no attempt by Mr Polhemus to link morality and economic interest in order to damn both will prevail. Such crude quasi-Marxism does not fit Trollopian categories.

Like its predecessor, *Doctor Wortle's School* (1881), also a short novel, ranks high in Trollope's overall achievement. Again, as in *Is He Popenjoy?* and *John Caldigate*, the idea of bigamy figures prominently, but by contrast with these novels, the bigamy here, though committed in ignorance, does turn out to be actual. What is important, however, is not so much the bigamy of Mr and Mrs Peacocke, but the attitude towards them of Dr Wortle, the clerical headmaster, in whose school Peacocke is an assistant. Thus Trollope does not hesitate to reveal the bigamy early in the story (I, ch. 3), and long before any of the principal characters know anything about it. Indeed, short though it is, *Doctor Wortle's School* slackens notably in interest in its later stages, and the romance of Mary Wortle, the doctor's daughter, with his old pupil, Lord Carstairs, serves only to divert and in no way to heighten that interest.

The fact of the bigamy is revealed by an American ruffian, Mrs Peacocke's brother-in-law, just before Peacocke himself has arranged to tell Wortle of it. It comes after the nobility of the Peacockes and their love for each other has been firmly established in the eyes both of the reader and of Wortle himself. As the world sees it, the Peacockes should have parted as soon as they realised that they were living in adultery, but that was to take no account of the 'situational ethics' of a relationship in which the woman had found the protective love of one man after experiencing the gross cruelty of another. That position is explored in an interview late in the book between Mrs Peacocke and Mrs Wortle, in which the former argues:

> 'I did do what was wrong. Would not you have done so
> under such circumstances? ...Wrong! I doubt whether it was
> wrong. It is hard to know sometimes what is right and what is
> wrong.'

The world, however, sticks by its conventional absolutes, whether through the malicious gossip of Mrs Stantiloup, the Bishop's concern for respectabilities or the impeccable but remorseless logic of the cleric Mr Puddicombe.

Prudence as well as conventional morality required Dr Wortle to get rid of Peacocke, for the sake of the parish, the school and his own family. That was his 'first conscience', 'But then there came that other conscience, telling him that the man had been more "sinned against than sinning", – that common humanity required him to stand by a man who had suffered so much, and had suffered so unworthily.' (III, ch. 9) Wortle himself is a 'character', a man full of self-esteem, convinced of his own rightness, with no time for what he regarded as canting pietism, a man who took some perverse pride in pursuing his own line. The Peacocke affair gives him chance to exploit this last propensity, not least in thinly concealed barbs against the over-careful Bishop. Thus, when the latter suggests the imprudence of Mrs Peacocke's remaining in a school house and the possible wisdom of her going into lodgings in Broughton, he receives as reply: 'The wife of some religious grocer, who sands his sugar regularly, would have thought her house contaminated by such an inmate.' (IV, ch. 11) Later, the Bishop unwisely draws Wortle's attention to remarks in a London gutter-press periodical, only to find himself meanly embroiled as a witness in a libel action, with Wortle magnanimously refusing to proceed. Trollope beauti-

163

fully combines in Wortle the nobility of quixotic generosity with the enjoyment of a power which delights in putting those to whom he is not well disposed into awkward situations.

Peacocke goes to America and gathers proof of the death of the first husband. All ends happily, but it is what has gone before and much earlier that matters, rather than the close of the tale. The novel is notable, too, for some of Trollope's finest dialogue. One example must suffice, an exchange between Mrs Wortle and Lady Margaret Momson, introduced with the sentence, 'The reader will remember that Lady Margaret was also the wife of a clergyman':

> 'The Doctor thinks that they [the Peacockes] are very much to be pitied.'
> 'The Doctor always was a little Quixotic – eh?'
> 'I don't think that at all, Lady Margaret.'
> 'I mean in the way of being so very good-natured and kind. Her brother came; didn't he?'
> 'Her first husband's brother,' said Mrs Wortle, blushing.
> 'Her first husband!'
> 'Well; – you know what I mean, Lady Margaret.'
> 'Yes; I know what you mean. It is so very shocking; isn't it.'
> (IV, ch. 11)

When he wanted, Trollope knew how to leave a character's own words to say more than enough.

Ayala's Angel (1881) is a long novel, far too long, about the love-affairs of several young persons. Ayala Dormer is herself the object of the attentions of her cousin Tom Tringle, Captain Batsby and Jonathan Stubbs. Her sister Lucy is faithfully loved by the artist Isadore Hamel, but financial considerations stand in their way, as they do also in that of Imogene Docimer, whom the penniless Frank Houston is, for most of the history of this tale, prepared to sacrifice for the wealthy Gertrude Tringle. Her father, Sir Thomas, guardian also of Lucy, is not prepared to make his money available to Houston, as he has to the husband of his elder daughter, the mean-spirited and critical Augusta, who has married an M.P. and son of a peer, the Honourable Thomas Traffick.

Ayala is searching for her angel, and of the three candidates *The Times*'s description cannot be bettered; 'Captain Batsby is preternaturally dull and uninteresting; Mr Thomas Tringle is preternaturally vulgar, and Colonel Jonathan Stubbs is preternaturally ugly.'

(16 July 1881) It is right in adding, 'We foresee from the first that Colonel Stubbs is destined to be the happy man.' Before that happens, however, we have read:

> Nothing could be more unlike an Angel of Light than Colonel Stubbs, – unless, perhaps, it were Tom Tringle. Colonel Stubbs, however, was completely unangelic, – so much so that the marvel was that he should yet be so pleasant.... She hoped she might meet him again very often. He was, as it were, the Genius of Comedy, without a touch of which life would be very dull. But the Angel of Light must have something tragic in his composition. (ch. 16)

The trouble is that Trollope does not show Ayala's struggles to discriminate at anything much below a superficial level, and Stubbs himself succeeds, it appears, less for his evident virtues than for the weakness of the opposition.

There are some amusing scenes in the book such as that in which, all unknowingly, the well-meaning but boorish Tom Tringle asks Stubbs to write a letter on his behalf to Ayala. As in others of the final novels there is some precisely conceived and convincing dialogue. The young men, of whom there are so many, are decisively differentiated, and among the rest Augusta Tringle and her father, no mere money-grabbing tyrant but a man who is hard pressed to keep up with the unpredictable antics of his offspring, are memorable. Stubbs himself was compared by a contemporary reviewer to Thackeray's Dobbin, 'gradually [impressing] you with a sense of his power as well as of his sterling worth'. (*Saturday Review*, 11 June 1881, LI, p. 756) He does, but what this reviewer missed and Thackeray so much intended was Dobbin's dullness. Stubbs is not the Genius of Comedy and Ayala is not all that much the romantic heroine.

The Fixed Period (1882), though short, is still longer than it needs to be. It is the least characteristic of all Trollope's work, an excursion into futuristic fantasy, set on the antipodean island of Britannula in 1980. It contains some references to mechanical novelties such as steam tricycles, catapult bowling machines and spring bats for cricket, but the main interest lies, as the title indicates, in a proposal for limiting the span of a human life and thus for euthanasia. The history is told in the first person by the President of the little republic, John Neverbend, who quickly informs us that he is 'an enthusiast'. The first victim of the new law will be his friend, Crasweller. There is a subsidiary love-interest centred around Eva Crasweller and involving Grundle, who supports the euthanasia in order to gain her father's property, and Jack, Neverbend's son, who in his love for Eva opposes his father's advocacy of the law. Crasweller seeks an extra year of life by arguing that his age has been mistaken, but eventually he acknowledges the truth and accepts his fate. He is being taken by Neverbend to be 'deposited' for his year's preparation for death when an English battleship arrives. The proceedings are halted and Neverbend is overthrown and sent into exile.

There is no real characterisation, the nearest to any such being the mania of Neverbend for the 'fixed period'. In the introduction he rises to real eloquence in his eulogy of the proposal, and he is never able to realise the human implications of either voluntary self-annihilation or bereavement. Trollope sustains this blinkered approach through his first-person narration, but in so doing he has sacrificed the possibilities that lay in Crasweller's contemplation of his own death and Eva's of her prospective loss. Nor does he convey sufficiently the horror of the idea in the eyes of the people at large. It is almost as though Shylock had been entrusted with Antonio's story. Appropriately, therefore, the greatest passion lies in Neverbend's surprised and scornful reaction to the arrival of the British gun-boat:

> These old men – the tanner and whisky-dealer, and the like – had sent home to Engand to get assistance against their own Government! These had always been a scum of the population – the dirty, frothy, meaningless foam at the top ... men who knew nothing of progress and civilisation. (ch. 8)

There is all a modern dictator's 'New Speak' in a tyrant long before our time. It is easy for Neverbend to argue that wars, armies and capital punishment are all usages of death by organised society (ch. 10); what he ignores is the degree of necessity that must be evident before any argument for death (or other social use of power) can be accepted. The support that he alleges from his own legislature is conspicuously not matched by the attitude of the people.

Marion Fay (1882) contains Trollope's most direct consideration of class-divisions and their effects on personal relationship. Both brother and sister, Lord Hampstead and Lady Frances Trafford, fall in love with apparently low-born commoners – Marion Fay and the Post Office clerk, George Roden. Their stepmother, Lady Kingsbury, actively opposes these liaisons, and she is supported by the mean and conspiratorial chaplain, Greenwood. In addition, a number of minor characters, Clara Demijohn from Paradise Row, the abode of Marion and George, and Crocker, his fellow-clerk, add their own contribution to the attempts to sabotage the relationships, particularly that of George and Lady Frances. The minor characters of Paradise Row though obviously intended as comic relief, are, in fact, rather tiresome. Crocker and Greenwood are better; they at least sustain an interest by what they will do and what will happen to them.

Trollope's theme is not unlike that which Gissing would attempt some few years later in *Demos*, but whereas Gissing's hero is low-born, brash and suddenly wealthy and his heroine, though well-born, comparatively impoverished, Trollope takes the simpler contrast of poor man and well-born woman. Lady Frances displays a firm determination to marry Roden and he for his part shows a delicacy towards her amid the difficulties of the situation. George's mother proclaims that 'unequal marriages are always unhappy' (II, ch. 2) and we could wish to know more of the background which enables her, quite credibly, to pronounce this judgment. Hampstead, moreover, despite his egalitarian professions (though he still hunts and goes to sea in his yacht), attempts a mild restraint on his friend's and his sister's love. When Hampstead is himself attracted to Marion, a possibly even more interesting set of complications seems likely to arise. She resists his advances, but a false report of his death brings her to acknowledge her love for him. Her resistance to his suit is strengthened by her awareness of her own poor health and likely early death. The approach of this event enables Trollope to reveal both in her and Hampstead a nobility of attitude that represents one of the high points of the novel. Her death, however, is in some ways an easy escape for Trollope, and the revelation that Mrs Roden's mysterious past really consisted in marriage to an impoverished Italian duke provides George with a nobility that resolves the problem of his relationship with Lady Frances. As Ruth ap Roberts has pointed out (1971, p. 155), the title being foreign and there being no wealth attached to it, Trollope is able to suggest how ridiculous is the insistence on status, but it remains obvious that he has taken the easy way out without making much of such ironic possibilities.

Lady Kingsbury is a hating and hateful step-mother, for ever envisaging Hampstead's death and the succession to the marquisate of her own eldest son, but her views on society have about them a consistency and depth that is not to be found among the other characters. Trollope calls her 'every inch an aristocrat', whereas the others possess nothing like her sincerity either in their socio-political views or in their passion for their beloved. Nor does Trollope, as Gissing does, link up the private and public lives of his characters. The coherence and interaction of these two which is such a marked feature of the Palliser novels is here entirely missing. Above all, he shirks the immense implications of Mrs Roden's belief that 'unequal marriages are always unhappy'. George at the end is promoted to a position appropriate to his rank and needs.

Kept in the Dark (1882), another of the shorter novels, centres on the accumulating ills that proceed from a single neglected opportunity. Cecilia Holt marries George Western. Both have previously had a broken love-affair, he jilted by a girl who marries Captain Geraldine, she driven to reject the captain's relative, Sir Francis Geraldine. He tells of his experience, she does not; he is thereby 'kept in the dark'. Cecilia sums up her problem to her sister-in-law, the understanding and reconciling Lady Grant: 'When he came to me with the other story and asked me to love him, was I to give him back his own tale and tell him the same thing of myself?' (ch. 8) The circumstances differed vastly. Sir Francis deliberately neglected Cecilia and obviously designed to neglect her still more after their marriage; but in a relationship that brings new hope and vitality to her Cecilia does not wish to disappoint Mr Western or to ruin her own renewed prospects. The dangers inherent in her silence are underlined by Lady Grant in the interview from which the quotation above is derived: 'How true he is, how affectionate, how honest; but yet how jealous!' (ibid.) Matters are not improved by an earlier unsatisfactory encounter between Western and Sir Francis, who now proceeds to engineer his revenge by a letter to Western revealing the past. Western thus sees that 'He had been deceived, and she was to him a thing altogether different from that which he had believed her.' (ch. 11)

The result is a breakdown of the marriage. Western decides to travel, leaving a provision for his wife at home. She insists in a letter to him that she has done nothing of which she should be ashamed: 'He must still be the master, and, in order that his masterdom might be assured, full and abject confession must be made.' (ch. 18) He exaggerates his wrongs to himself, and the situation is complicated by the revelation of her pregnancy. It is all very reminiscent of *He Knew He Was Right*, but without the intensity of that novel. Obstinacy is there, but it falls short of the monomania of Louis Trevelyan and the stubbornness of his wife. Thus it is possible for Lady Grant to play her part as mediator. Western is slow to believe her, and in the end Cecilia asks for forgiveness. That is the note on which the novel ends:

> No doubt to her mind, as she thought of it all, there was
> present the happy conviction that she had been more sinned
> against than sinning. She had forgiven whereas she might have
> exacted forgiveness. . . . Her strong desire to have him once again
> had softened her, and now she had the double reward. She had
> what she wanted, and was able to congratulate herself at the
> same time on her virtue. (ch. 24)

She has heaped coals of fire on his head and he, 'a man that loved justice even against himself' is led to acknowledge himself to have been 'cruel, stiff-necked and obdurate' and finally to ask forgiveness for himself.

In Sir Francis, Geraldine Trollope gets something of the raffish world of London clubs that we have seen elsewhere, but a closer parallel lies with Sir Hugh Clavering and his associates. Geraldine is a caricature, but he is also a baleful influence, and, in his limited way, a man of terribly unbalanced passions. In Western, Trollope explores a man of justice, unwilling to temper or test his ideals against experience. As a result, the novelist is able to sustain interest on a tenuous amount of plot-material by examining such a man under compulsion to do what he has been unwilling to do and by bringing out those facets of character which at once make both himself and the person dearest to him suffer. Thereby Trollope is able also to illustrate yet another instance of female nobility and suffering altogether out of proportion to the original error. Western and Cecilia Holt show Trollope delineating, within admittedly limited development, two sensitive characters enmeshed in a set of tragic circumstances. They are two characters, moreover, whom the reader acknowledges to be too good to be left at the mercy of such circumstances and about whom he has sufficient confidence in the novelist that he will find a way out for them. That confidence is sustained by the skilful dropping of hints and unobtrusive placing of signposts in which Trollope was a past master.

Mr Scarborough's Family (1883) was still being published serially when Trollope died. It showed, when others of the last novels suggested differently and so many readers were quick to agree, that his hand had not lost its ancient power. As elsewhere – *John Caldigate* and *Cousin Henry* are but two examples – Trollope resorts to a legal question for plot-interest. Whatever the inherent improbabilities, Mr Scarborough has, as we eventually discover, gone through two forms of marriage, and by producing evidence for the greater part of the story of only the latter of these he is able to suggest the disinheritance of his elder son and with it ensure the frustration of the Jew creditors who hold so many *post-obits* (i.e. bonds giving them a right to monies inherited) against Mountjoy Scarborough for his gambling debts. When these have been settled at a sum nearer their real worth than their face value, Mr Scarborough then reveals Mountjoy's legitimacy and re-establishes him as the heir to the exclusion of the younger and repulsively calculating Augustus. There is also the obligatory love-interest centering on their cousin, Florence Mountjoy, whose mother has destined her for Mountjoy Scarborough but who persists in loving Harry Annesley. Annesley himself also falls in danger of disinheritance by his bachelor uncle, Peter Prosper, as a result of malicious information received from Augustus Scarborough.

Augustus and his father are in the great tradition of Trollope's characters. Speaking of these two and of Mountjoy, Mr Grey, the family lawyer, places them thus:

> 'The father has been a great knave. He has set the laws of his country at defiance, and should be punished most severely.
> And Mountjoy Scarborough has proved himself to be unfit to have any money in his hands. A man so reckless is little better than a lunatic. But compared with Augustus they are both estimable amiable men. . . . Augustus is as dishonest as either of them, and is odious all round.' (ch. 20)

His dishonesty, however, keeps within the letter of the law; it consists in such acts as informing upon Harry Annesley and, for his own ends, paying off the Jews at less than they expect. Augustus passes for honest, but casts aspersions on those like Harry and

Mountjoy who, if less prudent, are really honest. He presumes too much on his inheritance and his father notices it.

Mr Scarborough manipulates the action from his death-bed and we derive a positive joy from his outscheming the schemer. He is not honest in the ordinary sense of the term and he delights in outwitting the law, 'a perplexed entanglement of rules got together so that the few might live in comfort at the expense of the many'. (ch. 21) He is one of the few, but typically this does not trouble him. He will use 'old father antic, the law' for his own ends, and as he does so, the reader feels that somehow his sense of justice based on personal relationships transcends the law.

> He had loved his son Mountjoy in spite of all his iniquities. ... He had endeavoured to love Augustus ... [but] his son laughed at him and scorned him, and regarded him as one who was troublesome only for a time.... Therefore he hated Augustus. (ch. 21)

After his death Trollope refers to Mr Scarborough's full-blooded capacity to hate; he goes on: 'But yet in every phase of his life he had been actuated by love for others', and he adds:

> Supremely indifferent he had been to the opinion of the world around him, but he had never run counter to his own conscience. For the conventionalities of the law he entertained a supreme contempt, but he did so wish to arrange matters with which he himself was concerned as to do what justice demanded.

Such indifference to the world and such a will to do justice require also another quality, that to which Harry Annesley makes reference in the next paragraph:- 'If you can imagine for yourself a state of things in which neither truth nor morality shall be thought essential, then old Mr Scarborough would be your hero. He was the bravest man I ever knew.' (ch. 58)

There is much in *Mr Scarborough's Family* to remind one of that play of Shakespeare's which also confronts the ideas of law and justice. Augustus often recalls Angelo, and Mountjoy is not unlike Claudio; Mr Scarborough manipulates like the Duke but, in addition, has qualities in dealing with the situation that lead us to admire him, for he is more a man and less a *deus ex machina* than his Shakespearean counterpart. Then there is Mr Grey, the lawyer, something of an Escalus, an ordinary man who sees through ordinary eyes, a man of conventional integrity who cannot understand the altogether eccentric integrity of Mr Scarborough. Trollope does not fail to exploit the dramatic possibilities of such ill-sorted characters in contact with each other. Witness Mr Scarborough's awareness of Augustus's real motives in paying off Mountjoy's creditors:

'It is a noble feeling on the part of Augustus; you must admit that, Mr Grey.' The irony with which this was said was evident in the squire's face and voice. Augustus only quietly laughed. The attorney sat as firm as death. He was not going to argue with such a statement or to laugh at such a joke. (ch. 20)

Beside this, we can almost forget the several love-affairs, comic like that of Peter Prosper and Miss Thoroughbung, futile like that of her father's partner, Mr Barry, with Dorothy Grey, slightly sordid like that of Mr Juniper and Amelia Carroll, or even serious and healthy like that of Florence and Harry Annesley, triumphing over parental and avuncular opposition, surviving not only Mountjoy but also the Foreign Office attaché gallant, Anderson. It will be sufficient to note that the women generally come out as more convincing, usually because more spirited, than the men. Florence Mountjoy indeed deserves her place in the succession of fine English girls created by Trollope. Her persistence in loving Harry matches that of Lily Dale refusing Johnny Eames, and with more reason. She is more impressive in her loyalty even than Dorothy Stanbury. The interest and variety of the love-scenes exceed those in many of the other novels, but they cannot compete with the power of the main plot.

An Old Man's Love (1884), the last completed work, is a miniature as fine in its way as its immediate predecessor. It tells of the love of William Whittlestaff for his ward, Mary Lawrie, her agreement to marry him, the re-appearance of her former love, John Gordon, and the conflict between Whittlestaff and Gordon which is eventually resolved when the former sensibly and generously agrees to concede Gordon's claim. There is a subsidiary interest in the love and eventual marriage of Gordon's friend, the Reverend Montagu Blake, and Kattie Forrester, a relationship that contrasts in its conventionality, unhindered progress and superficiality with that of Gordon and Mary Lawrie. Mention must also be made of the stoutly loyal and somewhat comic (at times pathetically) housekeeper to Whittlestaff, Mrs Baggett, who is determined to leave him, should he marry. She plays some part in his decision not to forsake his settled mode of life.

John Gordon resembles John Caldigate in making a fortune abroad to establish his claims at home. This time it is in South Africa, and no doubt relates to Trollope's visit there in 1877. He is, however, a rather ordinary and undistinguished piece of characterisation, and the same, too, can be said for Mary Lawrie. She, incidentally, represents a recurring relationship in the last novels, that of the stepmother and daughter. It occurs in *The Way We Live Now*, *Cousin Henry* and *Marion Fay* as well as here, and we find wards also in *An Eye for an Eye* and *Ayala's Angel*.

There is a sharpness in the encounters of Whittlestaff and Gordon, mixed in the last of them with a poignancy for Whittlestaff's loss. The novel is exactly titled; it belongs to him from the moment of early hope to that of final renunciation. A sadness marks the generosity which not only recognises the greater fitness of two young people joined together than of an older and a younger but which is also prepared to make provision for them. That altruism conflicts, however, in the moment of its origin with a sense of what others would say about his being jilted, a feeling of pride and a confidence in Mary's faithfulness. (ch. 11) Whittlestaff is sensitive enough to see Mary's undeclared unhappiness and he is man enough to be prepared to bear the world's scorn rather than to live with his own shame in taking one who really loves another. (ch. 21) He cannot concede her to Gordon without some hint of possible difficulties – that is natural enough. It is, in fact, his recognition of human verities which gives strength both to this passage itself and to the whole of Trollope's conception of Whittlestaff:

> 'O Mary! that would have made beautiful for me my future
> downward steps! But it is not for such a purpose that a young
> life such as yours should be given. Though he should be
> unkind to you, though money should be scarce with you,
> though the ordinary troubles of the world should come upon
> you, they will be better for you than the ease I might have
> prepared for you. It will be nearer to human nature. I, at any
> rate, shall be here if troubles come.' (ch. 23)

Trollope was always near to human nature.

9

Other Works

(Short Stories, Biography, Travel, Plays, Lectures and the *Autobiography*)

Adapting what Trollope applied only to the years 1859 to 1871, 'I feel confident that in amount no other writer contributed so much ... to English literature.' (*Autobiography*, ch. 15) To his forty-seven or so novels must be added a mass of miscellaneous and occasional writing, some of which has been noted in earlier chapters. (Page references to these works are to the first editions.)

To begin with, there are five collections of short stories — *Tales of All Countries* (1861) and its *Second Series* (1863), *Lotta Schmidt and Other Stories* (1867), *An Editor's Tales* (1870) and *Why Frau Frohmann Raised Her Prices: and Other Stories* (1882). Many of these are occasional in the sense that their origins seem traceable to incidents in Trollope's own life, not least to his travels. Many are set in foreign locations. To take only three examples, 'Returning Home' (*Tales of All Countries: Second Series*) with the decision to return by a different route from that by which the travellers had come, the consequent dangers of the river and sub-equatorial forest and the drowning of Mrs Arkwright is obviously related to a reference in the 'Central America' section of *The West Indies*; 'An Unprotected Female at the Pyramids' (*Tales of All Countries*) has a parallel in *Travelling Sketches*; and 'Aaron Trow' (*Tales: Second Series*), the story of an escaped convict, may well have come from the informant who told Trollope about the prison in Bermuda (*The West Indies*, ch. 22). The other main source of material was from Trollope's editorial experience. This produced 'The Adventures of Fred Pickering' (*Lotta Schmidt*) and *An Editor's Tales*, of which he wrote: 'There is not an incident in it the outline of which was not presented to my mind by the remembrance of some fact.' (*Autobiography*, ch. 18)

Certain stock situations recur. To take but one collection (*Lotta Schmidt*), there are rival lovers for the heroine's hand in 'Miss Ophelia Gledd' and the title-story, and rival loyalties of family and country in 'The Two Generals' and 'The Last Austrian Who Left Vienna'. Conflict of young girl and guardian, of a kind notable in such shorter novels as *Linda Tressel* and *The Golden Lion of Granpere*, occurs again in 'La Mère Bauche' (*Tales of All Countries*) and 'The Lady of Launay' (*Why Frau Frohmann*). There are one or two comic tales such as 'The Relics of General Chassé' (*Tales of All Countries*), where a cleric, trying on the leather breeches of the late famous general, finds that some lady-tourists have seized on his own broadcloth trousers and cut them up, thinking they were relics of Chassé, and 'Christmas at Thompson Hall' (*Why Frau Frohmann*), where – very improbably – a lady strays into the wrong bedroom and applies a mustard poultice to someone not her husband, but who later turns out to be her prospective brother-in-law. The end of this tale is foreseen long before it is ever reached.

This is a common fault with the short stories, though it must be said that in 'The Journey to Panama' Miss Viner's not marrying the narrator when she is free to do so and in 'Miss Ophelia Gledd' (both *Lotta Schmidt*) the heroine's final preference for the Englishman, Pryor, over the American, Hokins, in each case represent the unexpected. Trollope did not mind the reader's foreseeing in the novels, and in the novels, too, he can afford to be leisurely and spacious, but in the short stories such laxity often means an anecdote strung out at excessive length. Sometimes this is redeemed by the force of the latter stages. Thus in 'Lotta Schmidt' the scathing remarks of the immature Planken about his older rival, the musician Crippel, finally confirm Lotta in her appreciation of the latter's character against all the superficial advantages of the younger man. There is a rare concision in the sentence: '[Planken] said that Herr Crippel was too old to play the zither: too old! Some people are too young to understand.' (p. 38)

It would be wrong to claim that any of Trollope's short stories have the intensity that we associate with later, more dedicated practitioners of the art, but the better ones do maintain our interest throughout. In 'The Adventures of Fred Pickering' (*Lotta Schmidt*), for example, we are concerned for the outcome of Pickering's headstrong, but also wrong-headed, determination to become a writer. He makes an imprudent marriage against his father's wishes and leaves the law for journalism. He gradually becomes more impoverished and more irritable. His high ideas of his own literary skills lead him to resign one job and be declared unsuitable for another. He refuses payment for rejected work, even though his wife is pregnant and his savings are dwindling. It is only the prospect of the workhouse and not, as he so typically and impractically had thought, 'of some high-toned extremity of destitution' (p. 85) that brings him back to his senses, to Manchester and the lawyer's office. Likewise, though in a lower key, 'Why Frau Frohmann Raised Her Prices' is a tale of obstinacy, in which the hostess of the Peacock at Brunnenthal, benevolent but neither to be thwarted nor contradicted, resists economic pressures and sound advice in the interests of her poorer guests, even to the extent of seeking inferior supplies. She only surrenders when she finds that one of her regular visitors is now receiving a higher salary, and even then she retains the lower rate for some of her less wealthy visitors.

'Alice Dugdale' (*Why Frau Frohmann*) is a weaker version of something like the Jane Eyre–Blanche Ingram–Rochester triangle. Alice is the equivalent of Jane and Georgiana Wanless, a statu-esque but rather silent beauty, not unlike Griselda Grantly, that of Blanche. The Wanless family conspire to secure Major John Rossiter for Georgiana and the odds seem all in their favour. His father, however, the village parson, hopes that John will choose Alice. Because Georgiana has captured John's attention, Alice attempts to put an end to the relationship. The end, however, is predictable – 'the womanliness of the one, as compared with the worldliness of the other, conquered him completely'. (ch. 10) This tale illustrates something which, though often present, disturbs us less in the novels than it does here. We feel that in a situation as intimate as this we never get near enough to the characters. By contrast, in the novels we know them long enough. When Trollope has a character say, as he does here, 'I have gone through the fire and have come out without being much scorched' (ch. 9), we immediately realise that he is alleging experience which he has not shown.

The interest in 'Mary Gresley' (*An Editor's Tales*) is sustained by its emotional unity, a pervasive tone of tender sadness. Mary, in love with a curate of frail health and strict views, comes to the editor with a story, that of her own frustrating engagement and its likely outcome. He speaks better of it than it deserves and, though unable to accept it, agrees to help her with a new story. He also helps to place two others. Mary and her mother are living in genteel poverty and this together with her ill-rewarded effort develops the reader's sympathy for her. Her lover, Donne, away in Dorset, falls ill. She goes to him and promises, in compliance with his views, never to write a novel and indeed burns the one she has written. Donne dies, and eight years later Mary marries a missionary, going to 'some forlorn country' where she dies. Altogether a sad life and a sad tale.

'Malachi's Cove', one of Trollope's most impressive short stories, is in many ways a sport in his work. The setting, the characters, the action, the emotions are all unusual for him. Instead of middle-class figures in a Victorian drawing-room we find ourselves amid the harsh life of seaweed gatherers in a Cornish cove between Tintagel and Bosinney. There Malachi Tringlos or, more accurately, his granddaughter Mally pursues the trade.

> She was a wild-looking, almost unearthly creature, with wild-flowing, black, uncombed hair, small in stature, with small hands and bright black eyes.... She had no friends and but few acquaintances.... [It was] said that she was fierce and ill-natured ... a thorough little vixen. (p. 180)

A neighbouring farmer's son, Barty Gunliffe, trespasses on what she regards as her domain. There are harsh words. His skill does not match hers and he does not know the areas that are dangerous as the huge waves roll in. He falls in and Mally rescues him, but as she brings him, senseless, to safety, her grandfather predicts – accurately – that the incident will be misinterpreted and that, if he dies, she will be charged with murder. When Barty recovers, he reveals the truth; there is a reconciliation and, of course, an eventual marriage. The ending, however, is neither so trite nor so sentimental as such a bald summary might suggest, and the narrative of Barty's accident, danger and difficult rescue has about it an excitement unusual in Trollope. There is something similar in the description of the fight in the water in 'Aaron Trow'. A brief section from 'Malachi's Cove' must suffice for example:

> Straining herself down, laying herself over the long bending handle of the hook, she strove to grasp him with her right hand. But she could not do it; she could only touch him.
>
> Then came the next breaker, forcing itself on with a roar, looking to Mally as though it must certainly knock her from

her resting-place, and destroy them both. But she had nothing
for it but to kneel, and hold by her hook.... (pp. 198-9)

Besides his own *Autobiography* Trollope wrote four other works of
a biographical nature. The first of these was *The Commentaries of
Caesar* (1870) in a series on the classics for English readers, edited
by W. Lucas Collins, the clergyman in whose house Trollope was
staying when he wrote *Dr Wortle's School*. The other three were
Thackeray (1879) for Macmillan's English Men of Letters series, a
Life of Cicero (1880) and *Lord Palmerston* (1882) in the English
Political Leaders series.

The *Caesar* is a condensation of the ten books of the *De Bello
Gallico* and the *De Bello Civili*, mainly in the form of simple, fluent
summary but occasionally, particularly with speeches, giving the
original *in extenso*. Trollope acknowledges that he found the history
of the Gallic Wars more interesting than that of its successor –
'There is less in it of adventure, less of strange new life' (pp.
117-18), despite the fact that his accounts of actual battles are
extremely abbreviated. Indeed, Blackwood, the publisher,
complained on this point, only to be told that he 'could hardly
guess how great was the necessity of condensation'. (*Letters*, No.
446, 29 March 1870) Caesar was a man of destiny who, by contrast
with Pompey, 'knew very well what he meant and what he
wanted'. (p. 117) Apart from granting that Caesar abstained from
criticising the shortcomings of his subordinates, Trollope has,
however, very little to say in his favour. He finds him ruthless and
entirely lacking in compassion. He repeatedly employs the wolf-
lamb image from Aesop's fable on this subject. He marvels sar-
donically at the reputation for clemency that one so cruel as Caesar
had acquired. To quote only one example, there is his cutting off
the hands of those who fought against him at Uxellodunum and
turning 'the maimed wretches adrift upon the world' – but he had
spared their lives! 'This was perhaps the crowning act of Caesar's
cruelty, – defended, as we see, by the character he had achieved for
clemency!' (p. 115) Of Caesar's killing all but a quarter of the
368,000 migrating Helvetii, Trollope comments with heavy irony:
'Hereupon the Gauls begin to see how great a man is Caesar.' (p.
38) The present tense is used throughout, giving an aura of
vividness and immediacy that emphasises all the more the cool,
matter-of-fact manner in which Caesar's butchery is recorded. The
Trollopian estimate of Caesar, where it was not simply ignored,

roused much hostility. Sadleir records the note in one copy: 'How unjust is the Great Trollop [*sic*] to the Lion Caesar!' (Sadleir, 1961, p. 310)

Trollope loved Cicero as much as he hated Caesar: 'Had I been a Roman of those days I should have preferred Cicero with his memories of the past to Caesar with his ambition for the future' (I, ch. 3); and even Cicero's alleged insincerity of utterance he claimed was the product of his sincerity of purpose (ibid.). Of Cicero's wealth Trollope alleged that, unlike Caesar, he 'kept his hands clean'. (I, ch. 4) Cicero's legal advocacy might well make the worse appear the better cause, but in this he was no worse than any other lawyer. Trollope applauds Cicero's attempts at compromise in an age of political turmoil. (I, ch. 12) He even tries to excuse Cicero's all too evident self-pity during his exile (ibid.), and he sympathises with him in the increasing moral chaos of the last days of the Republic, reduced to 'Sed quid agas? Sic vivitur!' (*Epistolae ad diversos*, II, 15) 'Sic vivitur' – we remember that Trollope had just written *The Way We Live Now* and was only too aware of the difficulties of upright conduct in a corrupt society.

The latter parts of the *Life of Cicero* are devoted to the writings with special reference to Cicero's philosophy, ethics and religion and with particular emphasis upon the *De Officiis* with its distinction of 'honestum' and 'utile', whether a thing should be done or not, whether it is expedient or not. Trollope admired Cicero's morality, and, comparing him with Christ, remarked that 'a belief in that mystical part [of our religion] is not essential for forming the conduct of men'. (II, ch. 14) He admired him so much indeed that he counselled:

Read his works through from the beginning to the end
and you shall feel that you are living with a man whom
you might accompany across the village green to church,
should he be kind enough to stay with you over the Sunday.
(ibid.)

For Trollope, Cicero was a fine example of an English gentleman, less perfect in this regard than Plantagenet Palliser only because he had to come to terms with the evil of his time and place.

Over a quarter of the *Thackeray* volume is devoted to a gossipy survey of the subject's life. The remaining chapters cover the works with, perhaps surprisingly to us, separate treatment to the burlesques, the lectures and the ballads, whilst *Philip* and *Lovel the*

Widower are ignored, and only two pages are given to *The Virginians*. Even of the rest a good deal of the consideration consists of summary with a plentiful admixture of relaxed discursive comment. He thinks little of *The Four Georges* and he feels that Thackeray's range of authors indicated that he defined *The English Humorists* too widely. Of these latter he compounds Thackeray's own condemnation of Sterne with a piece of vintage Victorian stuffiness, comparing him with Goldsmith, of whom 'There are few among the young people who do not refresh their sense of humour occasionally from that shelf, Sterne is relegated to some distant and high corner. The less often that he is taken down, the better.' (ch. 7) For Trollope 'the object of a novel should be to instruct in morals while it amuses' (ch. 4) and *Esmond* is Thackeray's greatest work 'with its tale well told, its purpose developed, its moral brought home'. (ch. 5) With *Vanity Fair,* whilst arguing for the undeniable attractiveness of Becky and Rawdon, Trollope seems to perpetrate a contradiction on Dobbin, first saying that he 'does become the hero, and is deficient' and then claiming that he is 'as noble as any that [the reader] has met in literature'. (chs 3, 4) The opening biographical chapter has many shrewd observations about character, especially of that basic infirmity of purpose that afflicted Thackeray, whilst the final chapter on style illustrates Trollope's effective use of comparisons, not least with Scott, and the experienced voice of the practising novelist as in his remarks on conversation in the novel where 'in very truth the realistic must not be true, – but just so far removed from truth as to suit the erroneous idea of truth which the reader may be supposed to entertain'. (ch. 8) In other words, it must not be true, only look as though it is. Trollope's final verdict on his fellow-novelist is that, though he was no cynic, he was yet 'too thoroughly saturated with the aspect of the ill side of things'. (ch. 9) He had put it earlier: 'always ... encountering melancholy with buffoonery, and meanness with satire'. (ch. 1)

The other of his contemporaries that Trollope wrote about was a felicitous choice, for there was much in Palmerston that he admired. He recognised his faults – 'a man with whom it must often have been difficult for a colleague to serve' (p. 31), but he also cherished his virtues – a capable statesman, sound in principle and action. Coupling the name of Melbourne with that of his subject, Trollope wrote that 'though Whig statesmen, they were at heart Conservative'. (p. 80) That was approval from one who called himself an advanced conservative Liberal. Consistent with this,

Trollope applauds the position that Palmerston adopted: 'Throughout his career it was his object to repress the personal power of the occupants of thrones; but at the same time so to repress that power as to give no inch of standing ground to demagogues.' Perhaps with Disraeli in mind, he stressed Palmerston's solidity and predictability: 'He saw all things from a common-sense point of view. . . . His followers would always know what political teaching they were expected to follow.' (p. 46) He is the practical man of affairs:

> It was not because he was a good speaker, as is now generally the case, that he was chosen by one Minister after another . . . but because the office work was safe in his hands, and because he had shown that he would make fewer mistakes than another man. (pp. 25-6)

It was that same diligence and reliability, and not the more spectacular rhetorical talents, that he so much applauded in his own fictional political hero, Plantagenet Palliser.

To all these one other quality was added: 'He never quailed. . . . His courage was coarse and strong and indomitable, like that of a dog.' (p. 166) Trollope summarises at the end: 'He was bold, industrious, honest, strong in purpose as in health, eager, unselfish, a good comrade. He was at the same time self-asserting, exacting, never doubting himself . . . and confident against the world in arms.' (p. 200)

Over twenty years at the War Office and thirty as Foreign Secretary and Prime Minister, he looked mainly to England's position abroad, but his one brief period as Home Secretary found him diligent there also. His comment on the Chartist insurrection of 1848 that the constabulary would have 'mashed [the rioters] to a jelly' (p. 105) serves to complete a portrait that becomes what we would call more and more Churchillian as it goes along. In producing it, Trollope makes extensive use of Palmerston's letters, especially to his brother, and of periodicals, but it is – and Trollope would not have wanted it to be any other – finally an impressionistic rather than a systematic biography of a man whom he much admired. To end with one curious detail, it seems strange that Trollope should twice declare of a man who was nearly in the divorce court in his eightieth year that 'The world has heard of no trouble into which he got about women.' (pp. 9-10; cf. p. 26)

Trollope was always 'banging about' the world, from which experience he has left us four major travel-books, *The West Indies and the Spanish Main* (1859), *North America* (1862), *Australia and New Zealand* (1873) and *South Africa* (1878) and such lesser works as *Travelling Sketches* (1866) and *How the 'Mastiffs' went to Iceland* (1878), whilst Bradford Booth has collected twenty letters to the *Liverpool Mercury*, arising from Trollope's second journey to Australia in 1875, as *The Tireless Traveller* (Berkeley, 1941). This is to take no account of descriptions of foreign places which figure prominently in some of the novels. Of these that of Jerusalem and the East in *The Bertrams* is the most extensive.

All the volumes mentioned are about particular places with the exception of *Travelling Sketches* which, like the similar *Hunting Sketches*, is about people given to the pursuit. These cover those who travel 'because it's the thing to do', the lone traveller, the unprotected female tourist, the United Englishmen (i.e., young men travelling in groups), those in search of art and knowledge, the Alpine Club man and 'tourists who don't like their travels'. These vignettes are full of Trollope's acute observation and shrewd judgments – the unprotected female tourist is strong-minded, resilient, adaptable, found on the Nile, at Constantinople, in Spain, 'but her headquarters are perhaps at Jerusalem' (p. 35) (we remember Miss Todd of *The Bertrams*); the United English tourist is known by his hat which sets 'all propriety instantly at defiance;' he 'batters [it], and twists it, and sits on it, and rumples and crumples it till it is manifestly and undeniably indicative of its owner'. (p. 48) In the shadow of Whymper's death on the Matterhorn, Trollope argues strangely and even a little disturbingly that we are perhaps 'becoming too chary of human life', comparing the dangers of Alpine climbing with the unregarded dangers of sudden death on the battlefield; but it is at the end of this rather sombre essay that the only lyrical gleam in the whole work shines forth:

> The work [of the Alpine Club] is all pure – pure in its early
> practice and pure in its later triumphs. Its contact is with
> nature in her grandest attire, and its associations are with
> forms that are as suggestive of poetry to the intellect as they
> are full of beauty for the senses. (p. 97)

We can dismiss *The Mastiffs* briefly before going on to the other travel books. It is a short, illustrated (by Mrs Hugh Blackburn) account of a visit by a private party led by John Burns of Wemyss

Castle to Iceland in 1878. Burns presumably invited Trollope to act as 'our chronicler', as he describes himself. It tells of the voyage via St Kilda and the Faroes to Reykjavik and on to Thingvalla and the geysers. It is totally unremarkable, and such vividness as it possesses in the references to headstrong riding by the young ladies and to the party's spending a night in the church at Thingvalla could only be really appreciated by the participants themselves.

The West Indies and the Spanish Main is a different matter, though it is hardly 'the best book that has come from [Trollope's] pen'. (*Autobiography*, ch. 7) It covers his visit to Jamaica, Cuba, British Guiana, the other ex-British Caribbean islands, Panama, Costa Rica and Nicaragua. There are eight chapters devoted to Jamaica, about which he writes most knowledgeably, but the most memorable chapters are those (19 and 20) describing his ascent of Mount Irazu and his journey from San José to Greytown. He tells of slippery ground with his horse unable to maintain its foothold, of the infested *rancho*, the mist-shrouded final ascent, his feelings inside the cold dead crater, the explosions from the nearby live volcano with the smoke 'hot and thick and full of brimstone'. (ch. 19) Again, there is the ride through the forest along mud tracks where

> The bushes were so close upon me that one hand was required to guard my face from the thorns; my knees were constantly in contact with the stumps of trees, and when my knees were free from such difficulties, my shins were sure to be in the wars. (ch. 20)

Elsewhere, however, in this section Trollope bores us with a long enquiry as to the construction and profitability of railways and canals in the Panama zone.

Though he knew Jamaica best, he liked it little. He had high praise for British Guiana where 'life flows along on a perpetual stream of love, smiles, champagne, and small-talk. Everybody has enough of everything ... [under] a mild despotism, tempered by sugar'. (ch. 12) He contrasted the progressive commercial spirit of this territory and Trinidad favourably against the complacent conservatism of Barbados and the dispirited malaise of Jamaica. Much of the troubles of this last he ascribed to the short-sighted and restrictive coolie-immigration policies of the House of Assembly, in discussing which he questioned, with a prescience that latter-day constitution-makers have lacked, the suitability of British modes of government for colonial territories. He found the Jamaican planters 'the true aristocrat of the West Indies', not mercantile like those of Barbados and Guiana, but a man with 'the characteristics of an English country gentleman.... He has his pedigree, and his family house, and his domain around him.... They have county society, local balls, and local racecourses. They have local politics, local quarrels, and strong old-fashioned local friendships'. (ch. 6) These men had been reduced by slave-emancipation and free-trade and were now threatened by coloured ascendancy in the local legislature.

Trollope is critical of the blacks, considering them feckless, unstable, childish and lazy. He realises that this will lay him open to attack, but, with that plain commonsense and realism that always characterised him, he claims that 'It will avail nothing to humanity to call a man a civilised Christian if the name be not deserved' and, again, 'We are always in such a hurry; although, as regards the progress of races, history so plainly tells us how vain such hurry is!' (ch. 4) Whatever he thought of man, he did enthuse about the landscape; of Newcastle, the military station in the Blue Mountains, he was so enraptured as to say that a man might 'almost enlist as a full private ... of the line if one were sure of being quartered [there] for ever'. (ch. 3) Not so of Spanish Town, the capital, or of Kingston, or indeed of much else in Jamaica, where 'her roads are almost impassable, her bridges are broken down, her coffee plantations have gone back to bush, her sugar estates have been sold for the value of the sugar-boilers'. (ch. 9) Six years later came the Morant Bay rebellion and direct rule from London.

In *North America* he spells out, more than once, what he is not doing. He is not producing a traveller's guide: that will doubtless soon come from the publisher, 'Mr [John] Murray'. His work is, rather, an account of his own travels and what he thought of places and people as he found them. He was impressed by Niagara and depressed by Washington. Of the former he was lifted to well-nigh poetic utterance:

> To realise Niagara you must sit there till you see nothing else.
> ... At length you will be at one with the tumbling river
> before you.... The cool liquid green will run through your
> veins, and the voice of the cataract will be the expression of
> your heart. (I, ch. 7)

Autumn in New England was not so overpowering but equally

appealing with the trees in their 'bright rose colour, the rich bronze which is almost purple in its richness, and the glorious golden yellows'. (I, ch. 3)

It is a personal impression also that he gives of institutions and events. The last quarter of *North America* is devoted to the modes of government, law, finance and the like in the United States, and there are earlier chapters on Women's Rights and on Education and Religion. He had a high opinion of the progress made in educational provision, but detected a 'want of religion' (II, ch. 16) and with it a dominant materialism and dishonesty. He found, too, a general want of courtesy (II, ch. 14), pampering of children, especially girls, and assertiveness on the part of women. (I, ch. 14) One wonders what Kate Field, the future campaigner for Women's Rights, made of Trollope's conclusion to his chapter on the subject:

> Let women say what they will of their rights ... the question
> has all been settled both for them and for us men by a higher
> power. They are the nursing mothers of mankind, and in that
> law their fate is written with all its joys and all its privileges.
> ... That women should have their rights no man will deny.
> To my thinking neither increase of work nor increase of
> political influence are among them. The best right a woman
> has is the right to a husband, and that is the right to which I
> would recommend every young woman here and in the States
> to turn her best attention. (I, ch. 18)

As Trollope's visit took place in the winter of 1861-2, the Civil War could not help but figure largely in his impression. This was at the time when the Southern emissaries, Slidell and Mason, had been arrested on board ship bound for Britain and the strain between the Northerners and the British government was at its most severe. Though Trollope was pro-North, he makes it clear on more than one occasion that he was more pro-British. He felt that secession of the South was inevitable; and he saw that, despite their protestations, the Northerners did not want full political equality for the negro nor would anything induce them to give him 'social tolerance and social sympathy'. (II, ch. 3) He saw, too, the superior condition of the Kentucky slave over that of the English agricultural labourer, though recognising that the comforts of slavery could never compensate for the absence of freedom. He foresaw the helplessnesss of the negroes when once the patriarchal aspects of the slave-system were no longer there for them to rely on. (II, ch. 4)

The stupidity of philanthropists prevented them from seeing this and much worse from emancipation – 'Four millions of slaves, with the necessities of children, with the passions of men, and the ignorance of savages!' No wonder Trollope found in Wendell Phillips and those who advocated emancipation at a stroke 'no being so venomous, so bloodthirsty as a professed philanthropist'. (I, ch. 16) What they wanted represented a leap in the dark, everything that a doctrine of *festina lente* abhorred.

North America is too long, it lacks method and is both repetitive and digressive, but it is full of Trollope's inexhaustible curiosity and openness to new experience. It is candid but not deficient in generosity; it is full of its author's forthright prejudices, yet, at the same time, tolerant of other ways of life. It is the product of an interested and passionate personality. Yet Trollope himself thought that neither this nor his *Australia and New Zealand* (1873) was 'readable ... in the proper sense of that word'. (*Autobiography*, ch. 19) The latter he thought 'dull and long, [but] a thoroughly honest book ... the result of unflagging labour for a period of fifteen months.' [August 1871–October 1872] Recent scholars have found it a useful primary source, but its very thoroughness is daunting to the general reader. The country itself, Tasmania excepted, did not impress Trollope. Sailing down the Hawkesbury was exciting, he was struck by the beauty of Sydney Harbour and he had a good word for Melbourne, but, generally speaking, he found the landscape monotonous and the towns ugly. He did, however, admire the pioneering quality of so many Australians, whether in farming or gold-mining. He understood too why the miner, given his conditions of life and work, resorted to drink and gambling, 'an excrescence on his genuine industry' (ch. 27); he felt too for those who prospected to no avail – 'I can fancy no more heart-breaking occupation.' (ch. 19) Trollope's descriptions of the goldfields certainly indicate where the vividness of similar scenes in *John Caldigate* come from.

Accompanying his sympathy there was also his characteristic acuteness of observation. He recognised the two great social problems, the conflict of squatter and free-selector and the fate of the aborigine. Of the squatter, he noted, 'it is always pleasant to sympathise with an aristocracy when an aristocracy will open its arms to you', but he, none the less, felt that the free-selector, the man who had emigrated to farm on a much smaller scale than the squatter who occupied, but did not own, often thousands of acres, was 'the man for whom colonial life and colonial prosperity is especially intended'. (ch. 2) The contact of aborigine and white man had, he thought, resulted only in the former's degradation and deterioration; they had learnt many things, but 'we have been altogether unable to teach them not to be savage'. (ch. 38) The same, he felt, was true also of the Maori, though he found them superior in intelligence and courage to the aborigine. New Zealand, incidentally, evoked a more lively interest and presented apparently greater variety both in people and places than any of the Australian territories.

Trollope's more general opinions frequently appear. In the activities of Sir Julius Vogel in New Zealand he recognised the temptations for a government minister to spend money not so much for the public good as for his own political self-preservation, and in an age of increasing direct intervention by government it is worth noting the knowledge of human nature that lies behind his comment:

> Government cannot get the same work out of its workmen that is got by private employers. It cannot build a ship, or manage an estate, or erect a palace with that economy which a private master can ensure.... Scope for idleness produces idleness till it becomes the great blessing of the service that real work is not exacted.... A profuse expenditure of government money in any community will taint the whole of it with the pervading sin. (ch. 34)

Trollope's view of empire was not marked, however, by any similar political wisdom. He committed the error of believing, like many socialists in the latter days of the British imperial phase, that possession and glory of empire in no way benefited the workman: 'Will the ploughman between his stilts, with barely bread to eat and no shoes for his children's feet, be the better for it? ... ' (ch. 1)

Trollope's last major journey occupied five months in 1877 and out of it came *South Africa* (1878). He did not regard this part of the world as a colony, that is, a place to be colonised by emigrant Britons, but he did consider it an example of British imperial trusteeship - 'the condition of these people [the Kafirs] has been improved by our coming' (I, ch. 11), and he noted elsewhere that, rather than exploiting her colonies as Spain and Holland had done, England had been contented with the creation of new markets and the spread of her language, laws and customs. (I, ch. 16) Though the recent annexation of the Transvaal had provoked Trollope's journey, it was not this, but the native question which excited his greatest political concern. He identified four 'views of our duty' – hymns, land, the rod of iron, and the vote. (II, chs 9 and 17) Both in this book and in his remarks about the Maoris he had little faith in the first, while grants of land, he thought, would make the natives idle. The rod of iron he found abominable, and the vote was ridiculous for someone not then fitted to exercise it. Nevertheless, colour should not be a consideration, simply capacity: 'but we all know how impossible it is that any number of whites, however small, should be ruled by any number of blacks, however great'. (I, ch. 14)

The fertility and scenic beauty impressed Trollope, but he also told his son, 'South Africa is so dirty.' (*Letters*, No. 670) What is obvious is that he enjoyed the people and occasions in the country. His arrival in Grahamstown without his dress-suit, his old-man's nostalgic watching of a game of kiss-in-the-ring (I, ch. 10) or the mingled outrage and comedy which mark his account of a coach journey to Pietermaritzburg in the company of a man transporting a large and evil-smelling fish (I, ch. 15), all these evoke an intimacy that is all too rare in the Australasian volume. They also neatly summarise the variety of experience always likely to happen to a man with Trollope's omnivorous zest for life.

Trollope wrote the first of his two plays, *The Noble Jilt*, in 1850. Like *La Vendée* which he had just completed, it is set in French Revolutionary times and is now known merely as the prototype of the plot in *Can You Forgive Her?* and for the criticisms of it that Trollope puts in the mouth of Mrs Carbuncle in *The Eustace Diamonds*. (ch. 52) Margaret de Wynter jilts Count Upsel out of boredom with perfection and chooses Steinmark on his sister's urging, but he, though willing to have her as a mistress, will not marry her. She is finally reconciled to Upsel and marriage without passion. This part of the play is couched in pseudo-Elizabethan dramatic verse. The sub-plot of the widow, Madame Brudo, and her two suitors, Burgomaster van Hoppen and Captain Belleroche, is more lively and provides in the attempted elopement of the widow and the captain some comedy of disguise and exposure. (IV, ch. 3) Generally speaking, however, the characters are feeble and lacking in any credible motivation.

Trollope records the forthright criticism *The Noble Jilt* received when he submitted it to the actor-manager George Bartley. (*Autobiography*, ch. 5) His only other play, *Did He Steal It?*, though prepared at the request of a theatre manager, met no better fate. It is based on the Crawley story in *The Last Chronicle of Barset* with some slight transformations (Crawley, for example, is a school-master and Goshawk, the *alter ego* of Bishop Proudie, a magistrate and school trustee) and condensations (Captain Oakley, the equivalent of Major Grantly as Grace's fiancé, is the son of Mrs Goshawk by a previous marriage). The theatrical version is so much weaker than the novel. Crawley has lost much of his intensity and, though both he and the other main characters are well enough defined, they lack the cumulative effect that the more expansive form of the novel is able to develop. The dialogue, too, is sometimes stilted and artificial. (Cf. his own remarks on dialogue, *Autobiography*, ch. 12) Since much of this is applied by scissors-and-paste directly from the novel and since, further, Trollope's dialogue in the novels seems so natural, one realises how much art has concealed art in the medium in which he excelled. The dramatic form was too constricting: he needed space and leisure to develop what he had to say, even paradoxically in something apparently so dramatic as the history of Josiah Crawley.

Morris L. Parrish collected *Four Lectures* (1938), dealing respectively with the Civil Service, the United States at the time of the Civil War, 'Higher Education of Women' and 'On English Prose Fiction as a Rational Amusement'. There is nothing remarkable in them as lectures. They cover their subjects in a systematic, if at times pedestrian, manner. That on the Civil Service is informed with that fervour both of loyalty and criticism which Trollope manifested towards his own profession elsewhere. It repeats, for example, the old arguments about reliance merely on intellectual ability for promotion. The last of the four lectures skims over the history of the English novel and ends with a slightly extended critique of Scott and Thackeray. The contents of the American lecture are repeated in abbreviated form from sentiments in *North America*, whilst in 'Higher Education of Women' he comes out once more against women's rights and also against co-education. After repeated bantering remarks, he ends with nothing more than counselling 'steadfast adherence to fixed purposes made by yourselves on your own behalf'. (Parrish, 1938, p. 88) The moral note is typical. In this very lecture he counselled his hearers to choose their novels by the lessons they taught.

We come last to the *Autobiography* (1875-6). It ranks with the highest of its kind. Every writer on Trollope, and not least the present one, can do no other than draw extensively upon it. It supplies first-hand opinions about many of the novels and in long discursive digressions from its subject's history plentiful comment is provided about the writing and criticism of novels, matters of copyright law, the treatment of budding authors and the like. Here, however, I am concerned only to assess it as what it essentially is, the story of its author's life. This requires first that we identify what it is not. At the end he claims, rightly, that it is not 'a record of [his] inner life'. Women, wine, clubmanship, gambling – 'of what matter is that to any reader?' (ch. 20) His marriage, he asserted, was 'of no special interest to any one except my wife and me' (ch. 4), but he does devote a brief and tender paragraph, albeit anonymously, to Kate Field. (ch. 17) And if it is reticent about his inner life, it is little more effusive about his adventures. We do have mention of the encounter, half snub and half zany, with Brigham Young, the Mormon leader (ch. 19), but much else, as he says of his experiences as editor of *St Paul's* (ch. 18), must have gone into his novels and stories. He tells us of people he knew, but with the exception of a few authors (ch. 8) little about them.

Yet he can claim that in the busiest years (1859-71) 'few men, I think, ever lived a busier life'. (ch. 15) That life consisted of three hours each morning from 5.30 onwards writing '250 words every quarter of an hour', then to work at the Post Office, in addition to which he 'hunted at least twice a week . . . was frequent in the whist-room at the Garrick . . . lived much in society in London, and was made happy by the presence of many friends at Waltham Cross'. Even though the detail is missing, Trollope does effectively convey the sense of a ceaseless round and his own enthusiasm for it. In addition, the pugnacity of the man emerges not least from his account of his official life in the Post Office and the 'delicious feuds' he had with Rowland Hill – 'It was a pleasure to me to differ from him on all occasions' – and what consummate certainty informs the sentence that follows: 'And looking back now, I think that in all such differences I was right.'

In the latter parts of the book this individuality intrudes but rarely, and it might not have been very pleasant if it had. The first three chapters with their account of Trollope's painful and poverty-stricken early years are altogether different. With the vivid recollection of one who had been both a lonely and ill-treated child, he recalls the stigma of poor and dirty clothing, of other boys' taunts and the injustice of punishments he received. Such poverty may go far to explain the insistence he placed on the status and quality of a 'gentleman' (ch. 3); such loneliness, he recognised, explained his lifelong 'craving for love . . . a wish that during the first half of my life was never gratified'. (ch. 9) The irony is that, possessed with not a little of his father's fatal irascibility, Trollope's frequent impulsive reactions in later years often did less than endear him to those with whom he came in contact.

The *Autobiography* is a systematic account of as much as Trollope wanted us to know. It is most vivid on the early years, those that mattered most to its author and in all likelihood were the most vivid of his life. Within the limits of his time Trollope is frank and candid. Indeed, with the references to his methodical application to his writing and the statement of his receipts, he was too much so for many of his contemporaries. They must, however, have applauded his very Victorian gospel of work. (chs 7, 20) Above all, the *Autobiography* is a goldmine of comment on its creator's own writing. No other author has left us so large or broad a body of criticism of his work – and that, like all else of Trollope's, so sensible, honest and down-to-earth. These qualities leave us, though Trollope would not have relished the parallel, speaking of him in Antony's last words about Brutus – 'This was a man!'

10

Conclusion: An Estimate

> I have lived with my characters, and thence has come whatever success I have obtained. There is a gallery of them, and of all in that gallery I may say that I know the tone of the voice, and the colour of the hair, every flame of the eye, and the very clothes they wear. (*Autobiography*, ch. 12)

That is half the secret of Trollope's success. The other half, to match this intimacy with his characters, is what, in a letter to A. N. Monkhouse (8 February 1924), Joseph Conrad called Trollope's 'gift of intimate communion with the reader'. We feel, after reading him, that we are with a man we know and can trust, talking about people he knows and who through him we come to know. 'There is something so friendly and simple and shrewd about [him] that one is the better for taking a stroll with him.' (Stephen, 1902, IV, p. 179)

Unsympathetic critics have dismissed Trollope as ordinary. He is ordinary, but this is his strength. To extend the 1883 quotation from James briefly mentioned in the Preface: 'His great, his inestimable merit was a complete appreciation of the usual.' James then glosses this: 'He *felt* all daily and immediate things as he saw them.' (James, 1957, p. 91), and continues by referring to the way by which Trollope gratifies the taste for recognition rather than surprise. This is one of the grounds of confidence between himself and his reader and one reason why his world is so persuasive.

Another is that, for the most part, he writes of what Conrad called 'a highly organised, if not complex, society', in which certain standards were universally accepted and any decline from them open to unquestioning censure. In this sense, though I know that Dr Leavis would deny him the accolade, Trollope fulfils that critic's claim when he writes: 'A study of human nature is a study of social

192

human nature, and the psychologist, sociologist, and social historian aren't in it compared with the great novelists.' (1967, p. 25) In Trollope's society the values of responsibility, order, decency, cultivation were respected. Above all, as I have repeatedly tried to show, honesty was what mattered. Trollope had an uncompromising sense of moral purpose, but this does not mean that he felt it necessary to show his sympathetic characters as paragons of virtue. Indeed, many of them fall far short of that, and, conversely, in a famous passage of *The Eustace Diamonds* (ch. 35) he has told us of 'the persons whom you cannot care for in a novel, because they are so bad, [being] the very same that you so dearly love in your life because they are so good'. For Trollope people are only more or less imperfect. Thus there are those who are merely moderate, some of strong character like Archdeacon Grantly, some weak like Frank Greystock, whilst there are others magnificent in evil like Melmotte or mean and despicable like Lopez; and in a world where most are mainly normal, there can suddenly appear a Kennedy, a Crawley or a Louis Trevelyan. It might be objected that in a Harding there is a perfect person, and certainly one would not want to saddle so saintly a character with even the most minor degree of moral turpitude. What makes him convincing, and not just too good to be true, is, first, the element of introspection, uncertainty and weakness in withstanding the opposition which the Hiram's Hospital scandal provokes and, second, the views other people have of him and the judgements they make about him.

This directs us to the close-knit relationship in Trollope's work between character and plot. Henry James again is apposite:

> We care what happens to people only in proportion as we know what people are. Trollope's great apprehension of the real . . . came to him through his desire to satisfy us on this point – to tell us what certain people were and what they did in consequence of being so. That is the purpose of each of his tales; and if these things produce an illusion, it comes from the gradual abundance of his testimony as to the temper, the tone, the passions, the habits, the moral nature, of a certain number of contemporary Britons. (James, 1957, p. 95)

The phrase 'gradual abundance' is significant. Trollope accumulates detail. Events seem to follow a natural sequence. The events are often of the most minor nature in themselves. What matters is the attitudes they provoke. Thus a simple, even a chance, occurrence –

Rachel Ray seen with a young man – can initiate a whole set of malicious misinterpretations and family discords. The fact that Palliser does not like Major Pountney and that he has him in mind when Lopez's possible candidature for Silverbridge is brought to his notice has as much to do with his unrelenting opposition to Lopez as anything else. Trollope remorselessly exploits such detail. That remorseless exploitation may take the form of several versions of the same event or person from differing points of view. The chapter-title 'Phineas Dismissed' epitomises a frequent exercise.

Trollope extends his characterisation, not simply by our having several views of the one person but also because each of those views makes its own contribution to our understanding of the character who expresses it. This is an unobtrusive way by which to develop character, but it is again typical of Trollope's method, exploiting the normal and ordinary, the means by which we come to understand in life itself. This approach is further underlined by his dialogue, often so faithful as to seem tedious. Trollope, referring to this in the *Autobiography,* wrote: 'The writer may tell much of his story in conversations, but he may only do so by putting such words into the mouths of his personages as persons so situated would probably use.' (ch. 12) A similar unobtrusiveness marks his prose-style, so much so that critics complain of its neutral and even lifeless quality. 'We must be content with good homespun phrases which give up all their meaning on the first reading,' says Leslie Stephen. (1902, p. 178) Trollope himself asked for simplicity, ease and vigour; and in his study of *Thackeray,* he suggested that 'a novel should be easy, lucid and of course, grammatical'. (p. 184) Given the normal social world in which the novels are set, to have attempted anything more distinctive might easily have seemed mannered. To think of Thackeray or Dickens in this regard is to be reminded of their idiosyncrasies. Trollope had none such, or, if he had, it was only the occasional tendency towards passages of Carlylean lament, denunciation or address, and this mainly in the earlier novels.

Trollope had little aptitude for, or indeed interest in, plot. Of the Finn novels he wrote: 'As to the incidents of the story, the circumstances by which these personages were to be effected, I knew nothing. They were created for the most part as they were described. I never could arrange a set of events before me.' (ch. 17) These novels are some proof of this, for with theft, garrotting, a duel, two trials, murder, a brawl and a suicide they are sometimes more sensational than convincing. Even here, however, the truth or otherwise of the action seems to depend on that of character. The rancour between Bonteen and Finn is insufficient to associate the latter with the murder, even as suspect, whereas all Kennedy's previous behaviour presages the suicide that eventually occurs.

The people in whom we are principally interested are, however, nearly always more 'normal' than someone like Kennedy, and the difficulties they get into form his plots. A rash action by an otherwise admirable character, the pangs of conscience, the suffering involved both for the character and his or her close associates – that is one form in which we find Trollope developing his tale, as in *Framley Parsonage* and *Orley Farm*. The social pressures that disturb the peace or impede the progress of the protagonists provide another; *The Warden* and *Doctor Thorne* come to mind. Mistaken impressions of what people have done (*John Caldigate*) or may do (Eleanor Bold, Frank Tregear, Rachel Ray) are yet another.

Even the mere passing of years can be impressive. Trollope was the first to do what many, particularly of his twentieth-century, successors have imitated, namely, to write a series of novels largely about the same group of characters over a number of years. Of this process Trollope wrote: 'I had constantly before me the necessity of progression in character.' This in itself was a product of his intimacy with his creations:

> So much of my inner life was passed in their company, that I was continually asking myself how this woman would act when this or that event had passed over her head, or how that man would carry himself when his youth had become manhood, or his manhood declined to old age. (ibid.)

In some things characters may change with the years, but fundamentally they stay the same: 'The selfish man will still be selfish, and the false man false.' (ibid., ch. 10) Thus Archdeacon Grantly mellows, but he does not change. Thus, much as they have come to understand and appreciate each other over the years, Palliser and Glencora cannot even at the end forget her early near-elopement with Burgo Fitzgerald; they cannot forget, not just because it was an important event, but because they are what they are. That event illumines their characters, as they respond differently, but each characteristically, to the attraction of their daughter to Frank Tregear.

Looking forward is as important as looking back. The characters have a purpose which is progressively defined and which gives

195

power to the narrative, often in the sense of leading us to wonder not what will happen but rather how and when it will happen. The 'how' and the 'when' have much to do with the characters' own personalities and temperaments, but Trollope is no Henry James or even George Eliot. He does not probe the inner being of consciousness, nor does he laboriously examine the nuances of feeling or the minutiae of motivation. He paints with a much broader brush. How then can any critic claim that 'Of all the novelists of the nineteenth century he had perhaps the finest psychological grasp'? (P. Hansford Johnson, 1971, p. 30) Without necessarily claiming that exclusive superlative, one may perhaps suggest that the undoubtedly powerful psychological appeal in Trollope's novels is a product of his fine sense of the way in which people behave in society, what in an evocative phrase Mario Praz has described as Trollope's 'benevolently realistic estimate of human emotions, so full of shades and subtleties'. (1956, p. 261) Those shades and subtleties allow not only for what is evident but also for all that there is in life that lies above and below behaviour. In other words, Trollope often suggests as much as he states. A Lily Dale and a Laura Standish illustrate this as successful creations, just as, say, an Ayala Dormer does in her failure. Trollope may only appear to observe, but he saw far more than the merely obvious. His intimacy with his characters prevents him from saying too much, and his intimacy with his reader makes it unnecessary for him to say more.

There is no need for anything flamboyant. A low key will suffice, and hence perhaps the modesty of his definition of the novel as 'a picture of common life enlivened by humour and sweetened by pathos'. (*Autobiography*, ch. 7) Trollope's novels show 'common life' only in the sense that their subject-matter is the universal experience of love and family relationships in private life and of rivalries and struggle, sorrows and successes, in public affairs. There are the subtle variations of love, from the unhappiness of a Lily Dale or an Emily Wharton through the muted joys of a Glencora Palliser to the bliss of a Lucy Robarts or a Mary Thorne. There are, too, the endless permutations of family relationships – husbands and wives such as Palliser and Glencora, Louis Trevelyan and Emily, Kennedy and Lady Laura; mothers and sons like Mrs Clavering and Harry or mothers and daughters like Mrs Ray and Rachel; brothers and sisters with contrasting histories like the Dales or the Rays. In the public life we encounter the complications created by money, rank, property and marriage – or the lack of them, the struggles of a Finn, the problems of a Frank Gresham or the machinations of a Melmotte.

Trollope admired good blood. The gentleman was, he believed, the custodian of accumulated traditions of behaviour and belief. With his typical candour he wrote:

> I do not scruple to say that I prefer the society of distinguished people, and that even the distinction of wealth confers many advantages. The best education is to be had at a price as well as the best broadcloth. The son of a peer is more likely to rub his shoulders against well-informed men than the son of a tradesman. The graces come easier to the wife of him who has had great-grandfathers than they do to her whose husband has been less, – or more fortunate, as they may think it. (*Autobiography*, ch. 9)

But it was not just a matter of social preference. He found his subject-matter distilled and concentrated here:

> The English character with its faults and virtues, its prejudices and steadfastness, can be better studied in the manners of noblemen, in country houses, in parsonages, in farms and small meaningless towns, than in the great cities, devoted as is London to politicised gaiety, or as are Glasgow, Manchester, Birmingham and others like them, to manufactures and commerce. (*Australia*, ch. 30)

London, which does figure importantly, is largely a place of moral confusion. The country house and the small town are more characteristic Trollopian locations.

Sometimes this aspect of Trollope is used to suggest that he appeals simply to mere nostalgia. He does appeal to nostalgia, to the reader's regard for an established order of things in church and state, reflected in well-defined hierarchy and custom. The interest of the novels, however, derives also in this respect from the impression they provide of what Monsignor Knox called 'the twilight of an *ancien régime*', of an establishment under attack and in serious danger from forces without and failures within. Our admiration for those who are its reliable pillars becomes all the greater. The nostalgia is not, therefore, mere sentimentalism, but a proper regard and regret for the passing of much that was valuable.

Not least in this was what Trollope saw, accepted himself and represented in his firm sense of social proprieties and moral values.

His 'picture of common life [with] men and women walking . . . just as they do walk here among us' was the means he chose for

> impregnating the mind of the novel-reader with a feeling that honesty is the best policy, that truth prevails while falsehood fails; that a girl will be loved as she is pure, and sweet, and unselfish; that a man will be true, and honest, and brave of heart.

A little later, he writes: 'I have ever thought of myself as a preacher of sermons.' (*Autobiography*, ch. 8) The *Spectator* (27 October 1883) dismissed all this as 'morality of a very limited kind'. Whether it is limited or not, it is certainly fundamental.

'To enliven by humour and sweeten by pathos' was at once relief and reinforcement of this moral purpose. The discomfiture of Mrs Proudie, the suffering of Lady Mason or of Carry Brattle, the sad realisation of Mr Whittlestaff, the comic antics of Moulder and Kantwise, the comic attitude of Mrs Baggott, or the ridiculous pomposities of the American senator – these are but a random selection of humour and pathos, but they serve to remind us of the variety of each, variety both in kind and intensity. Trollope's detachment, balance and tolerance gave him a ready sense of the ridiculous. He employed satire where he thought it necessary, and sometimes, as in *The Way We Live Now*, it was satire of a sombre cast, but there is very little deep irony in his work. His criticism was usually too generous for that. He was aware, too, how quickly humour might be turned into pathos, satire into tragedy. There is much to laugh at good-naturedly in a Johnny Eames, but the end is sadness; there is much to criticise in a Melmotte, but the end, though just, is still catastrophe. This awareness of the proximity of differing states is again part of Trollope's sure grasp of the universal experience of life.

That he had his faults as a writer no sane critic would deny. At times he was prolix, slow-moving, and, as publication in parts and by serial encouraged, repetitive. At times the words seem to flow from the pen of an all-too-ready writer. Some of the later novels particularly show the craft, devoid of vitality. Despite his success, as Henry James noted, with the English girl, some of his heroines are rather lifeless, as indeed are some of his young men. He himself confessed of the Palliser novels that the politics interested him, and the love-element he felt he had to put there to meet the expecta-tions of his readers. Generally speaking, he is not concerned with the deepest springs of moral evil and of good. His people are not like that. If that is what we want, we must look elsewhere; and we must do the same if we are looking for the well-made plot.

'I do not think it probable that my name will remain among those who in the next century will be known as the writers of English prose fiction', Trollope wrote, adding with some accuracy, 'but if it does, that permanence of success will probably rest on the character of Plantagenet Palliser, Lady Glencora, and the Rev. Mr Crawley.' (*Autobiography*, ch. 20) *The Last Chronicle of Barset* and some of the Palliser series will always remain high in any estimate of Trollope's achievement. For comedy and the evocation of a particular ethos I would add *Barchester Towers* and, with some reservations, *The American Senator*; for its intensely critical spirit *The Way We Live Now*; for its breadth and psychological intensity *Orley Farm*; and, as a gem among the shorter novels, *Cousin Henry*. There are others with strong claims; *Mr Scarborough's Family* and *He Knew He Was Right* are obvious candidates.

Trollope was, in V. S. Pritchett's phrase, 'a man of liberal mind crossed by strong conservative feeling'. (1965, p. 114) As such, he possessed firm ground for judging and a spirit generous in doing so. Approached without predispositions, he offers a view of life, shrewd in observation, mature in understanding, wise in assessment and clear in its statement. He certainly had 'the gift of intimate communion with the reader'.

A Note on *La Vendée*

La Vendée (1850) was Trollope's only excursion into the field of historical romance. It followed the first two Irish novels and is quite different from anything else he wrote, and therefore can not really be considered as part of any group. It tells the story of the rising in La Vendée (the mid-west of France, in the Loire Valley, mainly near and in Saumur) against the revolutionary usurpers immediately after they had executed Louis XVI in 1793. Like Trollope's other early novels, it was a failure and, despite his own limited commendation, one must add, deservedly so.

The historical setting derives from the series of events beginning with the resistance to conscription and the raising of the flag of rebellion at St Florent, proceeding through the capture of Saumur, the despatch of Republican forces against the rebels and their ultimate defeat. Within this setting there are the love-affair of Henry Larochejaquelin and Marie Lescure and the unrequited love of Adolphe Denot for Henri's sister Agatha, which leads him first to treachery and then in the latter stages of the tale, when the fighting has moved to Brittany, to his rehabilitation in the disguise of the Mad Captain. He dies in the victory at Laval. The story does not cover the ultimate defeat of the Vendeans, but ends with the marriage of Henri and Marie.

Trollope, however, foreshadows the future in a sentence which is important for other reasons:

> Much fiction has been blended with history, but still the outline of historical facts has been too closely followed to allow us now to indulge the humanity of our readers by ascribing to the friends we are quitting success which they did not achieve. (ch. 34)

History was indeed very closely followed, too often tediously so, and this is one of the book's major faults. At times, in fact, it reads like a military history. Likewise, there are some overlong descriptions of places and houses – and a sermon! The characters do not take on much individual identity. Larochejaquelin and Lescure are very orthodox heroic members of the nobility and Marie is the proper equivalent in feminine character and attributes. Agatha, however, does possess some interest through her admiration for the original leader of the rebellion, the postillion Cathelineau, and his death-scene with her by his bedside has a certain power. The contrast of the Republican general, Santerre, with his own reputation and with his brutal colleague, Westerman, also brings a touch of surprise into the novel.

The mixture of history and fiction has not fused into a whole. Sometimes the obtrusiveness of the history is more obvious than at others. The passage on Robespierre followed by Eleanor Deplay's plea and its relation to the death of Marie Antoinette is one such. Trollope acknowledges that he has borrowed it from Lamartine's *The Girondists*. The greater fault, however, is the failure to make the fictional experiences of the characters more significant within the historical background. Too often the novel reads as passages of dialogue with an account of history. Trollope was not a second Scott, and it was good that he realised it.

Bibliography

Editions
The original dates of publication of the novels and other works are given in the text. There is no complete edition, but thirty-five are (or were) available in Oxford University Press's Worlds Classics series. References are given by chapter only, but where page numbers *are* given these refer to the 1st edition, except for:
Four Lectures (1938), ed. M. L. Parrish,
Hunting Sketches, (1952), ed. L. Edwards,
The New Zealander, (1972), ed. N. J. Hall,

Guides
Gerould, W. G. and J. T. (1948), *A Guide to Trollope,* Princeton.
Hardwick, M. (1974), *The Osprey Guide to Anthony Trollope.*
Sadleir, M. (1934), *Trollope: A Bibliography,* reissued 1964.

Letters
Booth, B. A. (ed) (1951), *The Letters of Anthony Trollope.* A new and much fuller edition is in preparation by N. J. Hall.

Biography
Escott, T. H. Sweet (1913), *Trollope: His Public Services, Private Friends and Literary Originals.*
Pope Hennessy, J. (1971), *Anthony Trollope.* Comprehensive biography with plentiful critical judgment.
Sadleir, M. (1961), *Trollope: A Commentary,* 1927, 1945 (revd); quotations from 1961 Oxford paperback. For long the standard critical biography and still useful for the careful and authoritative chronicling of Trollope's life.
Stebbins, L. P. and R. P. (1945), *The Trollopes: the Chronicle of a Writing Family.*

Criticism

Booth, B. A. (1957), 'Trollope's *Orley Farm*: Artistry Manqué' in R. C. Rathburn and M. Steinmann (eds), *From Jane Austen to Joseph Conrad.*

Booth, B. A. (1958), *Anthony Trollope: Aspects of His Life and Work.*

Cecil, Lord David (1934), *Early Victorian Novelists.*

Cockshut, A. O. J. (1955), *Anthony Trollope: A Critical Study.* Began the movement to rehabilitate the later Trollope.

Curtis Brown, B. (1950), *Anthony Trollope.*

Hansford Johnson, P. (1971), 'Trollope's Young Women' in B. S. Benedikz (ed.), *On the Novel.*

Helling, R. (1956), *A Century of Trollope Criticism,* Helsinki.

James, Henry (1883), 'Anthony Trollope', *Century Magazine,* July.

James, Henry (1957), *The House of Fiction,* ed. L. Edel.

James, Henry (1970), *Partial Portraits,* ed. L. Edel (original publication by James in 1888).

Leavis, F. R. (1967), *Anna Karenina and Other Essays.*

Polhemus, R. M. (1968), *The Changing World of Anthony Trollope,* Berkeley and Los Angeles. Studies the novel chronologically, but perhaps presses its thesis of Trollope's changing view of the world a little too strongly.

Pollard, A. (1968), *Trollope's Political Novels.*

Praz, M. (1956), *The Hero in Eclipse in Victorian Fiction.*

Pritchett, V. S. (1965), *The Working Novelist.*

Ray, G. (1967-8), 'Trollope at Full Length', *Huntingdon Library Quarterly,* XXXI, pp. 313-39.

Roberts, Ruth ap (1971), *Trollope: Artist and Moralist* (in USA *The Moral Trollope*). Persuasive account of moral structures in Trollope's work.

Skilton, D. (1972), *Anthony Trollope and His Contemporaries.*

Smalley, D. (ed.) (1969), *Trollope: The Critical Heritage.* Contains criticism from the nineteenth-century reviews. My quotations from contemporary reviews are drawn almost exclusively from this.

Stephen, L. (1902), *Studies of a Biographer,* IV.

Sykes Davies, H. (1960), *Trollope.* Essay in the British Council Writers and Their Work Series.

Background

Arnold, R. (1961), *The Whiston Matter.*

Bagehot, W. (1904 edn), *The English Constitution.*

Beckett, J. C. (1966), *The Making of Modern Ireland*.

Best, G. F. A. (1961-2), 'The Road to Hiram's Hospital', *Victorian Studies*, v.

Best, G. F. A. (1971), *Mid-Victorian Britain 1851-1875*.

Briggs, Asa (1954), 'Trollope, Bagehot and the English Constitution' in *Victorian People*.

Burn, W. L. (1964), *The Age of Equipoise*.

Chadwick, O. (1966), *The Victorian Church*, I.

Christie, O. F. (1927), *The Transition from Aristocracy, 1832-1867*.

Clark, G. Kitson (1962), *The Making of Victorian England*.

Escott, T. H. Sweet (1897), *Social Transformations of the Victorian Age*.

McDowell, R. B. (1956), 'Ireland on the Eve of the Famine' in R. D. Edwards and T. D. Williams (eds), *The Great Famine*.

Martin, R. B. (1962), *Enter Rumour*.

Nevill, R. H. (1925), *English Country House Life*.

Southgate, D. (1962), *The Passing of the Whigs, 1832-1886*.

Thompson, F. M. L. (1971 edn), *English Landed Society in the Nineteenth Century*.

Trench, W. Steuart (1966 edn), *Realities of Irish Life*, 1968.

Willoughby de Broke, Lord (1921), *The Sport of our Ancestors*.

Nineteenth-Century Fiction (originally from 1945 to 1949 *The Trollopian*) contains numerous articles on Trollope, details of which may be found (up to 1966) in *New Cambridge Bibliography of English Literature* and for subsequent years in *The Year's Work in English Studies*.

Index

(Quotations from the *Autobiography* and the *Letters* are so frequent and extensive that they are not included here. References to characters are not given by name, but are included under the book in which they appear. The reader may find therefore that a page listed under a title does not always specifically carry a mention of the title, but there will be reference(s) to characters in the book in question. All titles are listed under the main Trollope entry itself, the principal reference being shown in heavy type.)

Amery, Leopold, 75, 96
Arnold, Matthew, 49
Austen, Jane, 19, 68, 70, 126

Bagehot, Walter, 26
Balzac, Honoré de, 130
Baring-Gould, S., 118
Beckett, J. C., 9
Bentley, Richard, 6
Best, G. F. A., 57
Blackwood, John, 143
Booth, B. A., 23, 65, 70, 117, 119, 146, 182
Braddon, Maria, 6, 119
Bright, John, 77
Brontë, Charlotte, 3, 50, 92
Browning, Robert, 7

Carlyle, Thomas, 29, 30, 34, 55, 194
Carnarvon, 4th Earl of, 7
Chadwick, Owen, 57
Chapman Hall, 6, 68, 135
Church of England, 48-53

Cicero, 34 (see also *Cicero* under 'Trollope, Anthony: Works')
Cockshut, A. O. J., 122, 123, 134, 150, 155
Collins, Wilkie, 6, 119
Conrad, Joseph, 192
Constable Maxwell, M., 77, 78, 79
Cornhill Magazine, 6, 7, 32, 68, 118, 123, 135
Cunningham, J. W., 50
Curtis Brown, Beatrice, ix

Denison, G. A., 57
Derby, 14th Earl of, 30
Devonshire, Dukes of, 27
Dickens, Charles, x, 3, 40, 51, 55, 112, 139, 194
Disraeli, Benjamin, 34, 59, 181
Dobrée, Bonamy, ix

Edwards, Sir Henry, 77, 78, 79, 81
Eglinton, 13th Earl of, 59
Eliot, George, 7, 59, 134, 139, 196

205

Escott, T. H. S., 7, 50, 133
Examiner, 11-12, 70

Farnham, Lord, 9
Field, Kate, 6, 123, 131, 185, 190
Forster, W. E., 77
Fortnightly Review, 135

Gaskell, Mrs E. C., 20, 61, 133
Gissing, George, 167
Gladstone, W. E., 8, 30
Good Words, 135, 136
Gregory, Sir William, 3
Guildford, Earl of, 53, 54, 55

Hampden, R. D., 57
Hansford Johnson, Pamela, 196
Hardy, Thomas, 153
Harper's Magazine, 150
Hawthorne, Julian, 1
Headley, Lord, 9
Hill, Rowland, 7
Houghton, Lord, 7
Hudson, George, 27
Hutton, R. H., 143

Ireland, condition of, 9-12, 24

James, Henry, ix, 84, 85, 130, 139-40, 192, 193, 196, 198
James, Sir Henry, 7

Kennard, Captain E. H., 77, 78
Knox, R. A., 197

Lamartine, Alphonse de, 201
Leavis, F. R., 192-3
Lewes, G. H., 7
Longmans, 6, 29, 30
Lowe, Robert, 77
Lytton, Lord, 7

Maberly, Colonel, 5
Macaulay, Lord, 29
McDowell, R. B., 9
Macleod, Norman, 135, 136
Meetkerke, Adolphus, 2
Melbourne, Lord, 180
Merivale, John, 13

Mill, J. S., 102, 130
Millais, J. E., 7, 136
Monkhouse, A. N., 192

Nation, 139
National Review, 120
Newbolt, Sir Francis, 121
Newby, T. C., 6

O'Connell, Daniel, 10, 16
Osborne, S. G., 10

Palmerston, Lord, 9, 76 (see also *Lord Palmerston* under 'Trollope, Anthony: Works')
Parrish, M. L., 111, 189
Peel, Sir Robert, 114
Polhemus, R. M., 68-9, 70, 86, 101, 117, 123, 125, 142, 161, 162
Pope, Alexander, 34
Portland, 5th Duke of, 27
Praz, Mario, 196,
Pritchett, V. S., 199

Ray, G. N., 109, 135
Roberts, Ruth ap, 34, 41, 42, 156, 157
Robinson, C. F., 122
Ruskin, John, 34
Russell, Lord John, 30, 76

Sadleir, M., 1, 6, 18, 23, 29, 118, 136
St Paul's Magazine, 8, 30, 82, 190
Saturday Review, 68, 147, 152, 165
Scott, Sir Walter, 180, 189
Shaftesbury, 7th Earl of, 50, 51
Shakespeare, William, 4
Shakespearean characters: Angelo, 171; Antony, 191; Cawdor, 101; Claudio, 171; Duke (in *Measure for Measure*), 171; Escalus, 171; Hamlet, 32; Macbeth, Lady, 90; Othello, 117, 128, 129; Shylock, 166
Shelley, P. B., 90, 91
Simeon, Charles, 50
Smith, Elder, 6, 32
Smith, Sidney, 77
Southgate, D., 76
Spectator, 69, 109, 127, 129, 198
Spencer, Herbert, 7

'Spy', 1
Stephen, Sir Leslie, 192, 194

Tennyson, Alfred, Lord, 7
Thackeray, W. M., 7, 40, 50, 59, 79, 83, 115, 125, 165, 189, 194 (see also *Thackeray* under 'Trollope, Anthony: Works')
Thompson, F. M. L., 26, 28-9
Times, The, 55, 139, 158, 164
Trench, W. Stewart, 10
Trevelyan, Sir Charles, 111
Trollope, Anthony: appearance, 1; birth, 2; characters, view of, 193, 195; characterisation, methods of, 194, 196; death, 8; faults as a writer, 198; gentleman, idea of, 60, 73-4, 124, 137-8, 197; Harting, residence at, 8; hunting, 6, 12, 44; illness, 4; Ireland, 5, 8, 9 (see also *Examiner*, Letters to, below under 'Works'); London life, 7; marriage, 5; moral purpose in novels, 197-8; parents, 2; personality, 1; photograph, 1; plot, attitude to, 194-5; politics, 7-8, 75-9, 103-4; Post office, 5, 7; progress in characters, sense of, 195; publishing history, 6; *St Paul's Magazine*, editor of, 8; schools, 3; tone, 196; travels, 6-7, 8 (see also *Travelling Sketches* below under 'Works'); Waltham Cross, 6.

WORKS:
'The Adventures of Fred Pickering' **175-6**; 'Alice Dugdale', **176**; *The American Senator*, **41-6**, 198, 199; *Australia and New Zealand*, 182, **186-7**, 197; *The Autobiography*, **190-1**; *Ayala's Angel*, **164-5**, 173, 196; *Barchester Towers*, 6, 28, 50, 51, 52, **56-60**, 109, 198, 199; *The Belton Estate*, 135, **141-3**; *The Bertrams*, 109, **114-18**, 127, 140, 182; *Castle Richmond*, **18-21**, 23, 24; *Caesar, Commentaries of*, **178-9**; *Can You Forgive Her?* 75, **82-8**, 100, 150, 188, 195; *Cicero, Life of*, 178, **179**; *The Claverings*, 42, 52, **123-6**, 135, 169,

196; *Clergymen of the Church of England*, 49-50, 51, 52, 56, 135; *Cousin Henry*, 121, **160-2**, 170, 173, 199; *Did He Steal It?*, 88, **189**; *Doctor Thorne*, 6, 27, 31, 47, **60-4**, 109, 121, 195, 196, 197; *Doctor Wortle's School*, 39, **162-4**, 178; *The Duke's Children*, 8, 28, 82, 100, 101, **104-8**, 123, 195; *An Editor's Tales*, 174, 176; *The Eustace Diamonds*, 6, 82, **88-92**, 93, 188, 193; *Examiner*, Letters to the, 11-12; *An Eye for an Eye*, **21-3**, 173; 'Father Giles of Ballymoy', **12-13**; *The Fixed Period*, **165-6**; *Four Lectures*, **189-90**; *Framley Parsonage*, 6, 31, 50, **64-8**, 71, 109, 118, 195, 196; *The Golden Lion of Granpere*, 143, 144, **146-7**, 175; *Harry Heathcote of Gangoil*, **152-4**; *He Knew He Was Right*, 7, 94, **126-31**, 146, 155, 159, 169, 193, 196, 199; *How the 'Mastiffs' Went to Iceland*, **182-3**; *Hunting Sketches*, **44-5**; *Is He Popenjoy?*, 121, 131, **155-7**, 162; *John Caldigate*, **157-60**, 162, 170, 195; *The Kellys and the O'Kellys*, 6, **15-18**; *Kept in the Dark*, **168-70**; *Lady Anna*, 143, **147-9**; *The Landleaguers*, 8, **23-5**, 155; *The Last Chronicle of Barset*, **70-4**, 75, 88, 127, 146, 189, 193, 199; *La Vendée*, 6, 188, **200-01**; *Linda Tressel*, 6, 143, **144-6**, 148, 149, 150, 175; *Lord Palmerston*, 178, **180-1**; *Lotta Schmidt and Other Stories*, 174, 175; *The Macdermots of Ballycloran*, 6, **13-15**; 'Malachi's Cove', **177**; *Marion Fay*, **166-8**, 173; 'Mary Gresley', **176-7**; *Miss Mackenzie*, **139-41**; *Mr Scarborough's Family*, 121, **170-2**, 199; *The New Zealander*, **29-32**; *Nina Balatka*, 6, **143-4**, 145, 146, 148, 150; *The Noble Jilt*, 82, **188**; *North America*, 182, **184-6**, 189; 'The O'Conors of Castle Conor', **12**; *An Old Man's Love*, **172-3**, 198; *Orley Farm*, 6, 31, 33, 45, 109, **118-23**, 195, 198, 199; *Phineas Finn* and *Phineas Redux*, 8,

27, 31, 67, 77, 82, **92-9**, 110, 193, 194, 195, 196, 198; *The Prime Minister*, 28, 73, 75, 76, 77, 82, 94, **99-104**, 181, 193, 194, 196, 198; *Rachel Ray*, **135-9**, 141, 145, 148, 193, 195, 196; *Ralph the Heir*, 2, 7, 75, 77, **79-82**, 83, 148; *Sir Harry Hotspur*, 43, 135, 143, **150-2**; *The Small House at Allington*, 5, **68-70**, 93, 109, 196, 198; *South Africa*, 182, **187-8**; *The Struggles of Brown, Jones and Robinson*, 29, **32-3**, 109; *Tales of All Countries*, 174, 175; *Thackeray*, 178, **179-80**, 194; *The Three Clerks*, 5, 6, 29, 60, **109-14**; *The Tireless Traveller*, 182; *Travelling Sketches*, 174, **182**; *The Two Heroines of Plumplington*, **74**; *The Vicar of Bullhampton*, 28, **131-4**, 198; *The Warden*, 5, 6, 30, 31, 47-8, 53, **54-6**, 121, 193, 195; *The Way We Live Now*, 26, 27, 29, 30, **33-40**, 42, 43, 70, 71, 79, 99, 106, 109, 146, 148, 152, 173, 179, 193, 197, 198, 199; *The West Indies and the Spanish Main*, 174, 182, **183-4**; *Why Frau Frohmann Raised Her Prices and Other Stories*, 174, 175; 'Why Frau Frohmann Raised Her Prices', **176**

Trollope, Arthur, 2
Trollope, Emily, 4
Trollope, Frances (Fanny), 2, 4, 50, 136
Trollope, Henry (brother), 4
Trollope, Henry (son), 135
Trollope, Thomas A. (father), 2, 4
Trollope, Thomas A. (brother), 2, 4, 6
Tyndall, John, 7

Vanity Fair (periodical), 1
Vegel, Sir Julius, 187

Westminster Review, 40
Whately, Richard, 57
Whiston, Robert, 53, 55
Willoughby de Broke, Lord, 45

Young, Brigham, 150